THE

BEAST

ON THE

EAST RIVER

THE
BEAST
ON THE
EAST RIVER

The UN Threat to America's
Sovereignty and Security

Nathan Tabor

NELSON CURRENT
A Subsidiary of Thomas Nelson, Inc.

Published in Nashville, Tennessee, by Nelson Current, a division of a wholly owned subsidiary (Nelson Communications, Inc.) of Thomas Nelson, Inc.

Nelson Current books may be purchased in bulk for educational, business, fundraising, or sales promotional use. For information, please e-mail SpecialMarkets@thomasnelson.com.

Library of Congress Cataloging-in-Publication Data

Tabor, Nathan, 1973–
  The beast on the East River : the U.N. threat to America's sovereignty and security / Nathan Tabor.
     p. cm.
  Includes bibliographical references and index.
  ISBN 10: 1595550534
  ISBN 13: 978-1-59555-053-8
  1. United Nations—United States. I. Title.
JZ4997.5.U6T33 2006
341.23'73—dc22
2006021413

Printed in the United States of America
06 07 08 09 QW 9 8 7 6 5 4 3 2 1

CONTENTS

INTRODUCTION

THE GLOBE IS THE GOAL

The long war had left the countryside in ruins. The men and boys had been gone from the village for months or years, and only the women and small children remained. They scraped by as best they could, scavenging whatever meager scraps of food they could find, trying to fend off starvation for one more day. Many were sick and dying.

Then the foreign soldiers came. Many of them were drunk and cruel. The soldiers terrorized the people and plundered the village. They brutally raped the women, even the young girls, whenever they chose. Those who resisted were beaten or killed. If they screamed for mercy, it was in vain, for there was no one to hear or to help.

This sad scenario, or one like it, has been repeated too many times to count throughout the course of human history. From ancient times to the present day, in every part of the world, mankind's inhumanity and criminality has been documented. The carnage among armed combatants in time of war is terrible enough, but often the atrocities committed in the war's aftermath are even worse, for these innocent victims are the most weak and defenseless of all.

Most Americans are appalled at reports like these because they outrage our innate sense of justice. We instinctively feel that something must be done to help and protect these innocent victims. Unfortunately, there is another ironic dimension to this story that only aggravates our sense of righteous outrage: All too often, the dissolute soldiers who are committing these brutal crimes against women and children are the very ones who are charged with their safety and protection—the blue-helmeted, so-called peacekeeping forces of the United Nations.

Reports of brutal sexual misconduct by UN peacekeepers have surfaced periodically for more than a decade. But these charges have rarely been investigated thoroughly and exposed to the light of public scrutiny. That veil of secrecy and denial began to lift in May 2004, when major media sources first began to publish reports of alleged UN corruption and sexual scandal in the Democratic Republic of the Congo.

Those charges included the rape and sexual abuse of Congolese women in certain UN refugee camps staffed by UN soldiers and civilian employees. The UN Mission in Congo (MONUC) employs a large civilian staff, as well as about 10,800 peacekeeper soldiers from fifty countries. Fighting continues in war-torn Central Africa, despite a peace treaty signed in 2002, and the International Rescue Committee has estimated that the combination of war, famine, and disease kills thirty-one thousand civilians each month.

Heart of Darkness in Africa

The specific allegations, as reported by the *Independent* (London), initially centered around the sexual abuse of teenage girls who lived at the Internally Displaced People camp in Bunia, in the northeastern Congo, home to about sixteen thousand refugees. Many of these girls, some as young as thirteen, had already been the victims of multiple rapes by the various roving militia groups that had terrorized the region during the preceding six-year conflict commonly known as "Africa's world war." These militias regularly used rape and sexual violence as weapons of warfare.[1]

Desperate for food, both for themselves and in some cases for the babies they had birthed after being raped, each night these young girls would crawl under the wire fences that separated their compound from the UN soldiers' barracks, where they would sell their shrunken juvenile bodies for as little as two eggs, a banana, or a cake. Their willing but often brutal customers were usually the UN peacekeepers from Morocco or Uruguay.[2]

At first UN officials denied these serious charges, as the organization has habitually done with similar embarrassing revelations in the past. But that official denial merely fueled the flames of the scandal and led to further in-depth journalistic investigations by several Internet news services, as well as by prominent British and European newspapers. More and more evidence came to light revealing an ongoing pattern of corruption, abuse, and neglect by the UN's staffers and peacekeepers at UN outposts all around the world.

By November 2004, the UN Office of Internal Oversight Services had issued a confidential report that said its own "investigation into allegations of sexual exploitation and abuse of local Congolese women and girls found that the problem was serious and ongoing." Eventually more than fifty UN civilian staffers and peacekeeper soldiers in the Congo were charged with 150 separate crimes, the most serious being pedophilia, prostitution, and rape at gunpoint.[3]

In one instance, two Russian pilots based in Mbandaka reportedly bribed young local girls for sex with jars of jam and mayonnaise, then videotaped the sex acts they performed and sent the videos back to Russia. The Russians, apparently tipped off in advance, left the country before UN investigators got around to questioning them.[4]

At the remote Kisangani outpost on the Congo River, UN staffers from Morocco were found to have impregnated eighty-two local women and girls, and Uruguayan staffers fifty-nine more. Women there had given birth to hundreds of illegitimate children fathered by the UN peacekeepers. One soldier charged with rape was hidden in the barracks for more than a year. Major-General Jean Pierre Ondekane, a rebel commander who later became Minister of Defense in the postwar Congolese government, told a top UN official in July 2002 that the only thing the UN peacekeepers at Kisangani would be remembered for was "running after little girls."[5]

Pedophilia and Pornography

The most explosive charges centered on Didier Bourquet, a senior UN official from France who was stationed in the Congo as a logistics expert. The *Times* (London) reported that Congolese police arrested Bourquet at his home as he was allegedly in the act of preparing to rape a twelve-year-old girl who had been sent to him as part of a police sting operation. Bourquet had converted his bedroom into a studio for video-taping his sexual activities with young girls. His bedroom walls were covered with mirrors on three sides, with a remote-controlled camera on the fourth side. Some of Bourquet's pornographic videos were reportedly for sale on the open market in the Congo.

"It would be a pretty big problem for the UN if these pictures come out," one UN official told the *Times*. The British newspaper dubbed the pedophilia photo scandal "the UN's Abu Ghraib."

According to the *Los Angeles Times*, Bourquet's computer "reportedly contained thousands of photos of him with hundreds of girls. In one frame, a tear can be seen rolling down the cheek of a victim." An ABC News *20/20* segment broadcast on 11 February 2005 showed some of those sordid pictures to an astonished world.

Bourquet was sent back to France to stand trial on charges of sexual abuse and rape. His lawyer told the French court that "there was a network of UN personnel who had sex with underage girls," and admitted that Bourquet had done the same thing while on a previous UN posting to the Central African Republic. Many suspect that the Bourquet case was really just the tiny tip of a huge hidden iceberg.

Most of the sexual exploitation incidents specifically identified in the Congo apparently involved UN soldiers and staffers trading money, food, and sometimes jobs to local women for sex. Some say that it is just a case of prostitutes plying their trade in the world's oldest profession. But when the women in question are younger than eighteen, the core issue becomes pedophilia. Moreover, many women claim to have been forcibly raped by the soldiers, some of whom later gave them food or money to make the affair appear consensual, thus attempting to legitimize rape as prostitution.[6]

Zero Compliance with Zero Tolerance

Coming to light as it did at the same time that the multibillion-dollar Oil-for-Food scandal in Iraq was also grabbing headlines worldwide, the Congo sex abuse scandal was a great embarrassment for the UN. The widespread publicity surrounding the issue prompted a personal apology from UN Secretary-General Kofi Annan, who was under intense pressure to resign his position as head of the UN as the list of UN scandals grew longer every day.

"I am afraid there is clear evidence that acts of gross misconduct have taken place. This is a shameful thing for the United Nations to have to say, and I am absolutely outraged by it," confessed Annan. "I have long made it clear that my attitude to sexual exploitation and abuse is one of zero tolerance, without exception, and I am determined to implement this policy in the most transparent manner."[7]

Annan pledged to correct the problem, although he insisted that it was isolated to a relatively small segment of the UN contingent in Africa. Unfortunately, Annan had used virtually identical "zero tolerance" language previously, when a joint report in 2001 by the Save the Children organization and the UN High Commissioner for Refugees (UNHCR) had identified "widespread" problems of sexual abuse of refugees by UN personnel on the West Coast of Africa.

Ironically, that very same UN High Commissioner for Refugees, Ruud Lubbers, was forced to resign in early 2005 after being charged with sexual harassment by a fifty-one-year-old female administrator who claimed that he put his arm around her waist and pressed his groin against her. Lubbers, aged sixty-five, denied the charges, but four other women also filed similar claims of unwanted advances, and a UN internal investigation determined that he had engaged in a "pattern of sexual harassment" against female employees. Lubbers, who had served as High Commissioner since 2000, had previously been the Netherlands' prime minister from 1982 to 1994.[8]

Annan's official UN apology offers scant comfort to those who know how the organization operates. In the first place, the official UN regulations barring sexual relations with prostitutes and children under age eighteen apply only to UN staff employees. The UN has no authority whatsoever to discipline the soldiers in its peacekeeping forces, who are also immune from prosecution by local authorities. All the UN can do is send them back to their own countries for trial, where even the most serious charges are usually dropped, or at the very least drastically reduced.

Moreover, even where the official regulations do apply to UN personnel, they are so seldom enforced that they are widely disregarded by most. In fact, in another confidential internal UN report, Jordan's Prince Zeid Raad Al Hussein, a special adviser to Annan and the leader of one investigation, said candidly, "The situation appears to be one of 'zero compliance with zero tolerance' throughout the mission."[9]

Thus it appears that nothing very significant has been done to curtail what the *Weekly Standard* described in January 2005 as "a predatory sexual culture among vulnerable refugees—from relief workers who demand sexual favors in exchange for food to UN troops who rape women at gunpoint."[10]

Peacekeepers as Predators

Looking back over the past decade or so, we find that the same kinds of problems have plagued the UN all over the world—from Cambodia and

East Timor in Southeast Asia to Bosnia and Kosovo in Southeastern Europe; and on the African continent from Liberia, Sierra Leone, and Guinea on the west coast to Somalia and Ethiopia on the east.

Eyewitness accounts of violence and corruption, as well as rampant sexual abuse, are now being published with increasing frequency as those who know the truth are finding the courage and the voice to tell it. Many times the victims of these predatory crimes, especially the women who have been raped, don't readily come forward for fear of later reprisals.

The latest report of a victim who did come forward is from Haiti, where a twenty-three-year-old woman has reported to police that three UN soldiers from Pakistan forcibly raped her. The soldiers have disputed that claim, saying that she was a prostitute and they paid her for consensual sex. The soldiers "grabbed and pulled on my pants, had me lie down on the ground, and then raped me," the woman told a Haitian radio station. UN officials say they are investigating the incident.[11]

While many such "he said/she said" cases may never be resolved with certainty, some abuses and atrocities have been confirmed. The actions of certain UN troops in Somalia from 1995 to 1997, for example, are well documented—including acts of rape, torture, and murder.

WorldNetDaily, an independent Internet news service, published an article by Joseph Farah back in June 1997 detailing some of the UN's known abuses of power in Somalia by peacekeepers from various countries. The article, entitled "Those UN Peacekeeping Atrocities," is not for the squeamish: "In 1995, a group of Canadian paratroopers were investigated for torturing a Somali to death and killing three others," reported Farah. That's pretty mild compared to what comes next. Between 1995 and 1997, fifteen members of a Belgian regiment were accused of "acts of sadism and torture" against Somalis. One Somali child died after being locked in a storage container for forty-eight hours; he had been accused of stealing food. A Belgian sergeant was photographed urinating on the corpse of a Somali, whom he was later accused of murdering. Another Belgian soldier allegedly made a Somali, presumably a Muslim, eat pork, drink salt water, and then eat his own vomit. But that's not all.

"How sensational is this non-story?" queried Farah. "Yesterday, the *London Telegraph*, in a combined dispatch with AFP [Agence France Press], reported that Belgian troops roasted a Somali boy. Roasted him! And what was the sentence for this peace crime committed during an operation dubbed ironically 'Restore Hope'? A military court sentenced two paratroopers to a month in jail and a fine of 200 pounds."

Sadly, there was more to come; Farah hadn't even gotten to the Italian peacekeepers yet. One battalion commander reportedly sexually abused and then strangled a thirteen-year-old Somali boy. In 1993, Italian soldiers allegedly beat to death a fourteen-year-old boy who sold a fake medal. Then the finale: "Earlier this month, gruesome photos were published in a Milan magazine of Italian soldiers torturing a Somali youth and abusing and raping a Somali girl. Paratroopers claim they were specifically trained in methods of torture to aid interrogation. According to one witness, Italian soldiers tied a young Somali girl to the front of an armored personnel carrier and raped her while officers looked on," Farah wrote.

Questioned about these abuses, an Italian paratrooper reportedly replied, "What's the big deal? They are just n——— anyway."[12]

Brothels and Blood in Bosnia

Apparently those closest to the front lines of the UN operation know without question how thoroughly corrupt and incompetent the organization truly is, despite its lofty rhetoric and noble goals.

Kathryn Bolkovac was a former Lincoln, Nebraska, policewoman who worked for UN security in Bosnia as an employee of the American security company DynCorp. As part of her job, Bolkovac uncovered massive sex corruption, human trafficking, and prostitution rings in which UN officials and policemen were active participants. Girls as young as fifteen were sold into sex slavery to bar owners, where they were forced to dance naked and perform sex acts for their owners and bar customers. If they refused, they were locked up, starved, beaten, and raped.

In 2000, having failed to get any satisfactory investigative action by informing her immediate superiors, Bolkovac sent an e-mail to Jacques Paul Klein, the head of the UN mission in Bosnia-Herzegovina. In it she described the role of UN officials in exploiting the women they were supposed to be protecting from the sex trade.

Soon after sending the e-mail, Bolkovac was demoted and removed from front-line investigative police work. In 2001, she was summarily fired, allegedly over "time sheet irregularities." She denies that charge and says she was fired for exposing the corruption of the UN mission in Bosnia.

Bolkovac told a court in England that Mike Stiers, the deputy commissioner of the international police task force, had been flippant in dismissing the victims of the sex trade as "just prostitutes."[13]

Years before in Bosnia, UN soldiers stood by passively and did nothing while more than eight thousand Muslim men whom the UN had promised to protect were systematically slaughtered in the "safe area" of Srebrenica. There as elsewhere, the UN's corruption and incompetence were endemic, as eyewitnesses have testified repeatedly.[14]

Dr. Andrew Thomson, a liberal and a former UN employee, has coauthored a book entitled *Emergency Sex and Other Desperate Measures: A True Story from Hell on Earth*, which criticizes the organization's dismal record of failure at peacekeeping. He was fired by the UN for writing the following line of advice to the people of the world: "If blue-helmeted UN peacekeepers show up in your town or village and offer to protect you, run. Or else get weapons. Your lives are worth so much less than theirs."[15]

Dr. Thompson's coauthor, former UN human-rights lawyer Kenneth Cain, once worked as a human-rights observer in Somalia, Rwanda, Haiti, and Liberia. Cain has written a searing critique of both the UN organization and Kofi Annan's leadership of it, in which he observes that "while the media and conservative politicians and pundits have suddenly discovered that the UN has been catastrophically incompetent, this is very old news to anyone with the mud—or blood—of a UN peacekeeping mission on his boots."[16]

Cain sums up the matter in two sentences: "When the UN fails, innocent people die. Under Annan, the UN has failed and people have died." How many people? According to Cain, at least a quarter of a million in Liberia, and almost four times that many in Rwanda. "But if prevention of genocide and protection of the vulnerable are not core priorities on the left, what is?" he wants to know.

"If anyone's values have been betrayed, it is those of us on the left who believe most deeply in the organization's ideals. . . . The bodies burn today in Darfur—and the women are raped—amid the sound of silence from Annan. How many genocides, the prevention of which is the UN's very raison d'etre, will we endure before the left is moved to criticize Annan?"[17]

Rwanda Revisited

Perhaps the blackest blight on the record of UN peacekeeping operations in Africa is the 1994 massacre in Rwanda, in which an estimated one million of the minority Tutsi tribesmen were brutally murdered by their rivals, the majority Hutu tribe.

A powerful movie, *Hotel Rwanda* (MGM, 2004), graphically chronicles the many cold-blooded atrocities that were committed by the rampaging Hutus as the Belgian and UN troops stood by powerless to intervene. But to understand this act of wanton genocide properly, a little background is needed.

In 1990, Boutros Boutros-Ghali was Egypt's minister of foreign affairs. Part of his job was to sell weapons, and in that capacity he approved an initial $5.8 million arms deal with Rwanda. That sale opened the door to others, so that between 1990 and 1992, Cairo shipped $26 million worth of ammunition, grenades, rocket launchers, and mortar bombs to Rwanda. It was those arms that the Hutus later used to crush the Tutsis.[18]

When the wholesale slaughter began in 1994, Boutros-Ghali had moved up in the world—he was now the Secretary-General of the United Nations. The head of the UN's peacekeeping operations at that time was none other than Kofi Annan.

The UN Force Commander in Rwanda, General Romeo Dallaire, sent an urgent fax to Annan requesting permission to defend the helpless Tutsi refugees who were flooding into UN compounds seeking safety and protection. Annan's fax back to Dallaire ordered him to defend only the UN's image of impartiality and forbade him to protect the desperate Tutsis. Boutros-Ghali refused to intervene.

Later the UN troops were withdrawn completely from the scene of the carnage, leaving behind up to 800,000 hapless Tutsis, many of them bludgeoned to death with clubs or hacked into pieces with machetes by the bloodthirsty rampaging Hutus. The world watched for weeks as the bloodbath continued unchecked.

Finally, when the massacre was complete, the UN sent in more soldiers. "You are all late—weeks and weeks late!" Dallaire said with disgust.[19]

At a State of the World Forum panel discussion held in New York City in 2000, films of the Rwanda massacre were shown and the failures of the UN were discussed. Dallaire and others chose to lay the blame for the UN's fatal paralysis on the nations of the Security Council, who could not agree to act. "Every sovereign state that puts self-interest before humanity," Dallaire charged, "that's the dogma of the global market."[20]

But some may question whether the fact that Boutros-Ghali had been instrumental in arming the Hutus had anything to do with his refusal to defend the Tutsis, when he easily could have done so with the UN troops he already had in place.

Kofi Annan went right along with the program in 1994 and was rewarded two years later with his own promotion to Secretary-General. Since then, his record of success in UN peacekeeping missions has been just as dismal as Boutros-Ghali's was before him.

Is all of this mere coincidence, or is there a pattern emerging here?

The Seven Deadly Sins

King Solomon once said that there is nothing new under the sun. That is certainly the case when we consider the many scandals involving the sex, violence, and corruption associated with the United Nations' peacekeeping operations.

What strikes me as most ironic about the UN is the fact that this thoroughly corrupt organization has the audacity to hold itself up as the moral authority for the rest of the world. The UN purports to support and even guarantee universal human rights for all of mankind, but in reality it betrays, exploits, and victimizes those very people whom it most solemnly pledges to protect.[21]

This sad truth is, of course, obvious in the many dehumanizing UN actions that diminish rather than expand the human rights and freedoms (as well as the individual dignity and worth) of the people with whom the UN must interact on the basic local level. But the UN's elitist attitude is perhaps most succinctly expressed in two phrases that we have recently read: certain sets of people are dismissed as being essentially worthless because they are either "just n———" or "just prostitutes."

This blatant hypocrisy is evident to reasonable people of all political persuasions. Both liberals and conservatives can see that the UN doesn't deliver on its promises. We may disagree on whether those promises are worthwhile to begin with, but at this point that hardly matters, because we are dealing with a flawed, failed model.

I have sought to establish the fact that the UN today is at heart an arrogant, unaccountable organization—one that is basically out of control—for a very specific reason.

What we have seen, in discussing the failures of various UN peacekeeping missions over the past decade, is that the UN is characterized by corruption, negligence, and incompetence. In the coming chapters we will see how those same characteristics are manifest in every facet of the UN's operations, whether it be a global environmental policy through its Biosphere Reserves program, the attempt to establish binding international law and worldwide jurisdiction for its International Criminal Court, or the desire to establish a global police state and a UN standing army.

Because the volatile geopolitical situation is becoming increasingly complex and controversial, Americans are taking a renewed interest in the United Nations. However, much of the information now coming to light about the organization reveals a long-standing UN agenda that is at odds with the values and beliefs of most American conservatives—an issue of special concern since US taxpayers supply the lion's share of the UN's annual budget.

The Globe Really Is the Goal

What is most disturbing to me as an American citizen is the appearance that this fatally flawed and thoroughly corrupt organization really does want to rule the world. Further, there are a lot of very powerful people who agree it should do so and are trying to help it achieve that goal in the very near future.

If you happen to be rolling your eyes in disbelief, that reaction is perfectly understandable. After all, we are conditioned to regard such suggestions as conspiracy theories. However, this idea is anything but absurd, as the following chapters will demonstrate.

The UN strategists and global planners have a very specific agenda designed to accomplish their desired objective. It begins with the subtle indoctrination of our children over time through the outcome-based educational system, a process of dumbing-down and mental conditioning designed to make people think of themselves as citizens of the world rather than patriots of any one nation.

This agenda includes establishing control over our nation's vast wealth of national resources and private property through a stealth process of environmental regulations imposed by executive fiat without public or congressional approval. It also demands absolute control over 70 percent of the earth's surface through ratification of the Law of the Sea Treaty. It seeks to eliminate the private ownership of firearms and to establish a global police force that can enforce the dictates of an International Criminal Court—a tribunal that is not bound by the protections of our Constitution and Bill of Rights.

It also seeks the ability to levy global taxes, so that the UN will no longer be dependent upon the voluntary contributions of its members in order to fund its operations.

Once the United Nations has its own independent source of money, its own court system to declare what is legal and what is not, and its own army to enforce its edicts, it will then be a de facto global government, no matter what it may be called initially.

Those who promote this globalist agenda are very patient. Incrementalists, who know full well that their goals will not be achieved overnight, are confident of ultimate success and content with gradual gains. But the fact is they have been working diligently and patiently for more than sixty years to advance their world government agenda, and we are now entering the endgame on the geopolitical chessboard.

Today the World Federalist Association, the Commission on Global Governance, the United Nations Foundation, the Gorbachev Foundation and Green Cross International, and a host of other nongovernmental organizations (NGOs) are all working overtime to accomplish their globalist goals. They see world government under the UN as being "the last best hope of the world," and they see it coming into view.

One of the most transparently proglobalist propaganda films of the last decade is the 2005 Universal Pictures release *The Interpreter*, starring Sean Penn and Nicole Kidman. Actually filmed inside the Security Council and General Assembly chambers of the United Nations building in New York City, this movie clearly intends to tell the world that for all its faults, the UN is the one absolutely essential international organization in the world today, and our only hope for the future.

These people may be sincere, but I believe that they are sincerely wrong. I see their aspirations toward global government as being inherently evil and inimical to the best interests of the United States and the vast majority of its citizens. I believe that our uniquely American system of individual liberty protected by our Constitution is a precious, God-given heritage that must be preserved for our children and grand-children. And I believe that most Americans agree with me.

It is now time for America's elected leaders to do their jobs and protect America's interests from the clear and present danger that confronts us. The choice is simple: Either we boldly assert and preserve the national sovereignty of our free country, or we accept the ascension and inevitable authority of a world government over us.

The United States of America is the only nation on earth that can stop the UN's determined drive to global government, and it is without question in our own best interests to do so. Preservation of our personal liberty and national sovereignty is the only hope that our children will have for a better life in the future.

But we are already very nearly at the point of no return, and most Americans aren't even aware of the impending danger. This book is a call to immediate action—read its contents very carefully. What you will discover may surprise and anger you.

A Note about My Sources

Over the years, many books have been written on the general theme of one-world government, the new world order, and/or the United Nations. Most of these books have been of an alarmist religious nature, focusing on the allegedly conspiratorial and/or occult forces behind the UN's global agenda and the push toward global governance. Some have been marginally successful within certain niches of the reading public, but most of them either have been ignored by the mainstream media or dismissed by pompous pundits as the work of right-wing troglodyte conspiracy theorists.

The Beast on the East River touches on some of the same basic facts and ideas contained in those other works, because the facts are irrefutably true. But the primary emphasis of this book is on a commonsense analysis of how the current, generally anti-American agenda of the UN is fundamentally at odds with the values and beliefs of most conservatives in America today. I also intend to offer practical suggestions as to how we should respond to the threat that confronts our nation, in the enlightened self-interest of both our country and our posterity.

There have been a few books written quite recently by authors with impeccable credentials and experience who give some insight into both the operations and the goals of the UN. Most of these books, such as the aforementioned *Emergency Sex and Other Desperate Measures*, are highly critical of the UN.

Dore Gold, the former Israeli ambassador to the UN, has written an insider's account entitled *Tower of Babble: How the United Nations Has Fueled Global Chaos*. Gold argues that the UN is ineffective at preserving peace or impeding terrorism, and that it is also thoroughly corrupt.[22]

Another book critical of the UN is *Inside the Asylum: Why the United Nations and Old Europe Are Worse Than You Think*, written by former US undersecretary of defense Jed Babbin. He argues that the UN has been infiltrated by terrorist groups and that it openly pursues anti-American policies, all at the expense of the US taxpayers who foot the bill to keep the organization afloat.[23]

By contrast, *An Insider's Guide to the U.N.*, by Linda Fasulo, presents a pro-UN perspective. A UN correspondent for NBC News, MSNBC, and NPR, Ms. Fasulo is sympathetic to the ever-increasing responsibilities of the UN. According to *Publisher's Weekly*, "This book will be a useful source for those seeking in-depth information about one of the international community's most influential establishments at a time when its role and significance is very much in question."[24]

That seemingly innocuous statement is both accurate and highly informative. The United Nations is indeed one of the most influential organizations in the world today; its influence is rapidly growing; and its importance as the focal point of the "international community's" drive toward global governance cannot be underestimated.

However, it is equally true that both the UN's role and its significance are increasingly being questioned and in some cases challenged by growing numbers of Americans perceptive enough to grasp the logical consequences of this incrementalist international political process, and to be alarmed by it. This book has been written to help legitimately concerned American citizens understand the hard and unpleasant truth about the United Nations, the beast on the East River.

1

GLOBAL EDUCATION AGENDA

At its core, the United Nations today is in the education business. Its army of social change agents is working night and day to reshape the thinking of every person on the planet and to bring their mental attitudes into line with its global standards of political correctness, conformity, and obedience. They do this under the seemingly innocuous guise of "building peace in the minds of men."

The UN's greatest challenge has been to overcome the deep-seated attitudes of self-reliance, individualism, and independence that have permeated American thought and culture for generations. Many Europeans, considering themselves more refined and civilized than their transatlantic neighbors, tend to derisively dismiss all Americans as "cowboys" who are stubbornly clinging to an anachronistic frontier mentality. It is this perceived American attitude of antisocial isolationism and independence that the UN global planners are determined to change.

Americans, however, generally do believe in the value and benefits of education, and they like to think of themselves as being more knowledgeable than many of the less fortunate folks in the poorer nations of the world. Higher education has traditionally been seen as a trustworthy pathway to upward social mobility and success in life. Most parents want their children to learn and achieve more than they did, so they encourage them to study hard, excel in school, and seek more specialized training.

But most of these well-meaning American parents would probably be shocked to find out that, rather than learning to master the basic "Three Rs," their children are being indoctrinated from an early age in a set of values and beliefs far different from those of previous generations of Americans. Since its founding sixty years ago, the UN and its supporters have had the opportunity to influence the thinking of three generations of American school children, and the results of their efforts are sadly evident in the degraded culture that has evolved in our country over that same period of time.

Parents might be even more outraged to discover that, despite the massive amounts of tax money now being spent on the public education system in America, their children are in fact being sent out into the fiercely competitive global marketplace armed with an *inferior* education. To add insult to injury, it may be asserted that American school children are *intentionally* being dumbed-down.

Think about it. What if this academic mediocrity is not merely the sad result of bureaucratic inefficiency and teacher incompetence, but rather is actually a carefully crafted plot promoted by the United Nations to advance its globalist agenda of world government? The person leveling such an outrageous charge would probably be dismissed by most Americans as just another crackpot. Unfortunately—and as much as we all would like for it to be otherwise—an objective analysis of the facts supports just such a radical conclusion.

One primary goal of the UN is the re-education and indoctrination of American school children, conditioning them to think of themselves as global citizens rather than as nationalistic patriots. Does this serious charge sound implausible to you? Then consider the following statement from an official UN publication:

> As long as the child breathes the poisoned air of nationalism, education
> in world-mindedness can produce only rather precarious results. As we
> have pointed out, it is frequently the family that infects the child with

extreme nationalism. The school should therefore use the means described earlier to combat family attitudes that favor jingoism.[1]

It was exactly this kind of anti-American rhetoric emanating from the UN that prompted the popular conservative radio newscaster Paul Harvey to warn his listeners: "Through UNESCO, American children are influenced away from their national allegiance. American children are being indoctrinated with world government."[2]

The sad fact is that politically correct thinking has become an outcome valued more highly than individualism, creative independent thought, or academic achievement. There is an ever-growing emphasis on multiculturalism and a nonnegotiable demand that everyone display sensitivity and tolerance for diversity, which often covers a multitude of morally ambiguous situations that may be at odds with most Americans' opinions. In reality, these buzzwords are merely components in the so-called "gay rights movement" and have been pounded into our nation's psyche at the expense of the nuclear family and traditional family values.

The UN also promotes the specious secular humanist concept of "values clarification," where the moral emphasis is on relativistic situational ethics rather than any absolute standard of right and wrong. Homeschooling is seen as a threat, and parents all too often are viewed as subversive influences by the UN education establishment.

But before we begin to discuss the UN's global educational agenda in greater detail, it will be helpful for us to take a brief look at its labyrinthine, sometimes confusing, and often overlapping organizational structure.

Parsing the UN's Organizational Structure

The UN structure consists of six main divisions, or principal organs, and beneath these are literally dozens of other separate and specialized organizational entities.

Most people have heard of the UN Secretary-General, the Security Council, and the General Assembly, and are vaguely familiar with their respective functions, so we will discuss them only briefly at this point. The following are the main organs of the United Nations and a brief description of their functions and responsibilities.[3]

The *Secretariat* is the administrative bureaucracy that runs the day-to-day affairs of the UN from the organization's headquarters in New York City. Headed by the secretary-general and his extensive staff, the Secretariat presents the public face of the United Nations to the world at large. The secretary-general is appointed to a five-year renewable term by the General Assembly, with the approval of the Security Council. The operations of the Secretariat are carried out by numerous departments and offices.

The *UN Security Council* is the world's GloboCop: a permanent body responsible for dealing with breaches of the peace and acts of aggression worldwide. It is composed of five permanent member nations: the United States, Great Britain, France, Russia, and China. Each of these five permanent members has veto power over any proposed resolution for military intervention by the UN, as well as amendments to the UN Charter and applications for membership. The Security Council also contains ten nonpermanent members that are selected for two-year terms by the General Assembly, but these do not exercise veto power. The Security Council controls several subsidiary bodies, including the Military Staff Committee.

The *General Assembly* is the UN's version of a world parliament in which all member nations are represented equally. Its regular session in New York City convenes every year on the third Tuesday in September. The General Assembly is generally viewed as a worldwide public forum to facilitate discussion and make decisions on important political, social, or economic policy matters affecting the international community. Every member nation has one vote, and ordinary matters are decided by a simple majority vote. Important matters, such as budgetary issues, require a two-thirds majority. The General Assembly controls numerous subsidiary bodies, programs and funds, research and training institutes, and other entities within the UN.

While these three highly visible administrative and parliamentary institutions are of great importance, the real work of advancing the UN's long-term goals is carried out by other, less well-known but quite distinct branches of the organization, as established by the original UN Charter.

The *Trusteeship Council*, which operates under the supervision of the General Assembly, was established in 1945 to supersede the old mandate system of the League of Nations in administering the affairs of non-self-governing territories after the demise of European colonialism. Most of the trust territories once controlled by the Trusteeship Council have since become independent nations or merged with others. As a result, the Trusteeship Council has suspended its activities since November 1994. But there is a move recently afoot to reactivate the council to oversee the so-called common areas of the earth, such as the oceans, the arctic poles, and the atmosphere and space.

The *International Court of Justice*, a UN tribunal that meets at The Hague in the Netherlands, is composed of fifteen judges who are selected by the General Assembly and the Security Council. All UN member nations are considered to be members of the court, but at present its jurisdiction applies only to cases voluntarily submitted to it for resolution. The court normally addresses disputes between nations involving treaties, international law and obligations, and reparations, although it sometimes delivers advisory legal opinions to the various branches of the United Nations. Its activities and influence will be discussed in more detail later on.

Human Rights and Millennium Goals

In addition to the aforementioned UN bodies, the *Economic and Social Council* (ECOSOC) is also a distinct division, or what the UN calls a principal organ, whose functions are defined and authorized by

Chapters 9 and 10 of the UN Charter. Operating under the authority of the General Assembly, the council investigates a wide range of international economic and social problems and reports its recommendations for solutions to the General Assembly.

The Economic and Social Council's specific mandate—"with a view to the creation of conditions of stability and well-being which are necessary for peaceful and friendly relations among nations based on respect for the principle of equal rights and self-determination of peoples"—is to promote:

- Higher standards of living, full employment, and conditions of economic and social progress and development
- Solutions of international economic, social, health, and related problems; and international cultural and educational cooperation
- Universal respect for, and observance of, human rights and fundamental freedoms for all without distinction as to race, sex, language, or religion[4]

In furtherance of these lofty goals, since its inception, the Economic and Social Council has established a plethora of special commissions to study a wide variety of issues, ranging from narcotics to women's rights to statistics to sustainable development.

Thus, among the principal organs of the UN, the real radical change agent at work behind the scenes internationally is the Economic and Social Council.

In cooperation with more than three hundred non-governmental organizations (NGOs), the council schedules frequent conferences all over the world to discuss specific topics and to formulate policy recommendations. Much of the long-term agenda of the United Nations is contained in the plans, policies, and reports that result from these numerous UN conferences. Several of these very important contemporary issues will be the focus of analysis later in this book.

If, historically, the Economic and Social Council has one specific claim to fame, it would be the creation of the Universal Declaration of Human Rights that was adopted by the General Assembly in 1948. This widely misunderstood document is what the UN cites to justify its ostensible moral authority around the world. Since 1967, ECOSOC's own Commission on Human Rights has been authorized to monitor and investigate alleged human rights abuses worldwide, even among the more developed nations.

In addition to the functional and regional commissions that are under its direct control, the Economic and Social Council also works in close conjunction and shares overlapping authority with a variety of specialized agencies and permanent programs and funds inside the United Nations.

Within the UN's Byzantine organizational structure, a number of separate entities often are working simultaneously to accomplish the same goals, and knowing exactly where the authority of one entity ends and that of another begins can be a complex and challenging task, even for a seasoned UN observer. Keeping track of all the ongoing conferences, reports, and plans of action simultaneously being produced by these various organs, departments, and agencies would be a full-time job.

Currently, the UN's major international policy initiative, one that is being pursued by a plethora of UN agencies and commissions, is an ambitious set of eight Millennium Development Goals, which include long-term plans to eradicate poverty and hunger, achieve universal primary education, promote gender equality and empower women, reduce child mortality, improve maternal health, combat HIV/AIDS and other diseases, ensure environmental sustainability, and advance a global partnership for development.

The Millennium Declaration, which was issued in 2000 at the conclusion of the Millennium Summit in New York City, defines and articulates the UN's Millennium Development Goals. Because every one of the 191 UN member states has pledged to meet these goals by the year 2015, Kofi Annan has called the Millennium Declaration "a seminal event in the history of the United Nations."

The United Nations system

Trusteeship Council	Security Council	General Assembly

Subsidiary Bodies
Military Staff Committee
Standing Committee and ad hoc bodies
International Criminal Tribunal for the Former
   Yugoslavia
International Criminal Tribunal for Rwanda
UN Monitoring, Verification and Inspection
   Commission (Iraq)
United Nations Compensation Commission
Peacekeeping Operations and Missions

Subsidiary Bodies
Main committees
Other sessional committees
Standing committees and
   ad hoc bodies
Other subsidiary organs

Programmes and Funds

UNCTAD United Nations Conference on Trade and Development
> **ITC** International Trade Centre (UNCTAD/WTO)

UNDCP United Nations Drug Control Programme[1]

UNEP United Nations Environment Programme

UNICEF United Nations Children's Fund

UNDP United Nations Development Programme
> **UNIFEM** United Nations Development Fund for Women

> **UNV** United Nations Volunteers

> **UNCDF** United Nations Capital Development Fund

UNFPA United Nations Population Fund

UNHCR Office of the United Nations High Commissioner for Refugees

WFP World Food Programme

UNRWA[2] United Nations Relief and Works Agency for Palestine Refugees in the Near East

UN-HABITAT United Nations Human Settlements Programme (UNHSP)

Research and Training Institutes

UNICRI United Nations Interregional Crime and Justice Research Institute

UNITAR United Nations Institute for Training and Research

UNRISD United Nations Research Institute for Social Development

UNIDIR[2] United Nations Institute for Disarmament Research

INSTRAW International Research and Training Institute for the Advancement of Women

Other UN Entities

OHCHR Office of the United Nations High Commissioner for Human Rights

UNOPS United Nations Office for Project Services

UNU United Nations University

UNSSC United Nations System Staff College

UNAIDS Joint United Nations Programme on HIV/AIDS

NOTES: Solid lines from a Principal Organ indicate a direct reporting relationship; dashes indicate a non-subsidiary relationship. [1]The UN Drug Control Programme is part of the UN Office on Drugs and Crime. [2]UNRWA and UNIDIR report only to the GA. [3]The World Trade Organization and World Tourism Organization use the same acronym. [4]IAEA reports to the Security Council and the General Assembly (GA). [5]The CTBTO Prep.Com and OPCW report to the GA. [6]Specialized agencies are autonomous organizations working with the UN and each other through the coordinating machinery of the ECOSOC at the intergovernmental level, and through the Chief Executives Board for coordination (CEB) at the inter-secretariat level.

The United Nations system

PRINCIPAL ORGANS

| Economic and Social Council | International Court of Justice | Secretariat |

Functional Commissions

Commissions on:
- Human Rights
- Narcotic Drugs
- Crime Prevention and Criminal Justice
- Science and Technology for Development
- Sustainable Development
- Status of Women
- Population and Development

Commission for Social Development

Statistical Commission

Regional Commissions

Economic Commission for Africa (ECA)

Economic Commission for Europe (ECE)

Economic Commission for Latin America and the Caribbean (ECLAC)

Economic and Social Commission for Asia and the Pacific (ESCAP)

Economic and Social Commission for Western Asia (ESCWA)

Other Bodies

Permanent Forum on Indigenous Issues (PFII)

United Nations Forum on Forests

Sessional and standing committees

Expert, ad hoc and related bodies

Related Organizations

WTO[3] World Trade Organization

IAEA[4] International Atomic Energy Agency

CTBTO PREP.COM[5] PrepCom for the Nuclear-Test-Ban-Treaty Organization

OPCW[5] Organization for the Prohibition of Chemical Weapons

Specialized Agencies[6]

ILO International Labour Organization

FAO Food and Agriculture Organization of the United Nations

UNESCO United Nations Educational, Scientific and Cultural Organization

WHO World Health Organization

WORLD BANK GROUP

IBRD International Bank for Reconstruction and Development

IDA International Development Association

IFC International Finance Corporation

MIGA Multilateral Investment Guarantee Agency

ICSID International Centre for Settlement of Investment Disputes

IMF International Monetary Fund

ICAO International Civil Aviation Organization

IMO International Maritime Organization

ITU International Tele-communication Union

UPU Universal Postal Union

WMO World Meterological Organization

WIPO World Intellectual Property Organization

IFAD International Fund for Agricultural Development

UNIDO United Nations Industrial Development Organization

WTO[3] World Tourism Organization

Departments and Offices

OSG Office of the Secretary-General

OIOS Office of Internal Oversight Services

OLA Office of Legal Affairs

DPA Department of Political Affairs

DDA Department for Disarmament Affairs

DPKO Department of Peace-keeping Operations

OCHA Office for the Coordination of Humanitarian Affairs

DESA Department of Economic and Social Affairs

DGACM Department for General Assembly and Conference Management

DPI Department of Public Information

DM Department of Management

OHRLLS Office of the High Representative for the Least Developed Countries, Landlocked Developing Countries and Small Island Developing States

UNSECOORD Office of the United Nations Security Coordinator

UNODC United Nations Office on Drugs and Crime

UNOG UN Office at Geneva

UNOV UN Office at Vienna

UNON UN Office at Nairobi

Published by the UN Department of Public Information
DPI/2342—March 2004

9

According to Annan, the Millennium Goals "have unprecedented political support, embraced at the highest levels by developed and developing countries, civil society and major development institutions alike."[5]

We will look more closely at these Millennium Goals later. But for now we will turn our attention to what is perhaps the most controversial specialized agency within the United Nations organization—and one that is working closely with the Economic and Social Council to implement the Millennium Goals program.

UNESCO: Building Peace in the Minds of Men?

In the aftermath of World War II, world attention was focused on the daunting tasks of rebuilding our civilization in the wake of the war's widespread destruction, controlling the proliferation of atomic weapons, and setting up some kind of international oversight body that could guarantee the continuing peace.

Given those pressing priorities, the quaint notion of establishing a specialized agency within the UN that was to be solely devoted to sharing culture, encouraging education, and promoting international cooperation was probably seen by most as being maybe a good idea but not really a big news item.

The *United Nations Educational, Scientific and Cultural Organization* (UNESCO) was founded in 1945 in London at the behest of a group of academics who wanted to preserve and expand the literature and scientific knowledge of the developed world, and to share it with newly developing countries where education and literacy rates were abysmally low. But what started out as a seemingly inconsequential conclave of scholars and bureaucrats has today become the driving force behind the UN's long-term global education agenda.

Based permanently in Paris, France, UNESCO initially worked closely with the old International Board of Education (IBE), an educational research organization that had been founded by teachers in 1925 as part of the League of Nations. UNESCO and IBE co-hosted worldwide conferences on a variety of education-related topics until 1962, when the UNESCO General Conference established the Institute for International Educational Planning (IIEP). In 1969, IBE merged with UNESCO.

The stated goal of UNESCO is "to build peace in the minds of men" by encouraging education, promoting international cooperation, and facilitating shared culture among the nations of the world. Certainly it would be hard to find fault with such a noble-sounding sentiment; thus UNESCO met with warm initial support.

The preamble to the UNESCO constitution contains two corollary concepts that are at the heart of the Special Agency's mission:

1. Since wars begin in the minds of men, it is in the minds of men that the defenses of peace must be constructed.
2. Ignorance of each other's ways and lives has been a common cause, throughout history, of that suspicion and mistrust between the peoples of the world through which their differences have all too often broken into war.[6]

From these two basic philosophical premises flows the somewhat utopian assumption that if men are educated rather than ignorant, and familiar and friendly with one another rather than hostile and suspicious, peace will be the necessary and universal result. While this conclusion might seem both logical and desirable, it did not, in practice, always prove to be true.

Thirty years after the founding of UNESCO, one expert source on international education noted the failure of certain UN efforts and defined the problem as follows:

These "internationalizing" enterprises, even when they do quicken peoples' awareness of cultures other than their own, by no means necessarily result in understanding or peaceful disposition toward the cultures studied. There have been enough studies of prejudice and ethnocentrisms to show that teaching how other people live does not necessarily lessen prejudice or ethnocentricism. . . . Very little comes from a proliferation of activities built on the assumption that "even strange people can be friendly."[7]

That commonsense analysis comes from no less an authority than the *Encyclopedia Britannica*, which clearly is no foe of either the widespread dissemination of knowledge or the concept of international cooperation. However, notwithstanding *Britannica*, I would suggest that it is not merely the existence of prejudice and ethnocentricism that thwarts the attempts to produce world peace through global understanding. The real problems go much deeper than that.

"The implied presupposition is that peoples are nationalistic and governments go to war because they do not know each other well enough," explained Dr. Philip Bom, former economics professor at Regent University in Virginia Beach, Virginia. The late Hans Morgenthau, a preeminent international relations theorist, "realized UNESCO's misunderstanding of the nature of man and society, and of education and culture as tools for international peace," according to Bom. He taught for years:

> Irrespective of its great intrinsic merits, the program of UNESCO is irrelevant to the problem of world community because its diagnosis of the bars to world community so completely misses the point. The problem of world community is a moral and political and not an intellectual and esthetic one.[8]

It will be worthwhile to bear this thought in mind as we examine both the roots and the fruits of UNESCO.

Rotten at the Roots

According to the UNESCO website, this specialized agency of the UN not only serves as a "clearinghouse" for shared information but also functions as "a laboratory of ideas and a standard-setter to forge universal agreements on emerging ethical issues."[9]

Thus UNESCO clearly sees its mission as not only one of promoting universal education and disseminating vital information around the world, but also one of re-orienting the moral compass of the planet. But what is the ethical basis of UNESCO's claim to alleged superior moral authority?

The original director-general of UNESCO was Sir Julian Huxley, a noted British scientist and reputedly a brilliant intellectual. He was without question a distinguished choice to head up the UN's new global education organization. But Sir Julian was also a militant atheist and an ardent evolutionist who rejected all forms of religion and believed that UNESCO's guiding philosophy should be "a scientific world humanism, global in extent and evolutionary in background."[10]

Sir Julian unequivocally expressed these secular humanist views in his book, *UNESCO: Its Purpose and Philosophy*, written in 1948, a copy of which is proudly posted on UNESCO's website today.

"The world today is in the process of becoming one, and . . . a major aim of UNESCO must be to help in the speedy and satisfactory realization of this process," Huxley insisted.[11] He added that "political unification in some sort of world government will be necessary for the definitive attainment" of human evolutionary progress.[12]

But what about Huxley's basis for his secular humanist moral authority?

"It will be one of the major tasks of the philosophy division of UNESCO to stimulate, in conjunction with the natural and social scientists, the quest for a *restatement of morality* that shall be in harmony with modern knowledge and adapted to the fresh functions imposed on ethics by the world of today," Huxley wrote.[13]

Apparently for Huxley, then, modern human ethics originate in the mind of man and are situationally determined, rather than being grounded in any universal moral absolutes. Thus Huxley was an early proponent of the contemporary "values clarification" approach to morality that has become so common today.

He also advocated the use of psychological behavior modification techniques to help school children overcome their feelings of sinfulness, guilt, and repression.

"One other item which UNESCO should put on its program as soon as possible is the study of the application of psycho-analysis and other schools of 'deep' psychology to education," Huxley advised. "If we could discover some means of regulating the process of repression and its effects, we would without doubt be able to make the world both happier and more efficient." This repression-regulation process eventually "would mean an extension of education backwards from the nursery school to the nursery itself."[14]

Most Americans would recoil in horror from the idea of the state's imposing psychological behavior modification techniques on school children, beginning at birth and then conditioning them throughout the entire course of their lives to be compliant citizens under a global government. We would tend to see this whole conditioning process as an unacceptable attempt to bring us into subjection to a system of godless global totalitarianism.

But this is exactly what Sir Julian Huxley, UNESCO's first director-general, clearly advocated. And it is exactly what UNESCO is still attempting to do today.

Huxley, a Marxist sympathizer, proceeded to bring criticism upon himself and UNESCO by his appointment of several known Communists and Communist sympathizers—including Soviet officials—to key positions within the organization.

Planned from the Beginning

If Sir Julian Huxley had been the only person to express such Hobbesian authoritarian sentiments back in 1945, the long-term results of even his prestigious reputation and influence might have been minimal. Unfortunately, such was not the case. In fact, there was an active "international education conspiracy" afoot from the very beginning.

In America, the National Education Association, a teachers' union, had been pushing for a worldwide board of education for a quarter century or more. In 1920, the NEA established its own International Relations Committee designed to produce world understanding through cross-cultural education.

During World War II, Joy Elmer Morgan wrote a poem to celebrate the strategic alliance between the USA and the USSR, and to verbalize her hope for a coming world government. Elmer was the head of the NEA at the time, and her poem, titled "The United People of the World," was published in the December 1942 edition of the *NEA Journal*.[15]

After the war, Morgan continued to advance the theme of world government through her editorials in the same publication. In January 1946, she published "The Teacher and World Government," in which she openly declared:

> In the struggle to establish an adequate world government, the teacher has many parts to play. He must begin with his own attitude and knowledge and purpose. He can do much to prepare the hearts and minds of children for global understanding and cooperation. . . . At the very top of all the agencies which will assure the coming of world government must stand the school, the teacher, and the organized profession.[16]

In December 1946, Morgan published "Fundamentals of Abiding Peace," in which she again asserted the same globalist theme, and her view of the teacher's supremely important role in bringing it into being:

> The organized teaching profession may well take hope and satisfaction from the achievements it has already made toward world government in

its support of the United Nations and UNESCO. It is ours to hold ever before the people the ideals and principles of world government until practice can catch up with those ideals.[17]

Clearly, there was no question in this highly influential American educator's mind about the ultimate end that was destined to be achieved through UNESCO and the UN. Nor did anyone at UNESCO disavow Morgan's globalist gushings. In fact, they did exactly the opposite.

In June 1948, UNESCO conducted its Eleventh International Conference on Public Education in Geneva, Switzerland. Based on the results of that conference, UNESCO then published a ten-volume series of instruction manuals for teachers, entitled *Toward World Understanding*. Volume One of that series asserted that

one of the chief aims of education today should be the preparation of children and adolescents to participate consciously and actively in the building up of a world society . . . [and] this preparation should include not only the acquisition of skills, but more particularly *the formation and the development of psychological attitudes favorable to the construction, maintenance and advancement of a united world.*[18]

Volume Five of this teachers' series criticized parents for not being properly "world-minded" and for "infecting" their children with unacceptable attitudes of "nationalism, chauvinism, and sclerosis of the mind." The teachers' job would then be to "correct many of the errors of home training" that have produced "attitudes running directly counter to the development of international understanding."

The manual then warned the teachers that

as long as the child breathes the poisoned air of nationalism, education in world-mindedness can produce only precarious results. As we have pointed out, it is frequently the family that infects the child with extreme nationalism. The school should therefore use the means described earlier to combat family attitudes that favor jingoism.[19]

So here, almost sixty years ago, we find teachers intentionally being pitted against parents. Here, also, are the seeds of what we recognize today as outcome-based education, designed to indoctrinate children with state-approved, politically correct attitudes. Is it any wonder that parents sometimes find teachers insensitive to their wishes and concerns, when those teachers are being carefully trained to believe that their most important job is to correct the parents' negative influences upon their children?

While some UNESCO supporters were secretive about their early aims, others were more open and unapologetic. For example, the left-leaning magazine the *Saturday Review* wrote a pro-UNESCO editorial in 1952 that blustered:

> If UNESCO is challenged on the grounds that it is helping to prepare the world's peoples for world government, then it is an error to burst forth with apologetic statements and denials. Let us face it: the job of UNESCO is to help create and promote the elements of world citizenship. When faced with such a charge, let us by all means affirm it from the housetops.[20]

Some today may deny that these facts are true, but the historical record is clear. Others may assert that these events did indeed occur many years ago but have no relevance to today. Yet, six decades later, I have seen no evidence to support a credible claim that either the NEA or UNESCO has changed its original tactics and goals.

Cold War Treachery

Those who shared in the globalist vision of the UN and UNESCO wasted no time in putting their subversive anti-American theories into practice. By the early 1950s, a massive propaganda campaign was underway in America promoting the UN, both in school classrooms and in the major media.

However, this was also a period of time during which many Americans were challenging all such efforts to erode our national sovereignty. Congressional committees actively began to investigate whether or not there really were Communist moles entrenched within the vast bureaucracies of the US government.

When the American Legion, meeting at its national convention in Miami in 1955, passed a resolution banning the distribution of all UNESCO propaganda within the territorial boundaries of the US, the tide of public opinion began to turn against the UN. Former President Truman denounced the Legionnaires, saying, "The Legion doesn't know what it is doing. They have gone haywire in the last few years."[21]

In 1955, Congressman Lawrence Smith of Wisconsin, speaking from the House floor, publicly called UNESCO "a permanent international snake pit where godless communism is given a daily forum for hate, recrimination, psychological warfare against freedom, and unrelenting moral aggression against peace."[22] And in 1956, a Senate Internal Security Subcommittee reported that "by far the worst danger spot, from the standpoint of disloyalty and subversive activity among Americans employed by international organizations, is UNESCO."[23]

About the same time, Joseph Z. Kornfeder, a former top official in the Communist Party USA, renounced Marxism and spoke out against his former Soviet masters. Kornfeder gave a speech to a patriotic group in San Francisco, exposing the Communist influence in the UN. "UNESCO corresponds to the agitation and propaganda department in the Communist Party," Kornfeder explained. "This department handles the strategy and method of getting at the public mind, young and old."[24]

The 1950s and '60s marked the UN's heyday in America. By the '70s, the organization had begun to decline in public popularity, reaching its nadir in 1980 when Ronald Reagan was elected president. New conservative influences in the White House began to send signals of strong disenchantment toward the blue-green towers on the East River in New York City.

Americans were increasingly wearied and angered by the constant stream of vitriolic anti-Western and anti-American rhetoric emanating from UNESCO. The *Courier* newspaper, published by UNESCO, was filled with unabashed Communist propaganda promoting a new world economic order that defined prosperity along geographical lines and wanted to radically redistribute the wealth from the north to the poverty-stricken developing nations in the south.

Yet at the same time, UNESCO's corrupt socialist director-general, Amadou Mahtar M'bow of Senegal, wasted tremendous sums of money to finance his own opulent lifestyle, with no accountability to anyone. The last straw came when M'bow tried to impose a Communist-style New World Information Order (NWIO) on the Western world. This blatant UN attempt to license all journalists and to restrict media coverage of world events was too much for even the liberal mainstream media in America to accept.

When Ronald Reagan took the US out of UNESCO in 1984, citing the organization's corruption, waste, and hostility to Western values and American interests, few protested. But American patriots rejoiced.

Bill Clinton tried to rejoin UNESCO in 1994, but the new Republican majority in Congress refused to go along with the plan. Instead, Senator Jesse Helms orchestrated an effort to withhold paying America's regular dues to the UN until substantive changes were made in its wasteful and inefficient bureaucratic operations.

In 2002, citing the organization's purported reforms, President George W. Bush brought the United States back into the UNESCO fold, despite the objections of Rep. Ron Paul. "As a symbol of our commitment to human dignity, the United States will return to UNESCO," Bush declared in a statement to United Nations on 12 September 2002. "This organization has been reformed and America will participate fully in its mission to advance human rights and tolerance and learning."[25] Just a few months later, on 13 February 2003, US Secretary of Education Rod Paige participated in ceremonies to kick off UNESCO's Literacy Decade.[26]

In the minds of many, UNESCO has now been rehabilitated, and according to our president, we are once again as a nation willing to "participate fully in its mission." Whether that will be the altruistic humanitarian mission of its official public relations pronouncements, or the historic mission of reeducating and indoctrinating the youth of the world into support for world government remains to be seen.

Imposing Standardized Global Education

So much for the history of UNESCO. The question is, what is this controversial organization actually doing today? As we learned previously, UNESCO is working in concert with a variety of other UN commissions and special agencies to implement the UN's eight Millennium Goals by 2015.

According to UNESCO's website, the agency is also actively pursuing the goals promulgated by the General Assembly's 2002 special session on Early Child Care and Development (ECCD). Under a plan of action entitled "Create a World Fit for Children," UNESCO will seek to influence the policies of various national governments to produce positive action in at least six important areas.

In order to create a world fit for children, UNESCO proposes to:

1. Decrease illiteracy

2. Promote gender equality

3. Guarantee free and compulsory primary education

4. Eliminate child labor and fight poverty

5. Combat HIV/AIDS

6. Stop the sexual exploitation of and trafficking in children

Again, as we conceded earlier, it is difficult to find fault with these laudable goals. Every one of them is legitimate and worthy of support. The big question, however, is still this: what means will be used to accomplish these worthwhile goals? And also: What hidden ancillary agenda may be attached to these highly publicized efforts?

Those are questions that will be answered only with time and careful observation. There are some relevant observations, though, that can be made right now.

Based on my research, I am convinced that UNESCO's main focus at this point in time is neither the attainment of the Millennium Goals nor the "Create a World Fit for Children" goals. It is, rather, the completion of a much larger task begun years ago but still relatively unknown to most outside the educational establishment circles of government.

On 5 March 1990, UNESCO held a very important five-day conference at the remote location of Jomtein, Thailand. This meeting, the World Conference on Education for All (WCEFA), was officially sponsored by UNESCO, UNICEF, and UNDP (the United Nations Development Program). More than 150 nations sent delegates. Also participating were the World Bank, other UN agencies, and a number of NGOs. The WCEFA conference produced two important documents: *The World Declaration on Education for All* and *The Framework for Action to Meet Basic Learning Needs.*

According to veteran UN observer and John Birch Society senior editor William F. Jasper, "The Framework set forth six goals, which also just happened to be virtually identical to the controversial Outcome-Based Education (OBE) set out by then-President George Bush (CFR) [Council on Foreign Relations] in his 'America 2000' education plan."[27]

A scant eighteen months later, on 30 October to 1 November 1991, many of the same actors met again in Alexandria, Virginia. They were joined by representatives of various tax-exempt foundations as well as a number of cosponsors from business and government, including Apple Computer, IBM, the National School Board Association, the National

Federation of Teachers, the National Education Association, the US Department of Education, the College Board, USAID (US Agency for International Development), and others. This time their purpose was to launch an organization called the US Coalition for Education for All (USCEFA). Their slogan—and the eventual title of their conference report—was "Learning for All: Bridging Domestic and International Education."

The president of USCEFA is Janet Whitla, who is also director of the Education Development Center, Inc. According to Jasper, that company is "infamous for its pro-homosexual, pornographic, promiscuity-promoting sex education programs and globalist curricula. The Coalition is pushing to make UNESCO the global school board which will dictate education policy for the world."[28]

In 1992, President Bush and the US state governors adopted the WCEFA goals in their America 2000 education plan, almost verbatim. Anti-OBE activists across the country were outraged but essentially powerless to change the situation, which was presented to the unsuspecting American public as a *fait accompli.*

Today, just fifteen years into the EFA–OBE social experiment, we are all familiar with certain common buzzwords that we didn't hear just a few years ago. Words and phrases such as "outcomes," "accountability," "lifelong learning," and "no child left behind"—these are all part of the educational language legacy of OBE.

Critics of the OBE system charge that it is an inferior form of learning that does not stimulate the creative and intellectual potential of the student, but rather subjects the student to a Skinnerian-derived program of behavior modification. OBE is much more concerned with producing predictable, politically correct attitudes and actions than it is with stimulating academic or intellectual excellence.

OBE expert Charlotte Iserbyt offers the following explanation of what is at stake with the widespread advent of this OBE method into the American public education system:

Some are aware that Dr. Skinner was a militant atheist-humanist (a signer of the Humanist Manifesto and a winner of the "Humanist of the Year" award) and that he made some astonishingly totalitarian statements. What they don't seem to realize is that his whole philosophy and epistemology, which undergird OBE, are profoundly totalitarian in orientation and irredeemably hostile to Christian morality and individual liberty.

The real desired outcome of the OBE elitists is a deliberately dumbed-down, easily managed and controlled global workforce of compliant automatons. Any compromise with these totalitarian mind controllers is a bargain with evil and a sellout of our children's birthright of freedom.[29]

Thus it appears that from the original philosophy of irreligious "scientific humanism" propounded by UNESCO's first director, Sir Julian Huxley, to the freedom- and dignity-denying practical applications of B.F. Skinner's behavior modification techniques in the classrooms of America, UNESCO is continuing in its sixty-year quest for control of the minds of our children, in preparation for world government.

It seems obvious to me that UNESCO's continuing emphasis today is exactly what it has always been from its inception. And it is creeping ever closer to its goal. As of 2003, the World Bank has made a multi-billion-dollar commitment to provide significant funding for UNESCO's global Education for All program.

A Word to the Wise

It needs to be stated clearly that I whole heartedly believe that education is a good thing and ignorance is bad. I support good schools and the countless selfless, dedicated American teachers who stimulate our children to think creatively and independently, to excel, and to love learning. A good, solid basic classical education can help any person to achieve more of his or her full potential in life.

But what I am unalterably opposed to is the idea that an elite educational oligarchy, or an organized bureaucracy of teachers and administrators, should be able to secretly impose a one-size-fits-all educational curriculum on the whole world. An especially objectionable aspect of this scheme is the fact that traditional academic excellence is being sacrificed in furtherance of the larger goal of widespread mass indoctrination in politically correct attitudes.

This unconscionable substitution of political propaganda for classical curricula and revisionist myth for historical fact is the antithesis of true education and thus must be anathema to every legitimate intellectual.

I think it appropriate to close out this chapter with a "Word to the Wise" from William F. Jasper, a long-time researcher and journalistic analyst of UNESCO:

> The one-world architects at the UN have big designs for UNESCO: they intend for it to become a global school board that will set global academic standards, design and certify curricula, guide school accreditation standards, monitor national educational compliance with UN mandates, fund education programs—and much more.[30]

We will explore that "much more" in greater depth in future chapters.

2

GLOBAL LAND USE REGULATION AND SUSTAINABLE DEVELOPMENT

What do the Statue of Liberty, Independence Hall, and Monticello have in common? The average American with a smattering of historical knowledge might say that those historic sites are all symbolic of America's unique heritage of freedom.

Monticello, of course, was the home of Thomas Jefferson, the author of the Declaration of Independence. That seminal document was signed in Independence Hall (as was the US Constitution, a few years later). The Statue of Liberty is a symbol of the free nation under God that those founding documents created.

What about the Great Smoky Mountains, Yellowstone National Park, the Florida Everglades, and the Grand Canyon? These priceless natural resources are all managed by the US National Parks Service. They are among the most frequently visited natural recreation areas in America, where millions of American families vacation every year.

Would it surprise you to learn that every one of these unique American landmarks is also controlled by the United Nations? That is amazing but true.

Every one of the natural and historic treasures listed above—plus more than a dozen more in America—has been designated an official

World Heritage Site by UNESCO, which is headquartered in Paris, France. These sites are designated as protected areas under UNESCO's Convention Concerning the Protection of the World Cultural and Natural Heritage, a 1972 treaty that has now been ratified by 178 nations, including the United States, over the past three decades.

Sites included in the World Heritage program are considered to contribute "outstanding universal value to humanity" as part of our common world heritage. According to UNESCO, this designation currently includes 812 properties located in 137 nations.[1]

Who actually owns the World Heritage sites that make the UN's list?

That is a tricky "frequently asked question" that the UN artfully dodges and doesn't really answer. The World Heritage Center website responds vaguely, as follows: "While fully respecting the national sovereignty, and without prejudice to property rights provided by national legislation, the State Parties recognize that the protection of the World Heritage is the duty of the international community as a whole."[2]

That sounds to me like the UN is saying that it can step in at will to "protect" any one of these designated World Heritage sites whenever the "State Party" where the site is located isn't doing a satisfactory job of managing and maintaining it—as decided by the UN's international bureaucrats in Paris.

Yet another statement on the UNESCO website makes their true position clearer. "What makes the concept of World Heritage unique is its universal application," it explains. *"World Heritage sites belong to all the peoples of the world, irrespective of the territory on which they are located."*[3]

Somehow, the UN's strange idea that "all the peoples of the world" own Independence Hall, the birthplace of our American Republic, or the towering trees of Redwood National Park in Northern California just doesn't sit too well with me.

UN Biosphere Reserve Land Grabs

But, wait—there's more. In addition to those twenty World Heritage sites, there are also at least forty-seven locations in America that have been designated as UN Biosphere Reserves, which are vast parcels of land set aside for conservation and scientific study. Of these Biosphere Reserve sites, twenty-two are national parks and fifteen are national forests.

Symbolized by the Egyptian ankh, the UN's Man and Biosphere program is designed to help humans achieve a "balanced relationship with the natural world"—again, through the "sustainable use" of natural resources.[4]

UNESCO's 1968 Biosphere Reserve Conference began an insidious incremental process that culminated with almost fifty national treasures of the United States being added to the UN Biosphere Reserves program under the auspices of UNESCO. Some of these sites include the Statue of Liberty in New York Harbor, the Liberty Bell and Independence Hall in Philadelphia, and Yellowstone National Park. There are plans to add approximately seventy more US sites to that list.

What does all this mean in real life? Well, nothing, if you believe the UN.

"The idea that the United Nations is taking over US lands, private and public, is completely false. Neither the United Nations nor any other international body has any authority over public or private US lands which have received recognition as Biosphere Reserves. . . . Biosphere Reserves have no international or other authority," claims an "Open Letter" by Roger E. Soles, Ph.D., executive director of the US MAB program, on their website. Their list of common "myths" about MAB includes vehement denials that the program results in any "loss of sovereignty" or threat to private property.[5]

Others see it differently. Henry Lamb, executive vice president of the Environmental Conservation Organization and chairman of Sovereignty International, a pro-American organization, says that the operational guidelines developed by the UN are already effectively being enforced by the US government agencies that manage the World Heritage and MAB sites locally.

Lamb insists that the UN goals are secretly but effectively being accomplished by the administrative agencies of the US government, without either the oversight of the Congress or the consent of the American people.

> Neither Congress, nor any state legislature, has ever voted to approve any of the forty-seven UN Biosphere Reserves in the United States. International committees of bureaucrats, none of whom is elected, craft the management policy for millions of acres covered by these reserves. To comply with "international obligations," the United States conforms its management policy and, in some cases, its law to accommodate the wishes of bureaucrats that are completely unknown to the people who are governed by the policies. This reality is but a hint of what is in store for those governed by the rule of international law. Massive documents, such as the 1140-page *Global Biodiversity Assessment*, the 300-page *Agenda 21*, and the 410-page *Our Global Neighborhood*, all paint a picture of the international law that is being devised to govern the world in the 21st century.[6]

Later we will take a look at representative sections of the UN documents referenced by Lamb, because they lay out a detailed framework for future international control. But first we need to understand clearly how these Biosphere Reserves are set up.

Every Biosphere Reserve site consists of a legally protected *core area*, set aside strictly for conservation and research purposes; a surrounding *buffer zone*, where limited human activity is allowed; and a larger *transition area*, where humans may live and work, provided they do so in an environmentally responsible way.

But even outside the protected core area, normal human activity and land use that would otherwise be perfectly legal may be severely restricted whenever any protected site is judged to be "in danger."

For example, in 1995 President Bill Clinton got the UN to declare Yellowstone Park a "World Heritage Site in Danger." That gave him the so-called "international obligation" to close down a proposed gold mine about to begin operation on private property three miles away—despite the fact that the area had been mined for 150 years before Yellowstone Park was created, and that the Crown Butte Mines, which had just completed a prolonged and costly permit application process, had won an award for excellence in 1992.

Today, Yellowstone Park is still considered to be in danger, according to the UN, because of "year-round visitor pressure." Too many US tourists taking their kids to see Old Faithful, the global bureaucrats in Paris say.[7]

The president has the sole authority to approve these UN site designations. Congress has no oversight, and average American citizens have no input. Twice the House of Representatives has passed the American Land Sovereignty Protection Act or a similar bill requiring congressional approval before any more precious pieces of America can be designated as either UN Biosphere Reserves or World Heritage sites. But so far, the Senate has refused even to bring the measure up for a vote.[8]

Call me old-fashioned, but I still think Americans, not UNESCO bureaucrats, ought to control American land. Why are our elected leaders, both Republicans and Democrats, conservatives and liberals, allowing the UN to wield this kind of influence inside our nation's borders? US taxpayers should be outraged!

At least one conservative legislator, former Rep. Helen Chenoweth-Hage of Idaho, has forcefully expressed her opposition to the UN's environmental agenda, primarily because it subtly subverts the individual's right to own and control private property. In an article entitled "The United Nation's Big Green Machine," Chenoweth-Hage explains the subtle but very real danger of the UN's World Heritage and Man and Biosphere programs.

Working in collaboration with "green government" officials and eco-extremist groups, the UNESCO folks are helping effect policies that are gradually transforming these sites in ways that are detrimental to US interests, to the environment, and to the US citizens most directly affected. . . . However, the rights of all Americans are threatened by these policies and programs. . . .

Most of the socialist proposals pouring out of the UN today do not call for the outright abolition of private property. The collectivists who craft them are more clever than that. Nevertheless, that is where they are leading. They are using "green" fascism, actually, which relies on taxation and regulation, rather than overt expropriation, to destroy property rights. They are not so much challenging the right to own property *per se*, as they are making it increasingly difficult and onerous to do so. Holding title to the land is only one of the essential components of private property rights. Control of its use and disposition are equally important components.[9]

In the case of Yellowstone Park, for example, the UN bureaucrats were not content with merely closing down one nearby mining operation. Once they had gotten their foot in the door, according to Chenoweth-Hage, these international busybodies demanded the right to "review all policies involving mining, timber, wildlife, and tourism within an area of nearly 18 million acres surrounding the park"! One-quarter of that land is privately owned, but is considered to be part of the "Greater Yellowstone Ecosystem," and thus may be subject to arbitrary UN restriction in the future.

If anyone doubts what the UN's basic attitude is toward private property, one has only to look back thirty years to the official land policy articulated in the official *Conference Report* produced at the United Nations Conference on Human Settlements. This conference, commonly known as Habitat I, was held in Vancouver, British Columbia, in 1976. The preamble to agenda item 10, which defines land use policy, reads as follows:

> Land . . . cannot be treated as an ordinary asset, controlled by individuals and subject to the pressures and inefficiencies of the market. Private land ownership is also an instrument of accumulation and concentration of wealth, and therefore, contributes to social injustice; if unchecked, it may become a major obstacle in the planning and implementation of development schemes. The provision of decent dwellings and healthy conditions for the people can only be achieved if land is used in the interests of society as a whole. Public control of land use is therefore indispensable.[10]

This socialistic UN policy on land has not changed over time. In fact, almost everything the organization has done since then has served its ultimate goal: the eventual abolition of private property ownership as Americans have known it for four hundred years.

Jeane Kirkpatrick, former US Ambassador to the UN under President Ronald Reagan, has offered the following explanation for the socialist bent of the United Nations, especially where private property rights are concerned:

> In UN organizations, there is no accountability. UN bureaucrats are far removed from American voters. . . . Some come from countries that do not allow the ownership of private property. . . . What recourse does an American voter have when UN bureaucrats from Cuba or Iraq or Libya (all of which are parties to the [World Heritage] Treaty) have made a decision that unjustly damages his or her property rights that lie near a national park? When the World Heritage committee's meddling has needlessly encumbered a private United States citizen's land and caused his or her property values to fall, that citizen's appeals to these committees (if that is even possible) will fall on deaf ears.[11]

The rest of the world does not hold the same respect for private property rights, nor afford them the same level of protection, that we in

America traditionally have been privileged to enjoy. The global trend is toward ever greater governmental regulation and control, not toward greater individual freedom, responsibility, and opportunity.

Re-Wilding America: The One-Hundred-Year Plan

The foregoing is public information that is readily available. What is not so commonly known is the rest of the long-term plan, as envisioned by certain radical environmental activists who promote the philosophy of "deep ecology."

This warped ecocentric worldview holds among its cardinal tenets the idea that all life, whether human or animal, is of equal value, and that all human consumption above what is "vital" to basic human needs is immoral. Thus the population of humans, who are often viewed as destructive parasites, must decrease, and civilization as we know it must radically change in order to restore a proper natural balance to the planet.

The Wildlands Project, co-founded in 1991 by the EarthFirst! environmental extremist Dave Foreman, is devoted to "re-wilding" the North American continent by limiting all human activity and taking approximately 50 percent of the land mass of the United States of America back to permanent wilderness status—all for the protection of biological diversity.

Under this model of "biodiversity conservation," the various Biosphere Reserve core sites will eventually be connected to one another by vast tracts of roadless wildlife corridors that will allow wild animals to migrate unmolested between the sites. The transition areas where civilized human activity is allowed will be organized into "sustainable communities" that lie like small islands surrounded by oceans of wilderness.

The ultimate goal of those environmentalists who are most feverishly pushing the UN World Heritage and Biosphere Reserves programs is to establish "a regional reserve system which will ultimately tie the North American continent into a single Biodiversity Reserve." This vast new wilderness area will be called Turtle Island.[12]

"In North America, there is hope that our animals, our wild places, and our spirit of adventure will continue forever," proclaims the official Wildlands Project website. "Our vision is Room to Roam, and lots of it. We must connect parks and protected areas from Canada to Mexico, from the Pacific to the Atlantic."[13]

The self-described "group of conservation biologists and wilderness advocates" who comprise the Wilderness Project are unabashed about their one-hundred-year plan to re-wild America. And they are proud to proclaim that they are already winning, on a global scale.

> People called the vision delusional, a hallucination of romantics. More than a decade later, however, the basic concepts first proposed by the Wildlands Project are now mainstream. The idea of reconnecting and restoring wildlands on a continental scale has been widely adopted by conservation groups both large and small. Today, the Wildlands Project's vision can be seen working across North America and around the globe. Dozens of partner groups are actively turning the Wildlands Project's vision into reality in places as varied as Australia, South Africa, and Siberia.[14]

While most Americans might view as ridiculous the idea of destroying human civilization in order to preserve wild animals in a state of nature, there actually are a number of influential people and organizations devoted to just such a radical restructuring of American society, and indeed of all human life on earth as we know it.

Apparently this extreme ecocentric approach is consistent with the goals and environmental agenda of the UN, because according to one analyst, the Wildlands Project model is "also referred to as the principle design for biodiversity protection within Section 10 of the United

Nations' Global Diversity Assessment authorized under the UN Convention for Biodiversity."[15]

In fact, it was largely because this radical re-wilding agenda was revealed at the last minute, and the accompanying threat to the private property rights of individual American citizens was recognized, that the US Senate delayed a rushed September 1994 vote on the Biodiversity Treaty and ultimately refused to ratify it.

According to Senator Kay Bailey Hutchison of Texas, who opposed the treaty on the Senate floor, the potential impact on American citizens could have proven to be massive and devastating. Here is what she said, and what stopped the proposed treaty dead in its tracks:

> I am especially concerned about the effect of the treaty on private property rights in my state and throughout America. Private property is constitutionally protected, yet one of the draft protocols to this treaty proposes "an increase in the area and connectivity of habitat." It envisions buffer zones and corridors connecting habitat areas where human use will be severely limited. Are we going to agree to a treaty that will require the US government to condemn property for wildlife highways? Are we planning to pay for this property?
>
> Article 10 of the treaty states that we must "protect and encourage customary use of biological resources that are compatible with conservation or sustainable use requirements"—as set by the treaty. Whether our ranchers could continue to use public and private land for grazing could depend not just on the Secretary of the Interior's latest grazing rulemaking, but on whether grazing is considered a compatible use for conservation under the treaty. This bio-diversity treaty could preempt the decisions of local, state, and federal lawmakers for use of our natural resources. The details that are left for negotiation could subject every wetlands permit, building permit, waste disposal permit, and incidental taking permit to international review.
>
> We would be subjecting property owners to international review,

which would be yet another step in the already egregious bureaucratic processes, just to have the very basic permits necessary for the use of their own private property. [16]

While we are, of course, grateful for Senator Hutchison's accurate analysis of the danger posed by the UN's unconstitutional and virtually all-pervasive environmental agenda, and for the fact that the Biodiversity Treaty was not ratified that day, we still would be well advised to note the smug satisfaction implicit in the following statement on the Wildlands Project's website in 2005: "More than a decade later . . . *the basic concepts first proposed by the Wildlands Project are now mainstream*" (emphasis added).

If it is true that the previously radical idea of re-wilding, on both a continental and an international level, has now become an article of mainstream orthodoxy among most environmentalist activists, then our future under UN influence and control may indeed be bleak and threatening for human beings everywhere.

It may be helpful to our further study to try to understand just how this sad state of affairs has come to be.

A Brief History of the Greening of Planet Earth

We have come a long way since Teddy Roosevelt, an avid outdoorsman who wanted to preserve certain portions of our pristine national wilderness areas from the ravages of the Industrial Revolution, established the National Parks system more than a century ago. Roosevelt's desire to protect our natural heritage led him to propose unity among nations in environmental protection efforts. But the advent of World War I, the Great Depression, and then World War II all served to hinder those efforts from bearing fruit.

Nevertheless, two famous conservation organizations were established during the intervening years between the two world wars. In

1933, a wealthy socialist writer and conservationist named Bob Marshall created the Wilderness Society because he "believed that private ownership would certainly destroy America's forests." In 1936, the National Wildlife Federation was formed. These organizations have lobbied consistently for various environmental initiatives on both the national and international levels ever since.

Then in 1948, the famous British biologist Sir Julian Huxley, the new head of UNESCO, was instrumental in organizing a conference of environmental experts at Fontainebleau, France. The result of that conference was the creation of a loose-knit network of organizations collectively called the International Union for the Protection of Nature (IUPN), with headquarters in Brussels, Belgium. Their initial desire was ostensibly to protect the natural world from the ravages of modern warfare, and so the IUPN introduced the concept of environmental education to the UN.

A few years later, as the movement for European decolonization began to gain momentum, the IUPN abandoned Belgium and moved to Switzerland, changing its name to the International Union for the Conservation of Nature (IUCN). The group was small and poorly funded until the early 1960s, when growing awareness of the plight of overhunted wildlife in Africa—fueled largely by articles written by Huxley and published in the British press—led IUCN to establish the World Wildlife Fund (WWF) as an adjunct charitable organization in 1961.

The two groups shared office space on the banks of Lake Geneva. Soon the WWF coffers were overflowing with the charitable donations of kindhearted people worldwide, and the WWF was financing most of the operations of IUCN.[17]

Enlisting the aid of both the British and Dutch royal families, the WWF raised large sums of money over the next two decades. Working closely with one another, by the 1970s the two well-funded NGOs were able to exert disproportionately significant influence in directing the course of global environmental policy.

Flourishing under the leadership of Francois Bourliere from 1963 to

1966, the IUCN ultimately became a powerful force behind the International Treaty on Wetlands, signed in Ramsar, Iran, in 1971. That same year, Bouliere was appointed chairman of the first Man and Biosphere International Coordinating Council, which eventually resulted in the UN's global MAB program.

Throughout the 1970s, the WWF focused its efforts on raising money to save tigers in India and protect marine mammals such as whales, dolphins and seals. IUCN, meanwhile, established a traffic system to monitor the international trade in wildlife products. In 1973, the IUCN in Washington successfully promoted the UN's Treaty on Endangered Species, and afterward drafted global governing policy documents pertaining to wetlands, biosphere reserves, and endangered species.

In 1979, the IUCN was instrumental in persuading the Carter administration to launch the UN's Man and Biosphere Program in the US by means of an unpublicized US State Department agreement with UNESCO, which was ordered by the White House, even though there was no congressional approval of or authorization for the project.[18]

In 1980, both the IUCN and the WWF collaborated with the United Nations Environment Programme (UNEP) to publish a joint World Conservation Strategy. This document, which was later published in seven languages as a simplified version called *How to Save the World*, "recommended a holistic approach to conservation and highlighted the importance of using natural resources sustainably."[19]

A decade later, the same three organizations once again jointly published a major global environmental policy statement, *Caring for the Earth: A Strategy for Sustainable Living*. This important 1990 document emphasized the newest focus of the international environmental zealots: the recently recognized crisis of climate change and global warming, and therefore the necessity of reducing air pollution and the consumption of fossil fuels.

The WWF's website brags that the organization "played a part in pressuring governments to sign conventions on biodiversity and climate change at the United Nations Conference on Environment and Development," also known as the Earth Summit, held in Rio de Janeiro in 1992.[20]

The IUCN is also credited with being the author of the "sustainable communities" concept as well as the crucial Agenda 21 document—which has been called "a laundry list of recommendations designed to reorganize society around the central principle of protecting the environment"—that also emerged from Rio.[21]

Thus these two relatively unknown NGOs have been twisting arms worldwide to get the governments of sovereign nation-states to accept their latest version of revealed truth relative to fossil fuels, clean air, and global warming.

They have also been on the cutting edge of introducing to the world at large the most important environmental concept of the twentieth century: the brand new idea of sustainable development.

Understanding Sustainable Development

The primary vehicle being used by the UN to encroach on the sovereignty of independent nation-states is the so-called global environmental threat, and specifically the grim specter of global warming, which has only recently burst full blown upon the consciousness of the "international community."

In response to this dimly perceived common danger, now ostensibly confronting all mankind, a massive UN propaganda campaign has pronounced a moral claim upon the whole hearted allegiance of every enlightened, ecology-minded global citizen to the relatively new doctrine of sustainable development. It is a testament to the effectiveness of that global propaganda blitz that within a single generation, the focus of the entire world has shifted to so-called sustainable lifestyles.

From the smallest township to the largest city in America, citizens are constantly being barraged with exhortations to "think globally, act locally," as they faithfully recycle and employ best use practices in every facet of their lives, and strive mightily to practice tolerance, respect multiculturalism, and celebrate diversity. Still, very few people have connected this massive quantum shift in politically correct public perceptions and attitudes with an equally massive top-down global re-education effort by the UN, in the form of one international convention after another, each of which has generated at least one conference report, action plan, set of targeted goals, timetable for achievement, etc. These international gatherings are held in distant locations all over the world, so that it is hard for any single individual to keep up with all that is happening. Yet the cumulative effect of their mutually reinforcing conclusions is building into what appears to be a powerful edifice of international policy.

Twenty years ago, scarcely one American in a thousand would have heard of the now-popular buzzword "sustainability," or given much thought to others such as "endangered species," "greenhouse gases," or "biodiversity." Yet today a Google search for a "definition of sustainable development" produces 114 million responses. Here are just a few of those definitions.

- Improving the quality of human life while living within the carrying capacity of supporting ecosystems. (Caring for the Earth, IUCN/WWF/UNEP, 1991, www.interenvironment.org/wd1intro/glossary.htm.)
- Development that meets the needs of the present without compromising the ability of future generations to meet their own needs. It contains within it two key concepts: the concept of "needs," in particular the essential needs of the world's poor, to which overriding priority should be given; and the idea of limitations imposed by the state of technology and social organization on the environment's ability to meet present and the future needs. (Report of the Brundtland Commission, 1987, www.unisdr.org/eng/library/lib-terminology-eng%20home.htm.)[22]

- One of the factors which sustainable development must overcome is environmental degradation. (Wikipedia online encyclopedia, en.wikipedia.org/wiki/Sustainable_development.)

The fundamental idea here is one of frugality and the exercise of responsible stewardship. After all, most would agree that it is just common sense for people to live within their means. We shouldn't buy things on credit, for example, if we don't have a job and an income that will allow us to pay the bills when they come due.

This is the same basic principle involved in the idea of sustainable development. We should not deplete our finite resources today at the expense of ourselves or those who will come after us tomorrow. Again, this is one of those seemingly obvious propositions that is hard to condemn.

Unfortunately, conservation is not all that is involved with sustainable development, as defined by the UN environmentalists. Their definitions carry a lot of excess baggage.

The first definition above contains the loaded phrase "while living within the carrying capacity of supporting ecosystems." This implies that the maximum carrying capacities of those ecosystems is both finite and clearly defined. In some instances, that may be the case, but not always. And then there's the troublesome question of who defines the limits of those carrying capacities—the property owner whose land use is in question, or the UN expert who wants to regulate it on the basis of his own official agenda.

The second definition clearly indicates the desire by global planners to impose artificial limits on human consumption, in the same way that a dieter might strictly limit the daily intake of calories. It also seems to assign a moral superiority to the needs of "the poor," as opposed to those of all others.

Finally, the third definition implies that all "environmental degradation" is both predictable and avoidable, rather than being at times an integral part of the natural process of life.

It remains to be seen whether these official definitions of sustainable development will stand up to close scrutiny, rational analysis, and principled opposition by those who believe in personal liberty in the conservative American tradition.

What is becoming increasingly obvious, though, is the fact that this new environmentalist ideology is being systematically developed and has been disseminated by the UN for more than two decades.

Major Milestones along the Path of Sustainable Development

In 1980, the UN's Independent Commission on International Development, chaired by the former chancellor of West Germany, Willy Brandt (and therefore commonly known as the Brandt Commission), issued a report called *North-South: A Program for Survival*, which tasked the developed (northern) nations of the world with the responsibility for helping the undeveloped (southern) nations rise up out of poverty. This report contained the first real seeds of the sustainable development idea.

The UN World Commission on Environment and Development, also known as the Brundtland Commission, met in 1987 in Nairobi. Their conference report, *Our Common Future*, clearly defined sustainable development for the first time. Maurice Strong was a commission member.

The 1992 Earth Summit in Rio de Janeiro, chaired by Maurice Strong, produced a comprehensive plan of action called Agenda 21. Later in 1992, the UN created its Commission on Sustainable Development to advance the recommendations of Agenda 21. That same year Strong set up his own NGO, called the Earth Council, in Costa Rica to promote the idea of sustainable development among the various nation-states around the world.

In 1993, Bill Clinton signed Executive Order No. 12852, establishing the President's Council on Sustainable Development to promote the objectives of Agenda 21 in America. Jonathan Lash, president of the World Resources Institute, was co-chair.

The 1992 Convention on Biodiversity was *not* ratified by the US Senate in 1994, yet the Clinton-Gore administration voluntarily implemented the UN's recommended Ecosystem Management Policy to control all Man and Biosphere sites in America.

The UN's newly established Division for Sustainable Development held its first meeting in New York City in 1994.

In August 2002, ten years after the Earth Summit met at Rio, the World Summit on Sustainable Development was held in Johannesburg, South Africa. This convention reaffirmed the UN's commitment to implementing the global goals of Agenda 21 but also broadened its scope to include social justice and poverty eradication as key elements of sustainable development, and then developed specific action plans designed to produce measurable results. The UN has designated the ten-year period from 2005 through 2014 as the UN Decade for Education for Sustainable Development, under the auspices of UNESCO.

The point of this chronology is to establish beyond any doubt the fact that the UN has had an ongoing agenda of promoting the doctrine of sustainable development for at least the past twenty years. The environmental zealots and socialist land control regulators clearly have a vision for the future that is very different from what most Americans have known in the past, or would want to accept.

Henry Lamb has been studying and writing about the United Nations' socialist environmental agenda for as long as the sustainable development idea has been around. He has formulated the following concise summary of the ideological clash that looms ahead, and asks a question we would do well to ponder as we move to the next chapter.

Sustainable development is a concept constructed on the principle that government has the right and the responsibility to regulate the affairs of people to achieve government's vision of the greatest good for us all.

The United States is founded on the principle that government has no rights or responsibility not specifically granted to it by the people who are governed. These two concepts cannot long coexist. One principle, or the other, will eventually dominate. . . .

The question that remains unanswered is: will Americans accept this new sustainable future that has been planned for them and imposed upon them?[23]

3

GLOBAL WARMING AND GLOBAL ENVIRONMENTAL CONTROL

When former president Bill Clinton addressed movers and shakers of international business, finance, and politics at the World Economic Forum in Davos, Switzerland, in January of 2006, he reiterated his personal belief that climate change is the greatest threat facing our world today.

"First, I worry about climate change," Clinton told Klaus Schwab, the forum's founder, during an onstage discussion. "It's the only thing that I believe has the power to fundamentally end the march of civilization as we know it, and make a lot of the other efforts that we're making irrelevant and impossible." Clinton warned the influential crowd that the only way for humanity to avoid slipping into another Ice Age would be to launch "a serious global effort to develop a clean energy future."[1]

Clinton's comments were similar to those he had made a month earlier at the United Nations Climate Change Conference in Montreal, Canada. One of the largest international events ever held in Canada, the two-week-long UN conference attracted more than ten thousand delegates from around the world, primarily diplomats and environmentalists from more than 180 nations.

"There's no longer any serious doubt that climate change is real, accelerating, and caused by human activities," Clinton told the enthusiastic crowd. "We are uncertain about how deep and the time of arrival of the consequences, but we are quite clear they will not be good."

Speaking on the final day of the conference, Clinton sounded a hopeful note when he said that with a "serious disciplined effort" to develop alternative forms of energy for the future, "we could meet and surpass the Kyoto targets in a way that would strengthen and not weaken our economies."[2]

He was referring, of course, to the controversial Kyoto Protocol, which was largely negotiated by Vice President Al Gore in 1997 while Clinton was president. Although Clinton supported the international treaty, he never presented it to the Republican-controlled US Senate for ratification because he knew that the treaty was doomed to fail there.

Clinton has since criticized the Bush administration for renouncing the Kyoto treaty in 2001, rather than using White House clout to push it through the Senate. President Bush claims that implementing the treaty will seriously hurt the US economy, but Clinton says those fears are just "flat wrong." Clinton has emerged as a major spokesman for the Kyoto accord, promoting it through the Clinton Global Initiative climate-change program of his William J. Clinton Foundation.

So far, all of the world's major industrialized nations except the United States have accepted the Kyoto Protocol, which officially went into effect in February 2005, when Russia became the 156th country to ratify the pact. The treaty legally obligates thirty-five industrialized nations to reduce emissions from carbon dioxide and greenhouse gases to approximately 6 to 8 percent below their 1990 levels by 2012.

At the Montreal conference, the assembled delegates discussed even more stringent emissions control requirements to take effect after Kyoto expires in 2012. Many criticized the United States for refusing to participate in those negotiations.

"It's such a pity the United States is still very much unwilling to join the international community, to have a multilateral effort to deal with climate change," said the leader of the African group of nations, Emily Ojoo Masawa of Kenya.[3]

Liberal environmentalists in Montreal blamed the United States for hindering global progress toward bringing climate change under control. "When you walk around the conference hall here, delegates are saying there are lots of issues on the agenda, but there's only one real problem, and that's the United States," said Bill Hare of Greenpeace International.[4]

But US leaders point to the fact that the American government is spending upward of $3 billion per year on research and development of alternative energy sources and energy-saving technologies, and they argue that such voluntary efforts make a real and lasting contribution toward solving whatever environmental problems may exist. "I reject the premise that the Kyoto-like agreement is necessary to address this issue," senior US climate negotiator Harlan Wilson told the assembled delegates in Montreal.[5]

Even before the major Montreal conference, some prominent political figures who had previously endorsed the Kyoto Protocol had begun to express misgivings. British Prime Minister Tony Blair, for example, formerly a staunch advocate of Kyoto, had dinner with President Bush last summer and had hoped to convince him to accept the Kyoto treaty. Afterward, Blair said that it was "no longer productive to chastise Washington" for refusing Kyoto, according to news reports in the *Scotsman*.

Blair told the House of Commons that the Americans "come at this issue as much from the point of view of energy security and supply, as much as climate change." Noting the "limitations" of the Kyoto Accord, Blair said he hoped to develop "some sort of continuing process that locks in not just the US but those emerging countries, China and India in particular, without whom it is very difficult to see how we are going to make progress."[6]

Three months later, Blair made major waves at the ritzy inaugural meeting of the Clinton Global Initiative—which was similar to Mikhail

Gorbachev's State of the World Forums, both in format and in high-powered participants—which was held in New York City in September 2005.

"My thinking has changed in the past three or four years," Blair publicly announced. "No country is going to cut its growth" the way Kyoto would require. Blair said that he had come to realize that Great Britain cannot meet Kyoto's requirements without severely limiting its economic growth and thereby courting economic disaster. Nor could the Kyoto scheme possibly work without the cooperation of the larger developing countries that are currently excluded from the treaty, Blair insisted. China and India, especially, would never agree to shut down their newly emerging economies and so doom their countries to continued poverty.[7]

In discussing the concept of climate change, we have to realize that the topic is directly related to the concept of global warming. While most people have heard these terms, not everyone understands clearly what they mean. So to clarify these issues and to put these concepts into better perspective, we need to examine their history.

Where Did This New Idea Come From?

Bill Clinton has ominously warned that a phenomenon called extreme climate change—which is linked to and ostensibly caused by global warming—is "the only thing that . . . has the power to fundamentally end the march of civilization as we know it." He has further forcefully declared this phenomenon to be "real, accelerating, and caused by human activities."

Such serious warnings might well cause a reasonably prudent person to believe that immediate corrective action is required, especially if the dire warning comes from someone with respectable public credentials. When such alarming rhetoric comes from the former leader of the free world, it is especially hard to disbelieve or ignore.

So . . . is former president Clinton right or wrong? Is humanity really facing major global consequences by refusing to act immediately upon this perceived environmental threat? The answer to that question is vital.

The threat of global warming was virtually unheard of until 1988, when it burst upon the consciousness of the world literally overnight. The ripple effect of that bold new idea has generated far-reaching tides of public opinion in less than two decades. Today, practically every literate inhabitant of planet Earth has been exposed to the theory of global warming, and most people have come to accept the scientific validity of that theory as being the conventional wisdom of our time.

James Hansen, a prominent NASA scientist who specialized in using computer modeling to analyze the earth's climate, first introduced the concept of global warming in 1983 in an article in *Science* magazine. Hansen predicted that "the continuing increase in fossil fuel use would lead to about 4.5-degree Fahrenheit global warming by the end of the twenty-first century." The prediction made headlines and global warming theory was born, but little was done by other scientists to study Hansen's theory.[8]

Five years later, in June 1988 during a blistering heat wave that parched the country and partially dried up the Mississippi River channel, Hansen gave a brief fifteen-minute testimony to a joint House and Senate committee chaired by Senator Timothy Wirth of Colorado. Hansen displayed what has come to be called the "hockey stick" graph, which showed an anticipated sharply spiking increase in carbon dioxide levels in the earth's atmosphere. He told the committee that 1988 would set a new heat record worldwide and that he was "99 percent confident" that the "greenhouse effect" was the cause.

"It's time to stop waffling so much and say that the greenhouse effect is here and is affecting our climate now," Hansen told reporters after the meeting. Hansen's statements were controversial among climate scientists, most of whom initially believed that he had "gone beyond his data" and overstated his claims. But newspapers and scientific journals seized on the issue and propelled this new greenhouse effect into the consciousness of the average citizen. *Time* magazine even named "Our Endangered Earth" its "Planet of the Year" for 1988.[9]

That same year, under the auspices of the World Meteorological Organization (WMO) and the United Nations Environmental Programme (UNEP), the UN established its own Intergovernmental Panel on Climate Change (IPCC). The stated purpose of the IPCC, according to the Wikipedia online encyclopedia, is to study and assess the "risk of human-induced climate change." The IPCC does not carry out its own research, but rather analyzes and reports on the published research of others. The periodically issued IPCC reports form the basis for much of the current consensus on climate change among scientists. Three IPCC reports have been issued, with a fourth due out in 2007.[10]

The IPCC's *First Assessment Report*, issued in 1990, was largely inconclusive as to whether human activity in general, and the use of fossil fuels in particular, was having any significant impact on the earth's climate. According to the Executive Summary of the first working group report, the scientists concluded:

> We are certain of the following: *there is a natural greenhouse effect* . . . ; emissions resulting from human activities are substantially increasing the atmospheric concentrations of the greenhouse gases: CO_2, methane, CFCs and nitrous oxide. These increases will enhance the greenhouse effect, resulting on average in an additional warming of the earth's surface. The main greenhouse gas, water vapor, will increase in response to global warming and further enhance it.
>
> We calculate with confidence that: . . . CO_2 has been responsible for over half the enhanced greenhouse effect; long-lived gases would require immediate reductions in emissions from human activities of over 60 percent to stabilize their concentrations at today's levels.
>
> *There are many uncertainties in our predictions particularly with regard to the timing, magnitude, and regional patterns of climate change,*

due to our incomplete understanding of: sources and sinks of CHGs; clouds; oceans; polar ice sheets.

Our judgment is that: *global mean surface air temperature has increased by 0.3 to 0.6 °C over the past 100 years . . . ; the size of this warming is broadly consistent with prediction of climate models, but is also of the same magnitude as natural climate variability;* alternatively this variability and other human factors could have offset a still larger human-induced greenhouse warming. The unequivocal detection of the enhanced greenhouse effect is not likely for a decade or more.[11]

That 1990 report and its 1992 supplement became the basis for the UN's Framework Convention on Climate Change (FCCC), a nonbinding international environmental treaty that was produced at the 1992 Earth Summit held in Rio de Janeiro. The goal of this voluntary treaty was to reduce greenhouse gas emissions in industrialized nations to their 1990 levels by the year 2000. The FCCC, which went into effect in 1994, was intended "to achieve stabilization of greenhouse gas concentrations in the atmosphere at a low enough level to prevent dangerous anthropogenic interference in the climate system."[12]

Thus we see that within four years after James Hansen first popularized the term *greenhouse effect,* and despite there being no conclusive scientific evidence that human activity had actually produced any significant global warming, the United Nations had implemented a formal treaty to limit "dangerous anthropogenic interference" in the earth's atmospheric environment.

This set the stage for the IPCC's 1995 *Second Assessment Report,* which was finalized in 1996. This controversial report became the basis for the Kyoto Protocol, which, unlike the FCCC, is a binding treaty. The US Senate ratified the FCCC but has not voted on the Kyoto Protocol.

The Second Assessment repeated the findings of the 1990 report as to the extent of discernible global warming over the previous one hundred years, but nevertheless contained the following statement: "The balance of evidence suggests a discernible human influence on global climate."[13]

Some scientists associated with producing the Second Assessment argued that the report was changed by UN bureaucrats after the working groups had finished their tasks, and that the final version did not reflect a true consensus of their findings.

"We produce a draft, and then the policymakers go through it line by line and change the way it is presented. . . . It's peculiar that they have the final say in what goes into a scientists' report," British scientist Keith Shine complained to Reuters News Service on 20 December 1995.[14]

One particularly harsh critic was Dr. Frederick Seitz, who wrote, "I have never witnessed a more disturbing corruption of the peer-review process than the events that led to this IPCC report."[15] As the president emeritus of Rockefeller University and the past president of the National Academy of Sciences, as well as the director of his own Science and Environmental Policy Project, Dr. Seitz has the scientific credentials to criticize.

Dr. Rajenda K. Pachauri, chairman of the IPCC, unapologetically dismissed the complaints of the critics. "Firstly, the Panel as a whole must always respect and consider the specific perspectives of each member. But, more importantly, each member must respect and consider the perspectives of the entire Panel," Pachauri said. "Consensus is not something that happens by itself. It is an outcome that has to be shaped, and the only basis for shaping it is to follow the two cardinal rules that I have just mentioned."[16]

From these remarks, one might conclude that the UN bureaucrats do have a political agenda of their own to accomplish, and they may not be above bending the scientific data to their purposes to accomplish that political agenda.

Pachauri's admonitions notwithstanding, S. Fred Singer, president of the Science and Environmental Policy Project, strongly challenged the policy implications of the IPCC Second Assessment summary's

main conclusion: "The ambiguous phrase 'the balance of evidence suggests a discernible human influence on global climate' has been (mis)inter-
preted by policymakers to mean that a major global warming
catastrophe will soon be upon us," Singer warned.[17]

The Fear Factor and the Big Freeze

That implication of impending environmental disaster has, in fact, been
reinforced by the emerging emphasis on extreme climate change, which
allegedly could happen suddenly and unexpectedly. Some environmental activists have warned apocalyptically that the accumulation of these
greenhouse gases could cause the earth to overheat quickly, melting the
polar ice caps and causing the sea levels to rise enough to threaten
coastal cities worldwide.

Paradoxically, this unchecked global warming could actually trigger
a big freeze that could bring on a disastrous new ice age virtually
overnight. According to some predictive computer models, the global
warming process could affect the Gulf Stream Drift in the North
Atlantic, which in turn affects both land temperatures and ocean currents. If melting ice from Greenland and the Arctic were to dilute the
salinity of the seawater quickly enough, it might interfere with the
ocean's thermohaline circulation system, which operates like a huge con-
veyor belt to move warm water to the north and return it to the south
as it cools. Shutting down this current's circulation system could theoretically result in a massive freeze and the abrupt start of a new ice age.

"A global circulation of water between the surfaces and the depths
of oceans plays a major role in keeping the earth's climate congenial to
life," explains a synopsis on the website of the Institute of Science in
Society (ISIS). "But this circulation is unstable to global warming, with
catastrophic consequences."[18]

Such an apocalyptic scenario, if true, would be terrifying. Some have
been happy to hype the fear factor, and Hollywood has been equally

happy to help. The 2004 movie *The Day After Tomorrow*, for example, portrayed just such a scenario, with a heroic scientist (transparently modeled after James Hansen) whose sophisticated computer models have predicted an abrupt, literally overnight transition into a new ice age. The hero's warnings are repeatedly ignored by top elected officials (particularly an insensitive vice president bearing a close resemblance to Dick Cheney) who crassly put the nation's perceived economic interests before legitimate environmental concerns. The result is a massive human tragedy that could have been avoided, if only the inept politicians had heeded the sound advice of the noble scientific experts.

Here's some of the PR hype from the movie's promotional website. After promising "sensational, mind-blowing special effects" and a "spectacular roller coaster ride that boasts pulse-pounding action," the writer summarizes the plot this way:

> When global warming triggers the onset of a new Ice Age, tornadoes flatten Los Angeles, a tidal wave engulfs New York City, and the entire Northern Hemisphere begins to freeze solid. Now climatologist Jack Hall (Dennis Quaid), his son Sam (Jake Gyllenhaal) and a small band of survivors must ride out the superstorm and stay alive in the face of an enemy more powerful and relentless than any they've ever encountered: Mother Nature.

The movie is a fantasy. But some researchers say the prospect that global warming might be affecting the Gulf Stream is not only possible, but is actually happening today. According to Harry Bryden at the National Oceanographic Center in Southampton, England, researchers have found that the circulation of ocean currents between Africa and the east coast of America has slowed 30 percent from what it was twelve years ago.

Measurements in 1957, 1981, and 1992 found the current fairly stable, but noticeable changes were observed in 1998. An expensive new network of moored monitoring instruments in the North Atlantic is designed to keep track of any significant changes in the future. Researchers want to know if this is a temporary variation or part of a more serious trend. But most dismiss the idea that the current will shut down completely and trigger a big freeze.

"The only way computer models have managed to simulate an entire shutdown of the current is to magic into existence millions of tons of fresh water and dump it into the Atlantic," said Chris West, director of the UK climate impacts program at Oxford University. "It's not clear where that water would ever come from, even taking into account increased Greenland melting."[19]

James Hansen Warns of Dangerous Climate Change

While most research scientists do not seriously contend that a *Day After Tomorrow* scenario is likely to occur in our lifetimes, some do see a very real threat from global warming, and they insist that drastic remedial action is needed before it is too late.

In fact, James Hansen himself has argued recently that carbon dioxide levels are "now surging well above" the danger point, and if something isn't done quickly, the environmental damage could be irreversible. Rising CO_2 levels, he insists, "imply changes that constitute practically a different planet." One of Hansen's ardent supporters has written that those changes include "famine, pestilence and flood."[20]

Hansen made these and similar charges in a December 2005 speech to the American Geophysical Union in San Francisco, entitled "Is There Still Time to Avoid 'Dangerous Anthropogenic Interference' with Global Climate?" Hansen expressed his opinion that significant reductions in CO_2 emissions, particularly from automobiles, could be achieved with existing technology, and he called on the United States to take the lead. Ten days later he publicly released data that he said proved that 2005 was the warmest year in the past century.

Afterward, Hansen complained to the *New York Times* that his public comments on the dangers of global warming were being censored by the Bush administration. "Communicating with the public seems to be essential," Hansen told the *Times*, "because public concern is probably the only thing capable of overcoming the special interests that have obfuscated the topic."[21]

Hansen, now sixty-three, has been in the media spotlight for more than twenty years, since he first brought the global warming issue to the forefront of public policy. He joined NASA in 1967 with excellent academic credentials from the University of Iowa, where he studied under Dr. James Van Allen in the space science program. He has been the longtime director of the Goddard Institute for Space Studies (GISS) and is also affiliated with Columbia University. He has long been highly respected in his field.[22]

And yet Hansen's public statements over the span of his career have been inconsistent, ranging from the sensationalistic claims of the 1980s to the more moderate tone he presented in the early 2000s. In fact, some of the positions he has taken in the recent past have actually supported the claims that his critics have been making all along, namely: that there is no incontrovertible evidence that global warming is either a serious threat or that it is caused by human activity; that the IPCC's reports are skewed with bad data and that CO_2 emissions are actually on the low end of the spectrum; and that the climate's sensitivity to greenhouse gas warming is much lower than previously thought.[23]

In fact, in 1998 Hansen even wrote in the Proceedings of the National Academy of Sciences that "the forcings that drive long-term climate change are not known with accuracy sufficient to define future climate change."[24]

One of Hansen's perennial critics is Patrick J. Michaels, a senior fellow in environmental studies at the Cato Institute and the author of *Meltdown: The Predictable Distortion of Global Warming by Scientists, Politicians, and the Media*, which was published in 2004. Michaels took particular umbrage with Hansen's self-serving hypocrisy in telling the

New York Times on 8 February that "the foundation of democracy is . . . an honestly informed public."

Hansen has himself advocated the use of exaggeration and propaganda as political tools in the debate over global warming. In the March 2004 issue of *Scientific American*, Hansen wrote, "*Emphasis on extreme scenarios may have been appropriate at one time, when the public and decision-makers were relatively unaware of the global warming issue.* . . . Now, however, the need is for demonstrably objective climate forcing scenarios . . ."

In other words, Hansen thought the public should be subjected to nightmare scenarios regardless of the scientific likelihood of catastrophe, simply in order to gain people's attention. And further, that the lurid pictures that have been painted aren't objective after all. . . .

So now he says the time has come to tell the truth, and he is being censored. Why should we believe him now? What evidence can he give us that his opinions and statements about climate change are suddenly true, when he admits to having misrepresented the facts in the past? Was the public being "honestly informed" then? Hansen is far from alone in exaggerating climate change for his own political agenda. In 1989, at the same time Hansen was "emphasizing extreme scenarios," Dr. Stephen Schneider, now at Stanford University, opined in *Discover* magazine that "*we have to offer up scary scenarios, make simplified, dramatic statements, and make little mention of any doubts we might have.*" Hardly a recipe for encouraging an "honestly informed public."[25]

Other critics have pointed out that Hansen has publicly criticized the Bush administration repeatedly, even to the point of making a speech in Iowa, virtually on the eve of the 2004 election, in which he claimed scientists were being muzzled and voiced his intention of voting for John Kerry. It is also noteworthy that in 2001, Hansen was the recipient of the Heinz Award, which was presented by Theresa Heinz Kerry.[26]

The New Conventional Wisdom on Global Warming

But even though there is plenty of room to find fault with Hansen as a scientist, the global warming "movement" that he started two decades ago is still carrying the day in the public mind. According to Wikipedia, the scientific controversy has largely been decided in favor of Hansen's theories.

> There is an ongoing dispute about what effect humans have on global climate and what policies should be followed to mitigate any current detrimental effects, and prevent future detrimental effects. Although not fully settled, *the current consensus from the official scientific communities on climate change is that recent warming is largely human-caused. There is near consensus among scientists that global warming is already occurring due to greenhouse gases.*[27]

Belief in the factuality of global warming theory has become virtually an article of faith within the scientific and educational establishments, as well as among the UN environmental bureaucrats. In England, for example, the retiring president of the Royal Society has warned scientists to resist the "denial lobby" that does not accept the reality of climate change.

"Sadly, for many, the response is to retreat from complexity and difficulty by embracing the darkness of fundamentalist unreason," Lord May of Oxford said. He equated the danger of rejecting scientific orthodoxy on climate change with the threat posed by groups in America who want creationism to be taught in science classes. "By their own writings, this group has a much wider agenda, which is to replace scientific materialism by something more based on faith," Lord May explained. He urged scientists to resist both efforts to promote "intelligent design" and "other threats to scientific values." So pervasive is this politically correct mentality on climate change that scientists who disagree often feel ostracized by their peers. One such dissenter is Roger A. Pielke Sr., a climatologist at Colorado State University, who has recently resigned from a panel that is working on a government report on atmospheric temperature trends for the Bush administration.

"When you appoint people to a committee who are experts in an area but are evaluating their own work, it's very difficult for them to think outside the box of their own research," Pielke told the *New York Times*. Pielke believes that the publication of several papers by panel members in the 11 August online edition of the journal *Science* was an attempt to influence the final content of the panel's report.[28]

"[The report's] main focus is to explore why thermometers at the Earth's surface, especially in the tropics, have measured more warming than has been detected by satellites and weather balloons in the troposphere, the layer of the atmosphere where jetliners cruise," reported Andrew Revkin for the *Times*. "Dr. Pielke contends that changes in landscapes like the spread of agriculture and cities could explain many of the surface climate trends, while most climate experts now see a clear link to accumulating emissions of heat-trapping gases like carbon dioxide."[29]

The public at large generally seems to share in the newly established conventional wisdom about global warming, as well as its potential for causing extreme climate change. After Hurricane Katrina hit the Gulf Coast last September, Robert F. Kennedy Jr., head of the Natural Resources Defense Council, immediately blamed the severity of the catastrophe on global warming. "Now we are all learning what it's like to reap the whirlwind of fossil fuel dependence which [Mississippi Governor Haley] Barbour and his cronies have encouraged," Kennedy asserted. "Our destructive addiction has given us a catastrophic war in the Middle East and—now—Katrina is giving our nation a glimpse of the climate chaos we are bequeathing our children."[30]

Financier Warren Buffet, perhaps persuaded of the possibility that Kennedy might be right, has recently announced that his Berkshire Hathaway investment group will raise its rates on hurricane insurance because of the growing threat of climate change. The group lost $3.4 billion during the 2005 hurricane season in the United States. "We've concluded that we should now write mega-cat policies only at prices far higher than prevailed last year—and then only with an aggregate exposure that would not cause us distress if shifts in some important variable produce far more costly storms in the near future," Buffet explained.[31]

So from these examples it appears that a broad spectrum of modern society, from the scientific community to the environmental activists to the business and financial sector, has embraced the politically correct conventional wisdom on global warming.

Evangelical Climate Initiative Supports Global Warming Theory

A large segment of the evangelical Christian church apparently has bought into the conventional wisdom on global warming theory as well. A poll conducted in September 2005 by Ellison Research showed that 70 percent of evangelicals view global warming as a "serious threat" to our planet, and two-thirds are convinced that it is really happening right now. According to a WorldNetDaily report, the evangelical responders voiced the following opinions:

- 95 percent agreed with the statement: "God gave us dominion over His creation, so we have a responsibility to care for it."
- 84 percent agreed that reducing pollution is consistent with obeying the biblical commandment to love your neighbor.
- 51 percent felt the US government should pass laws to limit global warming, even though such measures might prove to be quite economically expensive.[32]

The poll was funded by the Evangelical Environmental Network, a new organization that has recently stepped forward to address the global warming issue. It is part of an expensive, well-orchestrated campaign called the Evangelical Climate Initiative, which will include radio and television spots and environmental educational events in churches and colleges.

In a statement issued in Washington on 8 February 2006 announcing the kickoff of the Evangelical Climate Initiative, a group of eighty-six influential evangelical leaders said that they are committed to fighting global warming because "millions of people could die in this century because of climate change, many of them our poorest global neighbors."[33]

The signers of the statement include the presidents of thirty-nine evangelical colleges, the leaders of parachurch ministries such as World Vision and the Salvation Army, the high-profile pastors of several megachurches, and others. Among the most prominent of these is Rick Warren, pastor of the Saddleback Church in California and best-selling author of *The Purpose Driven Life*, and *Christianity Today*'s editor David Neff and executive editor Timothy George.

Ted Haggard, pastor of the large New Life Church in Colorado Springs and current president of the National Association of Evangelicals, did not sign the statement because he said that he did not want to appear to be giving the organization's stamp of approval to the initiative. But Haggard told the *New York Times* that he personally supported the measure. "There is no doubt in my mind that climate change is happening, and there is no doubt that it would be wise for us to stop doing the foolish things we're doing that could potentially be causing this. In my mind, there is no downside to being cautious."[34]

"This is God's world, and any damage that we do to God's world is an offense against God himself," reads the statement issued by the Evangelical Climate Initiative. "The consequences of global warming will hit the poor the hardest, in part because those areas likely to be significantly affected first are the poorest regions of the world."[35]

Not all evangelicals agree with the Evangelical Climate Initiative campaign. Jerry Falwell, founder of the Moral Majority and president of Liberty University, has been outspoken in his opposition. Calling some of the signers "dear friends" who "acted prematurely," Falwell said he opposed their efforts "because I believe that global warming is an unproven phenomenon and may actually just be junk science being passed off as fact."

"In addition," Falwell continued, "I believe that so-called solutions to global warming—and particularly the Kyoto Protocol, which is the politically correct international agreement to fight greenhouse gas emissions—would devastate the American economy if adopted by our nation. Further, studies have shown that costly efforts to stem greenhouse gas emissions would barely reduce global temperatures."[36]

Paul Driessen, the author of *Eco-Imperialism: Green Power, Black Death* and a senior policy adviser for the Congress of Racial Equality (CORE), has pointed out that rather than helping disadvantaged people, the proposed legislation to reduce greenhouse gas emissions would actually hurt those who can least afford it. "By making energy less affordable and accessible, mandatory controls [on greenhouse gas emissions] would drive up the costs of consumer products, stifle economic growth, cost jobs, and impose especially harmful effects on the world's poorest people," Driessen explained.[37]

In fact, many prominent evangelical leaders of the conservative persuasion refused to sign the Evangelical Climate Initiative statement. In January of 2006, twenty-two of them wrote a letter urging the National Association of Evangelicals to refrain from endorsing the action because global warming is not a consensus issue and "Bible-believing evangelicals . . . disagree about the cause, severity, and solutions to the global warming issue."[38]

The signers of that letter included such conservative stalwarts as James Dobson, founder of Focus on the Family; Charles Colson, founder of Prison Fellowship Ministries; D. James Kennedy, head of Coral Ridge Ministries; and Richard Land, president of the Southern Baptist's Ethics and Religious Liberty Commission.

According to the *New York Times*, the expensive ad campaigns of the Evangelical Climate Initiative are being funded by large grants from several foundations, including the Pew Charitable Trusts, the Hewlett Foundation, and the Rockefeller Brothers Foundation.[39] This revelation has led to criticism by other evangelicals, because these left-leaning foundations generally support liberal causes that are not in line with biblical principles and values. Falwell points out that the Hewlett Foundation, which donated $475,000 to the ECI campaign, "routinely funds the Planned Parenthood Federation of America, the nation's chief abortion provider, the United Nations Population Fund, and other abortion-rights organizations." He also quotes Wendy Wright, president of Concerned Women for America, who calls the Hewlett Foundation "one of the most prodigious and unabashed funders of abortion causes."[40] According to author Brannon Howse, in 2001 the Hewlett Foundation contributed $600,000 to the International Planned Parenthood Foundation for "sexual and reproductive health services to adolescents in Brazil, Ecuador and Peru." Howse also cites evidence that Hewlett has contributed more than $2 million over the past three years to the Center for Reproductive Rights.

Not only the questionable science and the unholy associations of the ECI are being challenged, but also the underlying assumptions of their effort. Syndicated columnist Cal Thomas issued a pointed warning: "If evangelicals make the environment another 'cause,' they are likely to be as frustrated and disappointed as when they exercised misplaced faith in politics to cure other social ills," Thomas cautioned. "Should they desire a real effect on the planet, let them return to the eternal message that has been given them to share with a world that needs it now more than ever."[41]

The Report from Iron Mountain

Most people would be shocked to learn that many believe that a secret conspiracy to control people by means of a "fictitious environmental threat" was produced by our own US government more than forty years ago.

Right after JFK's radical disarmament initiative, Freedom from War, was announced in 1961, a powerful Washington think tank was allegedly commissioned with the task of convening a secret "brain trust" to come up with an alternative to war as a means of fulfilling certain needs in society during a period of permanent peace—a condition that had never before existed in recorded history.

According to revelations from someone who claimed to be a member, the group met periodically at a secret location for more than two and a half years. Their stated goal was to find ways to replace the economic, political, sociological, ecological, cultural, and scientific functions of war with alternatives that would maintain the stability of American society in time of peace.

When it was first published in 1967 by a division of Simon and Schuster, *The Report from Iron Mountain* was represented as being the official recommendation of that secret think tank study. Its principal suggestion was the creation of "fictitious global enemies" that would serve to keep the populace in line through fear. But these enemies would have to be credible.

> Credibility, in fact, lies at the heart of the problem of developing a political substitute for war. This is where the space-race proposals, in many ways so well suited as economic substitutes for war, fall short. The most ambitious and unrealistic space project cannot of itself generate a believable external menace. . . . Nevertheless, an effective political substitute for war would require "alternate enemies," some of which might seem equally farfetched in the context of the current war system. *It may be, for instance, that gross pollution of the environment can eventually replace the possibility of mass destruction by nuclear weapons as the principal apparent threat to the survival of the species.* Poisoning of the air, and of the principal sources of food and water supply, is already well advanced, and at first glance seems promising in this respect; it constitutes a threat that can be dealt with only through social organization and political power. *But from present indications it will be a generation to a generation and a half before environmental pollution, however severe, will be sufficiently menacing, on a global scale, to offer a possible basis for a solution.* . . . However unlikely some of the possible alternate

enemies we have mentioned may seem, we must emphasize that one *must* be found, of credible quality and magnitude, if a transition to peace is ever to come about without social disintegration. *It is more probable, in our judgment, that such a threat will have to be invented, rather than developed from known conditions.*[42]

When the book was first published, no one really knew for sure who had written it, and whether or not it was a true report or an anonymously written political satire. The book reached the best-seller lists and was translated into fifteen languages. Many people believed that it was an accurate description of a secret government plot.

Today *The Report from Iron Mountain* is widely reported to have been a hoax, written by Victor Navasky, editor of the liberal magazine the *Nation*. Since virtually every weblink on the Internet is now labeling it as such, and since Navasky claims authorship, perhaps we must accept that explanation.

Nevertheless, it is a very strange coincidence to observe what we are now living a little more than a generation and a half after the book first appeared. The global warming threat emerged just about one generation ago. The UN purports to offer us a peaceful world if we will just go ahead and follow through with those "complete and total disarmament" plans first proposed by JFK forty-five years ago.

Sometimes it's hard to tell the difference between fiction and reality.

Final Thoughts on Global Warming

Al Gore has received a lot of attention recently with his documentary film, *An Inconvenient Truth*, which merely adds fuel to the fire on global warming. Gore's politically correct environmental perspective is designed to persuade the general public that the danger of extreme climate change from global warming is serious and immediate.

Gore's critics charge that he overstates his case and is really just trying to ride the crest of the growing environmental consciousness wave into the White House in 2008. And there are a few uncomfortable facts that counter Gore's version of reality.

First, there's the fact that the climate scientists' sophisticated computer models of projected climate change are both inaccurate and unproven, and so the science doesn't really support the hype. There is a naturally occurring cycle of planetary warming and cooling that has been going on for millennia, and there is no conclusive evidence of imminent danger requiring immediate, drastic countermeasures.

Second, the leading proponent of the global warming threat is someone who has changed his story over time, and who eventually admitted to the limitations of his climate knowledge and predictive capacity, when at first he had claimed to be "99 percent certain" of his facts. James Hansen's 1988 prediction to Congress was wrong by 300 percent, and the implications of a scientific error that large are tremendous. Plus, he has subsequently admitted to fraudulently misrepresenting the seriousness of the problem merely to gain media attention.

Finally, the so-called experts who insist that climate change induced by global warming is happening now, and that humans are causing it, desperately want the general public to believe that *all* scientists feel the same way about the subject. But such is simply not the case.

Most of the scientists who promote the theory of global warming and its impact on climate change are fairly intelligent, well-educated individuals who believe fervently in their doctrine, pretty much as an article of faith, just as an evolutionist believes in Darwin and a Muslim believes in Mohammed.

For the most part, these scientists live, learn, and work within a closed circle of like-minded academics, and because they must "publish or perish," they periodically submit research articles to peer-reviewed scientific journals. So long as those articles don't violate any of the generally accepted articles of faith within their field, they will be published, and perhaps cited as a reference source by others. All of this establishes the scientist's credibility in his field . . . which leads directly to grants for research funds.

Scientists who write articles critical of the conventional wisdom on global warming don't get published, and therefore they don't get grants. Most of the many credible scientists who criticize global warming theory are retired professors who aren't vying for those coveted research funds. Their voices rarely get heard by the public.

So not only is the scientific evidence on global warming inconclusive to support the dire predictions made by folks like Hansen and Gore, but those who most ardently promote the idea have a vested interest—financial, political, or personal—in doing so. This is exactly the kind of "inconvenient truth" that many environmentalists hate to face. Thus they live in a state of denial and accuse those who point out these hard facts of being part of a disinformation campaign funded by "the polluters."

The jury is still out on global warming, and until the final verdict is in, we don't have to be intimidated by the scare tactics of these real life Chicken Littles who scream that the sky is . . . literally . . . falling in on us.

4

GLOBAL POPULATION CONTROL

The late Jacques Cousteau was well known as a world-renowned marine scientist and a generally personable kind of fellow. Many Americans will remember him as the articulate, informative host of a popular television program on ocean life, *The Undersea World of Jacques Cousteau*. But there was much more to Captain Cousteau's philosophy than his fascination with our incredible underwater world. In 1991, six years after he was awarded the Medal of Freedom by President Ronald Reagan, Cousteau was interviewed by the UNESCO *Courier,* and he discussed the topic of human population growth.

What Cousteau told UNESCO that day should be an instant and sobering reality check to every person now living.

> What should we do to eliminate suffering and disease? It's a wonderful idea but perhaps not altogether a beneficial one in the long run. If we try to implement it we may jeopardize the future of our species.
>
> It's terrible to have to say this. *World population must be stabilized and to do that we must eliminate 350,000 people per day.* This is so horrible to contemplate that we shouldn't even say it. But the general situation in which we are involved is lamentable.[1]

Eliminate 350,000 people per day! Was he serious? Unfortunately, the seemingly unthinkable ideas that the kindly captain espoused fifteen years ago are actually being accepted today by an increasing number of scientists and other self-described "experts" in the field of world population control. Cousteau himself died in 1997, at the ripe old age of eighty-seven—after marrying a younger woman and fathering two more children while in his eighties. But whatever his personal philosophical inconsistencies, Cousteau's publicly stated ideas still live on. We will return to a discussion of these disturbing ideas later on in this chapter. But for now, just keep his controversial quote in the back of your mind as you read what comes next. Here is an unpleasant but accurate thumbnail sketch of the current facts.

The UN is dedicated to achieving its goal of zero population growth (ZPG) by means of (1) propaganda and indoctrination in the developed world; and (2) a host of aggressive population control campaigns in Third World countries—even where such interventions are unwanted by the local populace. The ultimate UN goal is to establish a mandatory global population control similar to Communist China's one-child-per-family policy, which relies heavily on forced abortion and forced sterilization. In some cases women in Third World countries have actually been sterilized without their prior knowledge or consent.

Do those statements sound far-fetched to you? Well, at one time they sounded that way to me, too, before I began to do some homework on some of the most gruesome practices known to man. What I found is actually much worse.

The United Nations Population Fund (UNFPA) has been operating since 1969, and by 1995 it was funding state-sponsored birth control programs for women in 136 countries. The range of services offered includes providing condoms, contraceptive pills and IUDs, as well as abortion-based "family planning" services, often in conjunction with the International Planned Parenthood Federation (IPPF).

According to statistics released by the Alan Guttmacher Institute, a reproductive health foundation established by a former president of IPPF, there were approximately fifty million abortions performed worldwide in 1998, and about twenty million of those were legal. That means that thirty million illegal abortions are performed every year worldwide.

It's a death toll that's been in the works for a very long time.

Malthusian Theory and Margaret Sanger

Thomas Robert Malthus was a nineteenth-century English cleric and political economist who believed that the burgeoning human population was a threat to the future of the planet. In his "Essay on the Principle of Population," first published in 1798 and expanded in five later editions, Malthus wrote:

> All children born, beyond what would be required to keep up the population to a desired level, must necessarily perish, unless room may be made for them by the death of grown persons. . . . Therefore . . . we should facilitate, instead of foolishly and vainly seeking to impede, the operations of nature in producing this mortality; and if we dread the too frequent visitation of the horrid form of famine, we should sedulously encourage the other forms of destruction, which we compel nature to use. . . . But above all, we should reprobate specific remedies for ravaging diseases; and *restrain those benevolent, but much mistaken men, who have thought they were doing a service to mankind by projecting schemes for the total extirpation of particular disorders.*[2]

Malthus believed that human population growth was proceeding at a constant exponential rate, while food production was growing only arithmetically. Thus human consumption would quickly outstrip the earth's capacity for food production. The most merciful course of action, then, was not to seek to prolong or save human lives, but to allow wars, disease, and natural disasters to take their toll freely, thereby reducing the threat of future famine and starvation.

Malthus's dire predictions proved false, of course, primarily because he failed to factor in the increase in food supplies that would accompany the Industrial Revolution and the advances in agricultural methods and modern technology.

One wonders if Cousteau had read Malthus. We can be fairly certain that Margaret Sanger—socialist, radical feminist, and birth control activist—did, although she is better known now for starting the movement that ultimately legalized the use of birth control in the United States. She also founded the American Birth Control League (ABCL) in 1921.

Sanger temporarily "retired" from the birth control movement in 1942, in order to deflect public criticism of her stand on eugenics (a pseudo-science that purports to improve upon racial characteristics through breeding) from the organizations she had founded. Shortly thereafter, the ABCL changed its name to the Planned Parenthood Federation of America, relying on the new semantics of "family" association to soften its public image.

In 1952, allegedly because of an "alarm over population growth around the world," Sanger came out of retirement to found the International Planned Parenthood Federation, of which she served as president until 1959. During that time she was instrumental in securing major funding for the organization from the Ford and Rockefeller Foundations, as well as other major charitable trusts; her subversive influence continues today, not only in the United States but worldwide. Even Sanger's most supportive female biographer, Elasha Drogin, agrees with this assessment: "The influence of Margaret Sanger's International Planned Parenthood Federation on the contemporary world is so great," she writes, "that one can say its slogans and values have become exactly those of modern Western civilization and are rapidly becoming the morals which dominate the rest of the world. . . ."[3]

Many of the presuppositions and practices of the UN's global population control efforts are rooted in Neo-Malthusian theory and the race-based scientific eugenics that Sanger endorsed. And the licentious attitude of liberated sexuality that she personified has become the irreverent, values-free character of our godless, postmodern culture.

Exploding the "Population Bomb"

The Malthusian worldview resurfaced in 1968, in the form of a block-buster book entitled *The Population Bomb*. In this powerful polemic, Stanford University entomologist Paul Ehrlich, an expert in the study of butterflies, predicted food shortages and severe famines dead ahead as a result of human overpopulation.[4]

"The battle to feed all of humanity is over," Ehrlich proclaimed in his prologue. "In the 1970s and 1980s *hundreds of millions of people will starve to death in spite of any crash programs embarked upon now. At this late date nothing can prevent a substantial increase in the world death rate."[5]

His predictions were grim and large: "A *minimum* of ten million people, most of them children, will starve to death during each year of the 1970s. But this is a mere handful compared to the numbers that will be starving before the end of the century."[6]

Ehrlich urged swift government action to avert the crisis. "Our position requires that we take immediate action at home and promote effective action worldwide. *We must have population control at home*, hopefully through changes in our value system, but *by compulsion if voluntary methods fail."[7]

Some of the methods he considered were placing secret contraceptives in food supplies, adding luxury taxes on child-related products and toys, and giving "responsibility prizes" to couples who had no children for five years or to men who got vasectomies. In a suggestion reminiscent of some of Margaret Sanger's Parliament of Population, Ehrlich also advocated a Federal Bureau of Population and Environment to enforce strict population control guidelines.[8]

Ehrlich was especially critical of the "assorted do-gooders who were deeply involved in the apparatus of international food charity" to Third World nations that experienced chronic food shortages, because he believed that those countries would never be able to solve their hunger problems without instituting drastic population control measures. So when William and Paul Paddock proposed a ban on both public and private food aid to such countries if they refused to curtail population growth—with the clear implication that millions of people would therefore starve to death—Ehrlich endorsed the idea.[9]

Ehrlich compared the world's overpopulation problem to a malignant cancer that had to be cut out in order to save the life of the patient.

> A cancer is an uncontrolled multiplication of cells; the population explosion is an uncontrolled multiplication of people. Treating only the symptoms of cancer may make the victim more comfortable at first, but eventually he dies—often horribly. A similar fate awaits a world with a population explosion if only the symptoms are treated. *We must shift our efforts from treatment of the symptoms to cutting out the cancer.* The operation will demand many apparently brutal and heartless decisions. The pain may be intense. *But the disease is so far advanced that only with radical surgery does the patient have a chance at survival.*[10]

Fortunately for the world, Ehrlich's alarmist predictions—like those of Malthus 150 years before him—proved to be false. The alleged cancer proved to be non-malignant, and the patient survived without the "brutal and heartless decisions" that Ehrlich prescribed. Human population did indeed continue to increase worldwide, but thanks to human ingenuity and modern technology, so did plentiful food supplies. While there are pockets of famine in the world today, the problem most often is not an actual scarcity of food but rather government corruption and inefficient delivery systems. The biggest food problem in much of the world is not starvation but obesity.

Writing in the radical left-wing magazine *Ramparts* in 1969, Ehrlich also predicted that increased pesticide use in the United States would reduce the average American life expectancy to forty-two years by the year 1980, and that by 1999 the nation's overall population would drop to only 22.6 million people.[11]

As Michael Fumento of the American Enterprise Institute has pointed out, over the years Ehrlich has also predicted oil shortages, smog disasters, mineral depletion, and food shortages due to "human-induced land degradation." He even predicted that England would cease to exist by the year 2000. None of these things occurred.

But, like Malthus, Ehrlich's influence did not diminish merely because he was wrong. He became a world-renowned expert on the perceived problem of human overpopulation and has since received numerous scientific and environmental awards. Despite repeated prophetic failures, Ehrlich continues to write books that justify his past mistakes and to issue even more outrageous predictions of disaster for the future. And he is still regarded on the Left as a sage scientist rather than a false prophet of doom. Fumento explains why this is so: "Ehrlich will still garner those accolades because, while in reality he's always wrong, politically he's always correct."[12] And the widespread and willing adoption of the Malthusian worldview has led to chilling policy initiatives around the world.

US Foreign Policy on Population Control

On 24 April 1974, at the request of then-Secretary of State Henry Kissinger, the National Security Agency prepared the National Security Study Memorandum 200 (NSSM 200), entitled "Implications of Worldwide Population Growth for US Security and Overseas Interests." The final document was approved by Brent Scowcroft, national security adviser, and was marked classified and confidential.

From the following excerpt, it would appear that this secret US policy document closely followed the recommendations made by Paul Ehrlich six years prior, who had urged the linkage of vitally needed food aid to a poor nation's willingness to curtail its own population growth.

If future numbers are to be kept within reasonable limits, it is urgent that measures to reduce fertility be started and made effective in the 1970s and 1980s. . . . [Financial] assistance will be given to other countries considering such factors as population growth. . . . Food and agricultural assistance is vital for any population sensitive development strategy. . . . *Allocation of scarce resources should take account of what steps a country is taking in population control. . . .* There is an alternative view that *mandatory programs may be needed.*[13]

According to Dr. Stanley Monteith, a noted conservative researcher and radio talk show host, this secret memorandum outlined a "genocidal program" designed to seize control of the natural resources of Third World nations by limiting their population growth. NSSM 200 "recommended reduction in the growth of the world's population," Dr. Monteith writes, and "has been the basis of US foreign policy since that time."

As a result, Dr. Monteith asserts, "Half of the child-bearing women in Brazil have been sterilized, contraceptive vaccines were given to women without their knowledge, men and women were sterilized without their consent, and the US supported China's one-child policy."[14]

The World Bank soon began to tie development loans to family planning programs, even stipulating to the borrowers what percentage of each loan had to be used for population control. By 1980, this process was apparently well advanced, according to comments by Archbishop Peter Proeku Dery of Ghana.

"The World Bank denied loans to Ghana until my country agreed to institute a nationwide contraceptive and family planning policy," Archbishop Dery told the *National Catholic Register.* "There was also pressure to legalize abortion, although the Church and the people have so far been able to prevent this. For how long, I don't know. *The World Bank's attitude shows a total disregard for the beliefs of the people of the Third World.*"[15]

At the 1994 UN Conference on Population and Development, held in Cairo, Egypt, the dominant emphasis was on achieving sustainable development by limiting population growth worldwide. According to

Joan Veon, a researcher and author who attended that convention, "The World Bank put Third World countries on notice that future loans will be granted based on what that country is doing to reduce population."[16]

From these facts we may deduce that for many years our pragmatic policy makers in Washington have been using US economic clout to advance the questionable cause of worldwide population control. And as far back as 1969, that policy was being influenced by the Planned Parenthood organization.

It may be instructive to consider the content of a memo from Frederick Jaffe, vice president of the World Population division of Planned Parenthood, to Bernard Berelson, president of the Population Council. Entitled "Activities Relevant to the Study of Population Policy for the US," the memo advances a shorthand strategy that includes:

> . . . restructure family, encourage increased homosexuality, educate for family limitation, fertility control agents in water supply, encourage women to work, compulsory sterilization of all who have two children except for a few who would be allowed three, confine childbearing to a limited number of adults, stock certificate type permits for children, and payment to encourage sterilization, abortion, and contraception.[17]

This memo appears to be a laundry list of possible options that might be used to accomplish the express population control goals of Planned Parenthood. As is evident, some of those policies have been implemented already, either here or abroad. It makes one wonder if others might still be in the offering for the future, or perhaps even being conducted clandestinely at the present time.

Red China's Repressive Birth Control Regime

Many who believe that the earth is being threatened by burgeoning human population growth also believe that growth should be severely limited through government-imposed contraception, abortion, and mandatory limits on childbirth.

This type of authoritarian program is currently in effect in Communist China, where the nationwide "one-child policy" has been brutally imposed upon the people of that country for almost three decades, since 1979. Those who violate the policy by having more than the prescribed number of children may be heavily fined and lose their jobs. In some cases the Chinese government has destroyed the families' homes as punishment.

According to statistics from the Population Research Institute (PRI), Chinese women are forced to undergo approximately ten million abortions per year, whether they want to or not. If a woman is discovered to be illegally pregnant, she is forced to abort the child, even if the pregnancy is at an advanced stage.

Because of a cultural preference for male offspring, many Chinese couples regularly practice female infanticide by aborting their female fetuses, or allowing female babies to die after birth. This gruesome practice of "gendercide" has resulted in the death of at least fifty million Chinese girls.[18]

The controversial program in China has been coordinated from its inception by the International Planned Parenthood Federation and what was formerly called the UN Family Planning Association (now known as the UN Population Fund). For much of its tenure, funds from the United States have gone to support this population control project.

Currently, a US law known as the Kemp-Kasten amendment requires the government to deny funding to international organizations if forced abortion is involved. The Bush administration withheld $34 million from the UNFPA as a protest after the State Department determined in 2002 and 2004 that China was in fact coercing women to have abortions.

Secretary of State Colin Powell reported in 2004 that he had "determined that UNFPA's support of, and involvement in, China's population-planning activities allowed the Chinese government to implement more effectively its program of coercive abortion."

The Chinese government had denied forcing abortions on women, but evidence provided by PRI proved that they were lying. In fact, a PRI research team sent into China in 2001 even found that "the UNFPA population control officer's desk was located in the Chinese government's population control office."[19]

Steve Mosher, founder of the Population Research Institute and the author of *One Woman's Fight Against China's One-Child Policy* (1994), is perhaps the world's leading expert on international population control, and he calls the alleged overpopulation crisis a myth. Mosher is especially opposed to what he calls the "despicable" practices of Communist China, which he claims "have led to massive human rights abuses and undermined the health of women and children."

As the first American social scientist allowed to live in rural China from 1979 to 1980, Mosher witnessed first-hand the plight of pregnant women who were "hunted down by population control police and subjected to forced abortion for violating China's one-child-per-family policy."

Mosher pulls no punches in his candid assessment of the sordid situation in China.

> China's Communist government still enforces its population control program on its 1.3 billion subjects with a vengeance. Imagine living in a country where it is illegal to have more than one or two children. Imagine the incredibly oppressive nature of such a policy, which affects every single family in the country. If any family exceeds its quota, fines ranging from half to ten times the average annual household income can be imposed, the husband and wife could lose their jobs, and medical or educational benefits may be withheld from the couple's children.
>
> Isn't it odd to hear so little about this massive, systematic abuse of human rights from Western media organs, feminist groups, and

organizations that claim to stand for reproductive choice, such as International Planned Parenthood or the UN Population Fund?[20]

Nevertheless, many so-called pro-choice leaders in America want the United States to resume full funding for the UNFPA—despite the fact that in 1983 the UN Population Fund praised Chinese leader Qian Xinzhong for his brutal program that "implemented population policies on a massive scale."

The sad fact is, for years the UN's population control programs around the world have been solidly supported by such wealthy organizations and individuals as the Rockefeller, MacArthur, and Hewlett-Packard Foundations, as well as by billionaires like Bill Gates and Ted Turner. These folks have no problem with the Chinese forced birth control program.

Turner expressed the attitude of many when he said, "People who abhor the China one-child policy are dumb-dumbs."[21]

Sadly, a full decade before the Chinese set up their coercive system in 1979, the same idea was being publicly advocated here in the United States. Dr. Robert A. Harper told the American Psychological Association meeting in Washington DC in 1969 that the nations of the world should "remove the right to reproduce" from their people. The means by which this might be accomplished, Harper said, could include adding chemicals for temporary sterilization to the food and water supplies. But whatever the method used, the most important objective was that "the original removal of the right to reproduce would have to be done, whether or not it was with the individual's approval and consent."[22]

What Harper was advocating for America, then, was a state-mandated system of involuntary population control, imposed either by guile or by force, irrespective of the wishes and preferences of the people. This statist perspective on family planning is of course inimical to our long-standing American ideals of individual liberty and self-determination.

The UN's Global Population Control Agenda

The United Nations Population Fund (UNFPA) was created in 1966, the same year that Margaret Sanger died. For almost four decades, the UN has worked with the International Planned Parenthood Federation (IPPF) to promote family planning and birth control worldwide. A central feature of these population control programs has been the strong emphasis on abortion and sterilization, particularly among the women of Third World nations, although many of those traditional cultures have long held strong traditions of opposition to such measures.

The UNESCO Biosphere Conference, held in Paris in 1968, emphasized the "interrelatedness of the environment" and man's impact on it. The conference delegates concluded that most environmental degradation could be blamed on a combination of three factors: industrialization, urbanization, and human population growth. The Man and Biosphere Program, discussed previously, was one eventual result of this conference. So, too, was the later concept of "sustainable development."

One of the seminal documents in the history of environmentalism was a book called *Limits to Growth,* published by the Club of Rome in 1968. While this book did not specifically refer to the phrase "sustainable development," it did raise the bleak Malthusian specter of a world overburdened by excess human population, where millions would someday starve to death because the limited natural resources of the planet—including food, oil, and minerals—could no longer support them.[23]

Limits to Growth reportedly "has sold 30 million copies in more than thirty translations, making it the best selling environmental book in world history," according to Wikipedia.[24] But the book, which was allegedly "published as a publicity stunt with great fanfare at the Smithsonian in Washington," was immediately blasted in *Newsweek* by Yale economist Henry C. Wallich, who called it "a piece of irresponsible nonsense." Similarly, MIT scientist Robert M. Solow criticized the weak data upon which the book's predictions were based.[25]

Nevertheless, the weighty influence of the Club of Rome, which is composed of some very wealthy men from around the world, has served to make the Malthusian philosophical precepts of *Limits to Growth* the base of the UN's whole "sustainable development" program. The first Earth Summit, which was convened under the leadership of Maurice Strong in 1972, made global population control an important priority. At that time Strong was also a member of the Club of Rome.

Over the next fifteen years, a series of international conventions continued to advance the notion of living within our limits environmentally. In 1987, the phrase "sustainable development" was actually coined in the UN report *Our Common Future*, which emphasized "global solutions" to a number of interrelated problems.

Joan Veon has offered the following paraphrased definition of what sustainable development actually means to UN bureaucrats. It is simple and succinct.

> The world has too many people and not enough resources to feed and clothe them. If we do not reduce the population they will eat up and use all of the earth's resources and future generations will be left without any resources. The United Nations is the best global body to monitor, manage, and preserve the resources of the planet.[26]

Understanding this basic UN perspective on population control and sustainable development—flawed though it is—helps us to see where the UN is heading and why.

In 1991, the Council of the Club of Rome published another groundbreaking book, *The First Global Revolution*. This book advanced a new theory that identified humankind in general as the cause of all our earthly ills.

> In searching for a common enemy to unite us, we came up with the idea that pollution, the threat of global warming, water shortages,

famine, and the like would fit the bill. All these dangers were caused by human intervention. . . . *The real enemy, then, is humanity itself.*[27]

In 1992, Maurice Strong convened the second Earth Summit in Rio de Janeiro. That meeting reaffirmed the UN's ongoing commitment to global population control. The *Global Biodiversity Assessment* was the report that came from that conference.

"A reasonable estimate for an industrialized world society at the present North American material standard of living would be 1 billion," its authors reported. "At the more frugal European standard of living, 2 to 3 billion would be possible."[28]

What this analysis is saying, of course, is that the planet can support somewhere between one-fifth and one-half of its present inhabitants. So not only can we not add any more bodies to the planetary people pool, it would appear that a lot of us are just going to have to leave—immediately if not sooner.

1994 International Conference on Population and Development, Cairo

The 1994 International Conference on Population and Development (ICPD) was a watershed event at which the Vatican barely managed to stop, albeit temporarily, what Pope John Paul II called a "conspiracy against life" and a "culture of death."[29]

This conference can best be understood in its unique historical context. From 1970 onward, the US government had provided millions of taxpayer dollars to Planned Parenthood and other "family planning" organizations to promote birth control via counseling and contraceptives, both at home and abroad.

Domestically, this money had been authorized by Congress as part of the Title X appropriations of the Public Health Services Act. Internationally, the money was dispersed through the Agency for International Development; portions were also donated to the various UN agencies and programs that we supported on an ongoing basis. It would be difficult today to account for where all that money was spent thirty years ago.

After *Roe v. Wade* legalized abortion in America, Senator Jesse Helms of North Carolina introduced the Helms Amendment, which made it illegal for any US foreign aid money to be spent on abortions abroad. However, it did not prohibit organizations that provided abortions from receiving foreign aid money for other family planning purposes, so long as that money was not used specifically for abortion services.

According to research compiled by George Grant, Planned Parenthood was able to "skim the cream off of virtually every United States foreign aid package," including funds designated for International Population Assistance, the World Bank, the Agency for International Development, and the UNFPA. This amounted to "untold billions," Grant said, but no exact numbers were identifiable. On the rare occasions when Congress restricted such funds, Planned Parenthood would sue in court and get the money back.[30]

In 1984, President Ronald Reagan made it a policy of his administration that no US money would be given to international organizations that were either performing or actively promoting abortion as a means of birth control, anywhere in the world. Reagan's pro-life executive order set the general tone for the large US delegation to the UN's 1984 population control conference in Mexico City.

The Mexico City Declaration recognized the awareness of developing nations' need for family planning, and affirmed each nation's sovereignty in determining what population control measures it would accept or utilize. The declaration language also reflected a US-brokered compromise on abortion: "in no case should abortion be promoted as a means of family planning."

Planned Parenthood International was one of the groups adversely affected by Reagan's antiabortion Mexico City policy. Pro-abortion activists quickly dubbed Reagan's executive order the "Gag Rule," implying that it restricted their free speech rights to counsel women about abortions.[31]

But the beneficial effects of Reagan's efforts were merely temporary. In 1992 the avidly pro-abortion Bill Clinton was elected president, with strong support from the pro-choice feminists and the homosexual-rights activists. Clinton quickly changed his administration's policies to accommodate those groups.

On his first day in office, 22 January 1993, Clinton reversed Reagan's Mexico City policy and resumed funding for abortion providers abroad. By 1994, through a series of loopholes in the law, Planned Parenthood of America was actually receiving 34 percent of its annual domestic funding from the Title X program, and the pro-abortion juggernaut was rolling forward again.[32]

Clinton fully intended to change the results of the Mexico City conference. Thus the 1994 Cairo conference on population was expected, in the language of the pre-conference agenda document, to enshrine the right of women to "universal access to family planning and reproductive services," which pro-life advocates understood really meant funding for worldwide abortion as a means of birth control.[33]

Although it was technically a UN-sponsored event, the Clinton contingent dominated the entire conference. The on-site staff of Planned Parenthood included more than two hundred trained lobbyists and organizers. The US delegation was led by Timothy Wirth, the undersecretary of state for global affairs and a former one-term senator from Colorado. In the Senate, Wirth had focused his attention on population control issues and global warming theory, and was the first to give James Hansen a public forum to air his apocalyptic predictions about abrupt climate change in 1988. Wirth was a staunch advocate of abortion rights and a former board member of his local Planned Parenthood chapter.[34]

The Clinton/IPPF/UNPFA team went to Cairo expecting a cakewalk.

Virtually no evangelical Christians were on hand to oppose their well-laid three-year plan to establish a woman's right to abortion worldwide. But they had failed to reckon with an unflinching pope who knew how high the stakes were. The family unit was under assault, and the anti-abortion laws of the entire world were on the line. "The Holy See is well aware that the future of humanity is under discussion," a Vatican spokesman told the *New York Times*.[35]

Pope John Paul II sent a Vatican delegation of only seventeen members to Cairo to confront the combined diplomatic powers of the United States, Russia, Planned Parenthood, and the bloated UN bureaucracy of "population control careerists and the contraceptive and supranational financial interests that stand to benefit from their activities."[36]

Rep. Chris Smith, a pro-life congressman from New Jersey who attended the conference, later offered his firsthand account of what happened in Cairo.

> The final conference document, called *Programme of Action*, was, all things considered, a remarkable victory for global pro-life forces and the one hundred countries throughout the world that protect the lives of their unborn children.
>
> Led by a highly skilled and tenacious Vatican delegation, dozens of African, Central and South American countries joined Muslim states to resist abortion lobby bullying, despite vigorous opposition from the Clinton delegation at preparatory meetings in New York and Cairo.
>
> The final conference document affirmed all nations' "sovereignty" to protect and cherish the precious lives of unborn babies, and said that "in no case should abortion be promoted as a method of family planning."[37]

Because he stood up to the assembled might of the pro-abortion world and refused to back down, Pope John Paul II was named "Man of the Year" for 1994 by *Time* magazine. "For nine days the Vatican delegates, under his direction, lobbied and filibustered; they kept their Latin American bloc in line and struck up alliances with Islamic nations opposed to abortion," *Time* recounted. "In the end, the Pope won."[38]

The ramifications of this bitter struggle for "the future of humanity" still effect our lives. Twelve years after the Cairo conference, thanks to the Pope, the official UN position on abortion still remains what it was in 1984, thanks to Ronald Reagan: "in no case should abortion be promoted as a method of family planning."[39]

In 2001, on his first day in office, President George W. Bush signed an executive order reinstating Ronald Reagan's Mexico City policy as the controlling law that prohibits US foreign aid dollars from being spent to assist those who provide abortions.

But while these initial battles have been won, the global war is far from over.

Five years after Cairo, UN Secretary-General Kofi Annan explained the ongoing significance of what had happened there. "Since Cairo, the world does understand that we have to stabilize population," Annan declared in 1999. Moreover, the premise that women everywhere must have unhindered access to both birth control *and* abortion "seems blindingly obvious now," Annan continued. "But until Cairo the world did not fully understand it."[40]

According to the head of the UN, the language in the documents is not really the official UN position. Annan still believes that all women everywhere need to have legal access to abortion—whether the countries they live in agree to it or not.

Timothy Wirth was appointed by Ted Turner in 1998 to head up the media mogul's new United Nations Foundation. With this devoted disciple of Malthus at the helm of a $1 billion lobbying vehicle, there is little doubt that a determined push for both politically correct environmentalism and relentless pro-abortion advocacy will continue for the foreseeable future.[41]

So, for all the warm-fuzzy rhetoric about empowerment and equal rights for women, for all the high-minded scientific talk about sustainable development, for all the economic emphasis on eradicating poverty and improving quality of life—when all is said and done, the global struggle in the UN is still focused on population control through abortion.

5

WORLD TRADE AND GLOBAL
TAXING AUTHORITY

Under a wide variety of vague and intrusive environmental treaties, protocols, and regulations, the UN has effectively exerted its control over vast portions of the earth's surface. The next battleground in this fight will be over ratification of the Law of the Sea Treaty, which would cede control over most of the earth's oceans and undersea surfaces to the UN.

The inescapable conclusion is that the UN both desires and intends to transform itself from a voluntary forum of peace-loving nations into a sovereign, supranational world government. It seeks to usurp absolute political authority and acquire irresistible military power.

The US Can't Win with LOST

Legendary leftist music icon Bob Dylan presented a stark poetic contrast in the loaded lyrics to his hit song "Jokerman."

> Well, the Book of Leviticus and Deuteronomy,
> The Law of the Jungle and the Sea are your only teachers.[1]

To understand that contrast more fully, a little historical context is helpful.

First, "Jokerman" was a big tune on Dylan's *Infidels* album released in 1983, about the time that Dylan apparently became disillusioned with his brief but intense flirtation with "Born Again" Christianity. Thus the Law of Moses from the Old Testament has replaced the many New Testament scriptures and Christian ideals that had characterized Dylan's previous albums like *Saved* and *Slow Train*.

Next, Dylan strikes a decidedly secular note when he juxtaposes truth as being contained in either the Law of the Jungle or the Sea. Liberals desperately want the dumbed-down denizens of modern America to see the issue as a clear choice between the greedy violence inspired by self-interested nationalism ("the Law of the Jungle") and a more kindly spirit of cooperation for the common good of all mankind, as expressed in supranational communitarianism ("the Law of the Sea").

The dramatic dualism between ancient, sometimes anarchic "laws" that placed power in the hands of the man with the biggest stick or ship or gun and civilized modern law is exactly how today's globalists want to frame the ongoing debate on the disastrous Law of the Sea Treaty (LOST), which was first presented back in 1982 and is as of this 2006 writing pending in the US Senate for the second year in a row. The *real* bottom-line choice confronting those one hundred US Senators is one between the survival of the United States as a sovereign nation and the enthronement of the United Nations as a de facto world government.

What is LOST? Most folks have hardly heard of it. But the treacherous UN Convention on the Law of the Sea (UNCLOS), which would give control of over 70 percent of the earth's surface to the UN, has been around for almost three decades. It was painstakingly developed during the 1970s by radical leftists who wanted to sneak socialistic changes in through the back door by designating the world's oceans as the "Common Heritage of Mankind"—a concept that is Marxist to the core.

According to an in-depth report released by the conservative public policy organization America's Survival, Inc., LOST was the brainchild of Elisabeth Mann Borgese, the head of the World Federalists of Canada.

The youngest daughter of German novelist Thomas Mann, Borgese was a dedicated Marxist who longed for world government and saw the ocean treaty as the cornerstone of a socialistic "new international economic order," a global redistributionist idea that was prominent in the 1970s.[2]

She received the Environmental Prize from the UN Environment Program (UNEP) in 1987 for organizing the conferences that "served to lay the foundation" for the treaty. UNEP praised Borgese for recognizing the oceans as "a possible test-bed for ideas she had developed concerning a common global constitution."[3]

"The world ocean has been, and is, so to speak, our great laboratory for the making of a new world order," Borgese said in a 1999 speech. Known as the "Mother of the Oceans" by her UN supporters, Borgese died in 2002.[4]

"The name of Elisabeth Mann Borgese is probably unknown to most backers and opponents of LOST," said Cliff Kincaid, a prominent researcher for America's Survival. "But any analysis of the treaty and its impact has to take her life and influence over LOST into account."[5]

In addition to Borgese, other prominent individuals who were instrumental in drafting and negotiating the Law of the Sea Treaty in its early stages included Sam and Miriam Levering, a pacifist Quaker couple who founded the Neptune Society; Elliot Richardson, a self-described "radical moderate" career diplomat and cabinet member; and Louis Sohn, professor emeritus of International Law at Harvard University and one of the authors of the highly influential book, *World Peace Through World Law.*[6]

Serious Sovereignty Problems with LOST

In *Our Global Neighborhood,* the Commission on Global Governance suggests giving the UN Trusteeship Council new authority over the "global commons," which is defined as: "The atmosphere, outer space, the oceans beyond national jurisdiction and the related environment and life support systems that contribute to the support of human life."[7]

Thus what has been known for all of human history as the "high seas"—a vast expanse of water that belonged to no nation but was open to anyone with the ability to explore it—would now become the property of the world community, managed and controlled by yet another unaccountable United Nations bureaucracy.

UN Ambassador Jeane Kirkpatrick opposed LOST back in 1982 because she saw it as a threat to American sovereignty and national security, as well as a ploy to advance the new international economic order, and President Ronald Reagan rejected it.

According to Reagan's one-time political adviser Pat Buchanan, "Reagan saw this Law of the Sea Treaty for what it was: a joint scheme of the Soviet bloc, the Third World, and the United Nations to seize sovereignty over the oceans, mandate transfers of American technology, and get kickbacks from profits US companies might earn from mining and drilling. Reagan ordered it deep-sixed."[8]

But in 1994, after some minor renegotiations, Bill Clinton directed Secretary of State Madelyn Albright to sign LOST and then sent it to the Senate for ratification. There Senator Jesse Helms, who chaired the Foreign Relations Committee, courageously blocked the treaty for years. Nevertheless, LOST went into effect worldwide in 1995 with the support of 50 member nations; today, a total of 145 nations have signed onto the pact.

Now the Bush administration, which tried hard but failed to ram LOST through the Senate in 2004 and 2005, is back to try again. President Bush, apparently concerned about repairing America's unpalatable unilateralist image, "would certainly like to see [LOST] passed as soon as possible," said new Secretary of State Condoleezza Rice during her Senate confirmation hearings in January 2005.[9]

If LOST gains American support, an uncontested International Seabed Authority will regulate the oceans of the world through an operation called the Enterprise. The UN bureaucrats will have the power to regulate and tax all undersea mining activities—which could affect vast stores of minerals and up to 20 percent of the world's petroleum resources—and as a result will rake in trillions of dollars of revenue. In fact, in what University of New Brunswick ocean mapper David Monahan has called "the largest land grab in human history," they are already divvying up the ocean floor.[10]

The UN will also have the power to control shipping lanes and to restrict the movements of navies—possibly even banning the undersea operations of our US nuclear submarines—since the oceans would be reserved only for "peaceful purposes." UN bureaucrats could potentially control human activities on land, on inland waterways, and even in outer space too—all on the premise that these might pollute the oceans.

The UN, flush with its newfound potential tax wealth, might even float its own "blue hulls" navy to enforce the unappealable edicts of its international maritime courts, according to Dr. Peter Leitner, a long-time opponent of LOST. "There's nothing limiting the International Seabed Authority from going out and attempting to raise a navy, or have contributing member states contribute vessels or act on behalf of the Authority to enforce its rules," Dr. Leitner explains.[11] In fact, during the Clinton administration years, a "gold-plated think tank" called the Center for Naval Analysis had recommended that the United States actually donate the vessels for a UN navy.

Dr. Leitner, a senior strategic trade adviser to the Department of Defense, has been intimately involved in studying the severely flawed sea treaty for more than thirty years; he has been described by WorldNetDaily as the Reagan Administration's "in-house expert at the Government Accounting Office." In his 1996 book, *Reforming the Law of the Sea Treaty: Opportunities Missed, Precedents Set, and U.S. Sovereignty Threatened*, Dr. Leitner also warned about the mandated high technology transfers that the treaty required of those who operated under its authority.[12]

"This accord would constitute the most egregious transfer of American sovereignty, wealth and power to the UN since the founding of that 'world body,'" explains Frank Gaffney, president of the Center for Security Policy, a conservative think tank devoted to a strong US national defense. "In fact, never before in the history of the world has any nation voluntarily engaged in such a sweeping transfer to anyone."[13]

Senator Lugar's Stealth Campaign for LOST

Senator Jesse Helms used his powerful position as chairman of the Senate Foreign Relations Committee to block LOST for years. But since Helms' retirement in 2004, his successor seems to have a very different internationalist agenda. Senator Richard Lugar of Indiana took over Helms' seat, and he has been pushing hard to pass LOST ever since.

In February 2004, Lugar threw his support behind LOST and got his committee to pass the measure 19–0. A committee spokesperson said that the unanimous vote came "because the treaty has overwhelming support from the administration, the oil industry, environmentalists."[14]

Lugar had allowed only two days of testimony and did not call any witnesses who were opposed to the treaty. But conservative opponents learned of Lugar's ploy and vociferously objected, and Senate Majority Leader Bill Frist refused to bring the treaty to a vote before the full Senate.

Senator James Inhofe of Oklahoma responded by calling opponents of LOST to testify before his Environment and Public Works Committee on 23 March 2004. "I will fight to the bitter end to oppose ratification," Inhofe pledged.[15]

Nevertheless, in December 2004, the Bush administration published a US Ocean Action Plan that endorsed LOST. "As a matter of national security, economic self-interest, and international leadership, the Bush administration is strongly committed to US accession to the UN Convention on the Law of the Sea," the Action Plan declared. The document called for Senate approval "as early as possible" and described its commitment to "an ecosystem-based approach in making decisions related to water, land, and resource management."[16]

This vague reference to "ecosystem-based resource management" could include a federal program called the White Water to Blue Water

Initiative, or WW2BW. According to veteran UN researcher William Grigg, WW2BW is part of the larger Agenda 21 environmental scheme in which "the UN, acting as custodian of the planet, would regulate all human interaction with the biosphere."

This sustainable development partnership between government agencies, UN entities, NGOs, and radical environmental groups would ultimately affect every American citizen, regardless of where he or she lives, as well as every inland river and tributary. Why? "Because all waterways are connected, all activities—such as farming, manufacturing, and recreation—having any impact on those waterways would be brought under the UN's jurisdiction," Grigg explains.[17]

Grigg quotes Agenda 21 editor David Sitarz on what the ultimate result will be.

> Effective execution of Agenda 21 will require *a profound reorientation of all human society, unlike anything the world has ever experienced*—a major shift in the priorities of both governments and individuals and *an unprecedented redeployment of human and financial resources.* This shift will demand that a concern for the environmental consequences of every human action be integrated into individual and collective decision-making at every level. . . . [This will require cooperation and obedience] by farmers and consumers, by students and schools, by governments and legislators, by scientists, by women, by children—*in short, by every person on earth.*[18]

It seems strange that President Bush, while rejecting intense international pressure to accede to the demands for ratification of the Kyoto Protocol and the International Criminal Court, would embrace such a sweeping surrender of US sovereignty as LOST implies. Nevertheless, that seems to be the misguided direction in which he intends to steer the nation.

After eliciting Condi Rice's enthusiastic endorsement of LOST in January 2005, Lugar commented, "I cannot think of a stronger administration statement in support of the Law of the Sea Convention." Critics of the treaty expect Lugar to try to push it through the Senate again as soon as possible, but so far that hasn't happened—primarily because of the strong public show of opposition to LOST by conservatives.[19]

According to a report in the *Washington Times*, a 2005 C-PAC press conference of groups opposed to LOST "read like a who's who of the conservative movement." Groups represented included the Free Congress Foundation, the Freedom Alliance, the National Taxpayers' Union, Eagle Forum, Concerned Women for America, and Right March, among others.

"The conservative movement is opposed to the Law of the Sea Treaty and to the administration's support of the treaty," said David A. Keene of the American Conservative Union. Conservative columnist Pat Buchanan readily agreed. "It is a transfer of sovereignty, a transfer of taxing authority to a world body. It creates another instrument of world government," Buchanan told the *Times*. "I cannot understand how any conservative who believes in the sovereignty of this country and its continued independence can sign onto a treaty that constructs a New World Order."[20]

The fact is, America has everything to lose and nothing to gain from signing on to LOST. This agreement will give the United States no rights that we don't already possess, but we will effectively abdicate any legitimate claims that we might now be able to make as a sovereign nation. And if we do become a party to the treaty, we will immediately become liable for an assessment of 25 percent of the International Seabed Authority's budget, plus the potential liability for the expenses of American-based companies that choose to do business with the UN's new oceanic enterprise.

"Let's be frank: these international bureaucracies don't work," declared the Heritage Foundation's president Ed Feulner. "The UN is already dealing with a sex scandal in the Congo, genocide in Sudan, and the Oil-for-Food fiasco in Iraq. Why would we want to create more unaccountable international bureaucracies and put them in charge of our oceans?"[21]

Politicians of both parties, big oil companies, assorted UN bureaucrats, and wild-eyed environmental groups all want to see this flawed ocean treaty go into effect, for a variety of reasons. Some want political favor, some want increased profits, some want more power, and some may sincerely want to save the world.

But for Americans, our sovereign nation's very survival is at stake. This treaty was bad when Ronald Reagan rejected it in 1982, and it is just the same today. True American patriots will continue to fight against LOST—tooth and nail. It will take a two-thirds supermajority in the Senate to ratify this treaty. But unless at least thirty-four senators have the guts to stand up and say no to LOST . . . by the time you read this, it will be a done deal.

Constitutional Panic at the Law of the Sea Committee

On 20 January 2000, Senator Jesse Helms of North Carolina became the first sitting US senator in history to address the UN Security Council in New York. His speech was a blockbuster because, basically, he threatened that the United States would withdraw from the corrupt world body unless the UN cleaned up its money-wasting act and changed its power-grabbing ways.[22]

Although Bill Clinton—a former Rhodes Scholar and ardent globalist—was then president, Helms was the conservative GOP chairman of the Senate Foreign Relations Committee. In this capacity Helms had successfully blocked foreign aid funding for abortions overseas, withheld back dues from the UN because of its corruption, wastefulness, and anti-American slant, and stalled ratification of the Kyoto Protocol on global warming. Helms had also held the line for almost twenty years against Senate ratification of the Law of the Sea Treaty.

Perhaps some of the most interesting and enlightening reactions to Jesse Helms' UN speech were those that the general public most likely has never heard. They came in the form of a flurry of e-mails exchanged between members of the Law of the Sea Committee, both before and after Helms' address. I don't normally go out of my way to read other people's mail, but when I did a Google search for contemporaneous responses to Helms' speech, this series of e-mails came up. These comments shed a great deal of light on the concerns of those who wish to empower the UN as a world government, and for that reason I decided to share selected portions of them here, reproduced as they appeared.[23]

First came a general notice that Helms was going to speak and that the meeting was going to be open to the public and C-Span was going to broadcast it. Then, on the afternoon of Thursday, 20 January, following Helms' address, at 2:14 p.m., one Peggy Tomlinson at the Law of the Sea Committee sent out the following e-mail to undisclosed recipients, on the topic of "Helms-foreign relations committee."

> C-Span will cover the hearing of the Senate Foreign Relations committee tomorrow (Friday) morning at the Association of the Bar of the City of New York. I trust those interested saw the Helms speech at the Security Council this morning. Could we have some comments on his statement that treaties are binding on the US only as a matter of domestic law (ratification) and may be overridden by subsequent acts of Congress. Peggy Tomlinson

At 2:45 p.m. that same day, one Houston Putnam Lowry, apparently an attorney with Brown and Welsh, PC, of Meriden, Connecticut, replied as follows:

> Peg—I think there are US Supreme Court cases that I remember from law school that agree with him. Remember, the Constitution does not indicate how treaties are renounced . . . . While I don't always agree with him, he and his staff can research rather well.

Another response quickly followed at 2:52 p.m., this one coming from Francis A. Boyle, who turns out to be a professor of international law at the University of Illinois in Champaign-Urbana, Illinois.

A very complicated subject. I do not believe Helms is a lawyer. Certainly the best analysis would be found in the Restatement 3d on Foreign Relations Law and Professor Henkin's second edition of Foreign Affairs and the US Constitution. fab.

At 3:11 p.m., Professor Boyle sent along the following comments under the subject heading "P.S. Helms-foreign relations committee."

P.S. We do have the Supremacy Clause that makes treaties the Supreme Law of the Land under Article IV of the Constitution. So we do not have the UK system where treaties must be implemented by Parliament in order to be effective domestically. As for the notion that statutes can supersede treaties, have a look at Meese v. PLO, where Judge Palmieri refused to enforce a statute that clearly would violate the Headquarters Agreement. You might want to try my book that discusses some of these matters. fab.

The professor then discusses a book that he has written, entitled *Defending Civil Resistance Under International Law*. The book description reads, "Provides legal information to individuals to help them design a legal defense for actions of civil resistance intended to halt destructive government activities that violate international law. Has a special section relating to nuclear weapons activities."[24]

The following day, Friday, 21 January, Professor Boyle writes again briefly at 9:48 a.m.

I heard the full text of Helm's speech on the radio last night. Reminded me a bit of the Nazi arguments at Nuremburg—we are only bound by international law to the extent we feel bound. fab.

There you have it, then: American patriots who believe in sovereignty, liberty, and the Constitution are really just like Nazis, the good professor says.

There was no correspondence over the weekend, but at 10:46 p.m. on Wednesday, 26 January, attorney Lowry sent out a forwarded message that is described as a "cross post from *SeaWeb*," on the subject: "*SeaWeb*: NYT Report on Helms Speech."

> Senator Helms has spoken to the UN Security Council, and has raised strong rejoinders from the representatives of the most important allies of the US.
>
> The full story can be seen at http://nyt.com/library/world/global012100helms-un.html.
>
> The NYT story does not indicate that Helms spoke about his opposition to the 1982 Convention on the Law of the Sea, although that is one of his most important "contributions" to US foreign policy. His appearance there also points up the degree to which Congress rather than the President has seized control over US policy toward the UN.

Immediately thereafter, Lowry sent another forwarded message with the subject heading "*SeaWeb*: A comment on and a quote from Jesse Helms' UN Speech."

> There is no question that our esteemed Senate Foreign Relations Committee chairman has delivered a provocative speech to the Security Council. *It is a speech that attacks head on a real, not imagined issue, for there are indeed those in and outside of the UN who do hold that the UN has non-consensual authority over sovereign states.*
>
> This authority has been supported primarily on criminal and humanitarian grounds. Helms presents a legal theory that would allow the UN (or presumably other enforcers) to defend human rights inside sovereign borders without fracturing *his theory of the UN as a body of sovereign states, not a body with authority over states* (emphasis added).

This last writer then posts a link to the *New York Times'* transcript of Helms' speech, and also quotes the concluding paragraphs of that speech, noting that "the gist of his main point is contained in this brief quotation from his summary paragraphs."

There are several important facts to be gleaned from this spate of internationalist e-mails, some of which are more important than others.

Among the minor points worth noting is the fact that at least some of these folks are devoted to providing a spurious legal defense for those who would subvert the legitimate acts of the US government through unspecified "actions of civil resistance."

Equally noteworthy is the fact that even their legal authorities are fairly fuzzy on the Constitution. They clearly seem bent on finding a way to circumvent it rather than, like Helms, trying to preserve, protect, and defend it and to enforce its legal provisions. They do, however, give Helms grudging credit for doing his homework.

In another way, though, these Law of the Sea folks are quite perceptive. While most of the major media and virtually all of the UN delegates were focused on the relative non-issue of US arrears dues payments and demands for reform, Peggy Tomlinson zeroed right in on the most important thing that Helms had to say to the Security Council—the fact that international treaties are *not* perpetually binding contracts, but are merely documents subject to later revocation by Congress.

"Thus, when the United States joins a treaty organization, it holds no legal authority over us," Helms told the Security Council. Note those words well: *no legal authority.* That is an important idea.

"We abide by our treaty obligations because they are the domestic law of our land, and because our elected leaders have judged that the agreement serves our national interest," Helms explained. This statement implies a logical corollary: if our elected leaders should come to judge that those agreements no longer serve our national interest, we are free to change our minds and revoke those treaties.

Tomlinson immediately realized that if Helms' assertion is correct, and if enough Americans ever come to realize this fact, the whole internationalist game plan bites the dust. Why? Because their entire endgame strategy is built around maneuvering the United States into an untenable political position where, under international pressure, it voluntarily gives away the precious national sovereignty that no one else on earth has the power to take from it by force.

Hence the panic at the Law of the Sea Committee when Helms proclaimed this fundamental truth about sovereignty to the world at large. These globalists have been working behind the scenes to accomplish their long-desired goal of ratifying the Law of the Sea Treaty—which in their minds is clearly a righteous cause that will "secure the rule of law over two-thirds of the planet." Yet they clearly recognize their potential legal peril if global treaties are judged to be something less than sacrosanct.

Finally, the last two forwarded posts from *SeaWeb* plainly identify two other major obstacles to the internationalists' global governance agenda. One is the inconvenient fact that Congress does indeed have the power to limit and to some extent control our foreign policy commitments, and that the president does not have a free hand to do whatever he may please.

Moreover, it is interesting to note that these folks have apparently adopted the new globalist perspective on national sovereignty, which they accurately describe as "a real, not imagined issue." They characterize Helms as someone who holds a "legal theory" that views the UN "as a body of sovereign states, not a body with authority over the states." Obviously, they see these things quite differently than Helms.

The last forwarded *SeaWeb* e-mail clearly states that "there are indeed those in and outside of the UN who do hold that the UN has non-consensual authority over sovereign states." This basically means that they think they can tell Americans what to do, without our permission, whether we agree with them or not.

In the globalists' own words, then, this question of national versus global sovereignty is the fundamental issue confronting both our nation and our world, and this battle over the Law of the Sea Treaty is where the line in the sand must be drawn.

What about a Worldwide IRS?

In 1962, the US State Department financed a study entitled *A World Effectively Controlled by the United Nations*. That report outlined what would be needed for a viable world government to function: it would need a mandatory universal membership, the compulsory global jurisdiction of its courts, and an ability to use physical force to enforce its will. One of the UN's "principle features," stated the report, would be "enforceable taxing powers."

Most American citizens would be happy not to have to think about the taxman's hand in their pockets any more than they absolutely have to. Most think they pay out too much money in taxes, and most agree that the IRS today is out of control. There are over thirty thousand pages of tax code, and it generally requires an accountant or a tax service to file your taxes. Wouldn't it be nice if we could simplify the tax code and eliminate the IRS?

Good news! The United Nations wants to do that for us.

However, this creates another problem. The UN wants to create its own global IRS. Yes, you read that right: the UN wants to control and impose a wide array of taxes, and ultimately to tax even your income.

That's because the UN has its sights set on becoming a bona fide global government within the next few years. According to "the most trusted man in America," the famous CBS news anchor Walter Cronkite, "We must strengthen the United Nations as a first step toward a world government."[25]

Any sovereign government must have the money to finance its operations. As long as the UN has no independent source of funding, it has not much more status than a beggar or a charity case. But once it can collect its own taxes as a matter of international law, and it no longer has to rely on the voluntary contributions of nation-states, the UN will quickly emerge as a global ruling authority with its own overpowering military force.

"Once the United Nations has independent financing, and an adequate stream of revenue to maintain its own standing army, it will be the world government that has been the dream of globalists for the entire century," insists UN expert Henry Lamb.[26]

A number of creative taxation ideas have been advanced to accomplish that goal. Back in 1972, Yale economist James Tobin proposed that the UN impose a tax of 0.05 percent on all foreign currency exchange transactions, but the idea never gained traction. Then the United Nations Development Program (UNDP) began pushing the Tobin Tax in its 1994 *Human Development Report*, ostensibly as a way to slow down greedy international currency speculators and redirect their unearned profits to benefit the most poverty-stricken countries on the planet.

Today nearly $300 trillion is exchanged annually on open currency markets around the world. Dollars are sold for British pounds. Japanese yen are converted to euro. If such a Tobin Tax were imposed on all international currency transactions today, the UN would rake in $1.5 *trillion* per year—or about one hundred times its current annual budget.[27]

In 1993, the Ford Foundation produced a report called *Financing an Effective United Nations*, which recommended that the UN should also have the authority to tax international airline traffic, shipping, and arms sales. The co-chairman of the group that produced that report was Paul Volker, one-time head of the Federal Reserve System. "The standard of living of the average American has to decline," Volker famously said back in 1979. "I don't think you can escape that."[28]

Then in 1995, the UN-funded Commission on Global Governance suggested that the UN should collect levies from those who use "flight lanes, sea lanes for ships, ocean fishing areas, and the electromagnetic spectrum."[29]

Global taxation zealots at the UN also smell a powerful opportunity in the Internet. The UNDP's 1999 *Human Development Report* called for a tax of "one US cent on every 100 lengthy e-mails." The tax, proponents say, would "raise funds that would be spent to narrow the 'digital divide' between rich and poor" nations.[30]

The highly touted Millennium Declaration of 2000 promised that the UN will reduce poverty, hunger, and HIV-AIDS by 50 percent by the year 2015. It is also supposed to see to it that everyone in the world has clean drinking water and access to basic education. Needless to say, we're still a long way from those laudable, if perhaps unreachable, goals.[31] But the Millennium Declaration also affirmed that, to accomplish those goals, the UN has the moral right to extract resources from wealthy nations such as the United States, partly through a carbon tax on fossil fuels like aviation fuel, gasoline, coal, oil, and natural gas. Such a tax would allegedly combat global warming, while theoretically the revenue could be redistributed to poorer nations. But this carbon tax would also drive up the price of gas for cars and trucks, home heating fuels, plastics, and countless other products for consumers worldwide.[32]

All of these tax schemes are still in the works today, and many of them were discussed at the UN's International Conference on Financing for Development, which was held in Monterrey, Mexico, in 2002. Rep. Ron Paul says the real goal of that conference was to "consider the best ways to shake down rich nations for money."[33]

The Tobin Tax on international currency transfers remains the first step currently favored by globalists who want to establish the legitimacy of the UN as a worldwide taxing authority. But, according to Congressman Paul, the UN's ultimate goal is worldwide income taxes. "The Tobin Tax is not the only idea being considered," he insists. "Some have suggested taxing airline travel or carbon emissions. *The ultimate goal is an income tax, which will be imposed after we've swallowed the idea of UN taxing authority.*"[34]

The UN's High Level Panel on Financing for Development worked for two years after the 2000 Millennium Summit to produce a "consensus" report that would be accepted in Monterrey. The final result was a 101-page document designed to establish UN control over a broad spectrum of economic activity worldwide.[35] Among the ideas discussed during the course of that conference was a tax on "speculative cash flows," or international currency exchanges, and the confiscation of the proceeds of drug trafficking, which would be placed into an "international humanitarian fund." Also considered was a global lottery and the forgiveness of debt for the sixty or so HIPCs, or Heavily Indebted Poor Countries, mostly in Africa.[36]

The four major financial proposals contained in the seventy-two-page pre-conference consensus-building report were:

1. Assure that developed countries contribute 0.7 percent of their GDP (Gross Domestic Product) to development aid for developing countries into a "common pool" for distribution by the United Nations.
2. Create a Global Economic Security Council as proposed by the Commission on Global Governance.
3. Create an International Tax Organization.
4. Establish an "adequate international tax source," namely, the Tobin Tax on currency exchange, and a global tax on carbon (the use of fossil fuels).[37]

All of these ideas survived in one form or another in the vaguely worded final document. How they will ultimately be implemented— and enforced—remains to be seen, but for now, more than 150 nations of the world have agreed that these Robin Hood–type, tax-the-rich schemes should become the global economic reality of the future. According to one press observer, "The Monterrey conference was about a massive new drive for wealth redistribution, via both foreign aid and global taxation. The United States can never give enough to satisfy the adherents of the international socialist creed."[38]

Henry Lamb warns that the issue of global taxation by the UN is not just theoretical but real, and that the threat is not merely trivial but critical.

The jury is still out on the issue of which way the United States will go on the issue of global economic control by the UN. Most Americans will never know the issue is on the table until after the decisions are made. The media is not likely to address the issue, nor is it likely to be a topic of congressional debate.

These events are taking place in other parts of the world, with decisions being made by officials who are not elected by anyone. No elected official in the United States has any authority to alter or veto these decisions. The world is moving swiftly toward Global Governance. . . .

If Congress does not intervene—quickly and powerfully—it will be too late. *If the UN gets the independent financing it covets, and has designed in the report of the High Level Panel, the United States will cease to exist as a sovereign nation.* It will become nothing more than just another state at the mercy of a world government.[39]

The burden of all taxation falls on both taxpayers and consumers. It's time for the US taxpayers to host another Boston Tea Party for the United Nations.

Free Trade Idols: NAFTA, CAFTA, FTAA

In 2005, our representatives in Congress approved the controversial Central American Free Trade Agreement, also known as CAFTA, by a narrow margin of 217–215 in the House of Representatives. But to get CAFTA through the House, President George W. Bush had to twist arms and cut deals until long after midnight on the day of the vote.[40]

This hotly contested trade legislation expands the so-called Free Trade Zone previously established a decade before between the United States, Mexico, and Canada by the North American Free Trade Agreement (NAFTA). The law removes trade barriers between the United States and the six Central American nations of Costa Rica, El Salvador, Nicaragua, Guatemala, Honduras, and the Dominican Republic.

The highly controversial CAFTA trade pact was negotiated in early 2004 with the strong backing of the Bush administration. Its supporters knew they didn't have the votes to ram it through Congress before the 2004 presidential election, but after Inauguration Day 2005, GOP lawmakers were mercilessly pressured by the White House to pass CAFTA as soon as possible.

The way they got the job done was reminiscent of the tactics employed by Bill Clinton and his Republican co-conspirators to pass NAFTA back in 1993—which passed by a wider margin of 234–200, but only after a bitter fight from passionately determined opponents. Here's the way NAFTA opponent Pat Buchanan described the tawdry affair at the time:

> In the end they had to buy it. In the end they won the bidding war, not the battle for the hearts and minds.
>
> All week long we were witness to an astonishing spectacle—the open selling of America by men and women entrusted with her governance. For 72 hours Congress was like the "pit" in the Chicago commodities market when word hits that the corn harvest will be 20 percent smaller than expected. It will be a long time before the stench of bribery leaves the Capitol building.
>
> The president's men won not by giving their countrymen the vision of a better future, but by buying up their representatives with deals on tomatoes, peanut butter, sugar, citrus, trade centers, C-17s, and development banks.[41]

Sadly, the way Clinton had to do it in 1993 was the same way Bush had to do it in 2005. He had to buy his costly political victory, selling out the economic future of America in the process. I had expected nothing less from Clinton, but I had thought better of Bush before that day. I was wrong.

Twelve years after NAFTA went into effect, as CAFTA was coming up for its crucial vote, Buchanan held up the failed NAFTA record and predicted what would be in store with CAFTA:

In 1993, Republicans, by four to one, signed on to NAFTA. They believed the promises that our $5 billion trade surplus with Mexico would grow and illegal immigration would diminish. They were deceived. The NAFTA skeptics were proven right. The US trade surplus with Mexico vanished overnight. Last year, we ran a $50 billion trade deficit. Since 1993, 15 million illegal aliens have been caught breaking into the United States. Five million made it, and their soaring demands for social services have driven California to bankruptcy. As for Mexico's major exports to us, they appear to be two: narcotics and Mexicans.[42]

Facts are facts, and it's hard to argue against the unpleasant but obvious truth.

I personally believe that the passage of this CAFTA legislation was a tragic mistake for America, for the same reason that NAFTA was twelve years before—because both treaties undermine the American economy and ship American jobs overseas, all just to fill the coffers of the callous multinational corporations that, like a rich man with a poor strumpet, benefit from their intimacy with America but don't love and respect her.

I also believe that the idolatrous worship of so-called free trade within the ranks of nominal conservatives in the Republican Party is a modern-day golden calf that will ultimately bring an economic curse upon our country. I realize that is a highly inflammatory statement, so let me clarify my position.

I, too, firmly believe in free trade in the sense that the great classical liberals of yesteryear—visionary statesmen like Adam Smith and John Locke—understood the term. But I also believe in *fair* trade, and that is the real issue at stake today.

Honest competition is the beating heart of capitalism, and I endorse it. But as a small businessman responsible for running my own family-owned company and meeting a payroll every week, I know firsthand just how hard it is for American businesses to remain competitive when the global playing field isn't level.

International treaties ratified within the past two decades have established the General Agreement on Tariffs and Trade (GATT), the World Trade Organization (WTO), and the North American Free Trade Agreement (NAFTA). The net result of *all* of these ill-advised documents has been to diminish the productivity of the United States, severely limit our national sovereignty, compromise our borders, subject our people to the non-appealable dictates of an unfriendly international tribunal, impoverish many of our communities, and transfer ever-increasing portions of our national wealth abroad.

All of these objections apply equally to CAFTA, as do the outright deceptions used to lure the United States into these internationalist entanglements. Even the "free trade" label is misleading. As with NAFTA before it, the CAFTA pact will *not* promote free trade but rather highly regulated trade, subject to the rules of the WTO—which has already proven itself to be biased against and hostile toward American interests.

These and other dangers of CAFTA were well-documented by William Norman Grigg in "CAFTA: Exporting American Jobs and Industry," published in the 18 April issue of the *New American* magazine.[43]

That is why I am especially pleased with the unequivocal statements made by my own congresswoman Virginia Foxx, who was an outspoken opponent of CAFTA. When somebody suggested that we might lose the tiny Central American market to China, and so "a vote against CAFTA is a vote for China," Representative Foxx was not persuaded.

"While I don't want to lose our markets to China, the fact is that it was NAFTA that nearly wiped us out—and CAFTA would do more damage than NAFTA ever did," Representative Foxx told the *New American*. "Most of the people in my district are very opposed to CAFTA for economic reasons," she continued, but she noted that her own misgivings were rooted in her desire to preserve American independence. "I have concerns about our involvement in any kind of international arrangement of this sort that undermines our sovereignty—whether it's NAFTA, CAFTA, the WTO, or certainly the United Nations."[44]

Perhaps the greatest danger from CAFTA is that its globalist sponsors really do view the treaty as a stepping-stone to a hemispheric EU-type union under a planned Free Trade Area of the Americas—another major expansion of NAFTA—and eventually the establishment of a real global government. That might sound like an overstatement, were it not for the fact that the same thing has been said before by many prominent people who are in a position to know.

Let's consider for a moment just a sampling of those, starting with Henry Kissinger, former secretary of state and national security adviser to Richard Nixon. Here's what Dr. Kissinger said about NAFTA at the time it was being debated:

[NAFTA] will represent the most creative step toward a new world order taken by any group of countries since the end of the Cold War, and *the first step toward an even larger vision of a free trade zone for the entire Western Hemisphere.* . . . [NAFTA] is not a conventional trade agreement but the architecture of a new international system.[45]

Dr. Kissinger, arguably one of the most intelligent and influential people on the planet, clearly told Americans in advance that NAFTA was "not a conventional trade agreement." Instead, it was to be "the architecture of a new international system." What kind of system was it intended to produce? A "free-trade zone for the entire Western Hemisphere," or a hemispherical federation like the European Union.

Mexican president Vicente Fox said exactly the same thing in 2002. "Eventually, our long-range objective [with NAFTA] is to establish with the United States, but also with Canada, our other regional partner, an ensemble of connections and institutions similar to those created by the European Union," Fox admitted in Madrid.[46]

And Vicente Fox's progressive idea got strong support from an unexpected source: the supposedly conservative editorial page of the *Wall Street Journal.*

Reformist Mexican President Vicente Fox raises eyebrows with his suggestion that over a decade or two NAFTA should evolve into something like the European Union, with open borders for not only goods and investment but also people. He can rest assured that there is one voice north of the Rio Grande that supports his vision. To wit, this newspaper.[47]

What about the World Trade Organization? Well, the same bunch of GOP reprobates—Dole, Gingrich, and Company—who had sided with Clinton to deliver NAFTA in 1993 did the same thing for WTO a year later.

Newt Gingrich, who was the incoming Speaker of the House, admitted that approving WTO amounted to "a very big transfer of power." Gingrich told his congressional cohorts in a committee meeting, "We need to be honest about the fact that we are transferring from the United States at a practical level significant authority to a new organization. This is a transformational moment."[48]

Gingrich was right. Over the past decade, NAFTA and WTO tribunals have overturned US laws and court rulings. And American leaders have meekly complied with our new foreign masters.

Next on the horizon is the FTAA, which President George W. Bush has promised to bring into being come hell or high water. This new entity, to which CAFTA was merely a necessary stepping-stone, would expand the NAFTA/CAFTA framework throughout all of South America, so that the entire Western Hemisphere would at last be just what Henry Kissinger predicted it would become: a huge regional trade zone spanning two continents. Like the European Union, we may become the Union of the Americas.

While FTAA might still face stiff resistance in the House, its globalist architects are desperately working to push the scheme through Congress, sooner rather than later. The key to defeating any such regional expansion of CAFTA is to let our representatives in Congress know that their constituents are informed about and opposed to FTAA, and that we will be watching to see how they vote on this crucial "trade pact." It's not too much to say that the long-term survival of our sovereign Republic is at stake with the FTAA vote, whenever it comes.

6

GLOBAL JUSTICE AND THE
INTERNATIONAL CRIMINAL COURT

The One-Worlders on the Left Coast love to promote the United
Nations. The most blatantly pro-UN movie ever to emanate from
the liberals in Hollywood is *The Interpreter*, a 2005 Universal Pictures
production that was actually filmed inside the United Nations building
in New York City, with the personal blessing of Kofi Annan.

Nicole Kidman, the heroine, plays the role of a seemingly innocent
UN interpreter who inadvertently overhears an assassination plot against
the controversial leader of a war-torn African nation. Sean Penn plays a
skeptical Secret Service agent charged with finding the plotters and foiling
the crime before it can be carried out on the floor of the General Assembly.

But as it turns out, Kidman has a secret history as part of the rebel
resistance movement opposing President Zawani, the intended assassination victim. Having since forsaken armed resistance for diplomacy,
she has left her home in Africa and moved to New York to work for the
UN. When confronted with her own violent past, Kidman passionately
declares, "I believe in this place. I believe in what it's trying to do."

That is the primary message of the movie: the UN is an indispensable forum for mediating the crises of the world. The only alternative is
an endless cycle of violence, blood, and death all around the world. We
all need to "believe in" the UN.

The movie's subplot is more subtle but every bit as relevant: the International Criminal Court (ICC) is the equally indispensable tribunal for dispensing justice to global thugs like Zawani. In the end, the evil dictator must answer to the world for his crimes against humanity, because his case has been referred to the ICC by a unanimous vote of the Security Council. For those familiar with contemporary politics, the implications of such unanimity are tremendous, because the vote indicates that the United States has at long last dropped its obdurate opposition to the international tribunal.

The International Criminal Court Is Dangerous

Clearly, the Hollywood liberals want us to believe that the UN is great and the International Criminal Court is good. But I personally believe that the ICC is incredibly dangerous, both to the sovereignty of the United States and to the rights and liberties of US citizens. In fact, I consider it to be one of the *most* dangerous of the UN-affiliated organizations.

Some may be skeptical of my warnings about the ICC. After all, it is responsible for prosecuting crimes against humanity, war crimes, and other atrocities. Who could object to that, except maybe a reactionary conspiracy theorist?

No sane person—and certainly no Christian, including me—believes that war crimes or other crimes against humanity should go unpunished. That is not my objection to the ICC. My objection is not to the end result; it is to the means employed to achieve it.

The problem with the ICC is the agenda of those who created it and the mechanisms that they have set up, whereby the court can become a vehicle to subvert national sovereignty and to impose its own trans-nationalist agenda.

The ICC is an international institution in which unaccountable foreign judges may someday sit in judgment of American citizens without regard for certain fundamental protections accorded by our Bill of Rights, such as the right to a speedy trial, trial by jury, and petition of habeas corpus. What's more, the ICC's global prosecutor has virtually unlimited power to enforce criminal laws, many of which are as yet undefined.

Add to this volatile mix the growing tendency to homogenize all laws globally, so that new international standards may eventually replace the settled and customary laws of individual nations, and what we have is a potentially explosive situation.

For those of you persuaded of the dangers of the UN generally, or the ICC specifically, let me warn you that believing this in a general way is not enough. If we are to avoid the coming dangers inherent in American acquiescence to the ICC agenda, US presidents and legislators will need to take certain actions, and refuse to take others, to keep our national sovereignty safe.

As we consider this subject, it may be helpful to remember that the idea of such a tribunal is a fairly recent development. How has the civilized world managed to deal with such crimes all this time without the ICC? After all, the ICC was only authorized by the General Assembly, subject to ratification by sixty countries, on 17 July 1998, and it came into existence on 1 July 2002. The Court did not officially open in The Hague until 11 March 2003.[1]

At this point, to avoid possible confusion, I should point out that the ICC is an entirely different entity from the UN's International Court of Justice (or World Court), which also customarily meets in the Netherlands at The Hague. The World Court exists to settle disputes between nations, generally regarding treaties or other questions of international law, and not to try individuals for criminal violations.

Searching for Sources in Law Journals

It will be helpful to start by examining some "deep background" on the ICC. To do so, I will examine some sources that are widely regarded as being reputable: the writings of law professors.

Why dig into the obscure and sometimes arcane writings of law professors? Well, there's the rather obvious reason that courts engage in lawmaking and those who teach law might be best suited to tell us what the courts are up to.

But there is a more important reason. Law professors are required by their law schools to produce a steady stream of scholarship. Most legal scholarship is published in academic journals called law reviews. And over the years some very strict standards have arisen that are universally followed.

Some of this scholarship is objective. But most of it is not. The thing that makes law review articles such a rich source of information is that they must be extensively documented—a hundred-page article could easily have over four hundred footnotes—and that each and every footnote has been checked by someone else for accuracy before being put into print. Law students all across America spend hours "cite checking" the articles that will be published by their schools and bringing errors to the author's attention, as well as requiring them to add additional documentation.

But even more importantly, the pro-UN articles published in law journals are a great source for finding out facts. The things that we know to be great dangers are the very things that those on the other side tend to tout as great triumphs. They are not trying to hide these things: they are strenuously advocating for them or bragging about their accomplishments.

To begin with, the ICC was created when enough nations ratified a document called the Rome Statute of the International Criminal Court.[2] It is usually referred to as either the Rome Statute or the Rome Treaty. It was created at a conference with the rather pompous-sounding name of "United Nations Diplomatic Conference of Plenipotentiaries on the Establishment of an International Criminal Court," held in Rome in June 1998.[3]

The Emerging Threat of Transnationalism

Transnationalism is a very important term, and it can mean many different things. The term *transnational law* was put into usage by a law professor named Philip C. Jessup. One of his most widely quoted definitions states that transnational law is "the law which regulates actions or events that transcend national frontiers . . . includ[ing] both . . . public and private international law. . . ."[4]

This definition, on its face, covers an enormous amount of law. It could cover the Law of Nations, a biblical concept that our Founding Fathers believed in and actually wrote into the Constitution. It could cover private international transactions. But it can also cover what some have called the transnationalist movement.

Professor Jessup, now deceased, was one of the prime movers and shakers in the transnationalist movement. He served as professor of international law at Columbia University from 1946 to 1961. However, his connection to the "dark side" of transnationalism is readily apparent through his lifelong involvement with globalist institutions. According to the Modern History Project, he was a trustee of the Institute for Pacific Relations, a delegate to the Bretton Woods Conference in 1944, a delegate to the UN Organizing Conference, a US delegate to the UN General Assembly, president for one term of the American Society for International Law, and a judge on the UN's World Court.[5]

However benign Jessup's definition may sound, and no matter how loudly some may protest that transnationalism is the same as the US founders' Law of Nations, don't be fooled. Given that Jessup coined this term and had the affiliations noted above, it is no surprise that others have taken up his mantle and that today there is a full-blown transnationalist agenda.

One of the most important contemporary players is Harold Hongju Koh, the current dean of Yale Law School. Koh never misses an opportunity to preach the transnationalist message. On the law school's website, in an open letter to prospective students, Koh prioritizes this message. Even before would-be students are accepted, Koh seeks to get them excited about the transnationalist ideology. He identifies it as one of three great challenges at Yale Law School, writing:

> **First, globalization**: Many law schools have waved the "globalization" banner, but no law school has truly asked and answered the question: "What does it mean to have a genuinely global curriculum, faculty, student body, and program in the 21st century?" At Yale Law School, we have already integrated an international perspective into many of our core courses. We also have a huge array of internationally focused programs, including the Schell Center on International Human Rights, the Corporate Law Center, the Middle East Legal Studies Seminar, the China Law Center, and our Global Constitutionalism conference.[6]

Can you guess how Yale law graduates will view the UN, the World Court, and the International Criminal Court? What about American sovereignty? By the time they graduate, some will undoubtedly be active soldiers in the transnationalist army.

Perhaps more alarmingly, many will gain employment as state and federal law clerks, where they will write judicial opinions for judges. (Most judicial opinions in this country are written by law clerks and just "touched up" by the judges before they are issued.) Others will take positions in various branches of government.

But most will go on to the regular practice of law. Neither they, nor their clients, nor the judges they practice in front of, will know that these new generation lawyers are actually pawns in the hands of the transnationalists.

And make no mistake: the transnationalists want to capture every law school in America. The vast majority of law schools in this country belong to an organization called the American Association of Law Schools (AALS). At its 2006 annual meeting, much of the AALS's agenda was dedicated to transnationalism. One of its two major emphases for the entire first day was "Integrating Transnationalist Perspectives into the First Year Curriculum."[7] Dean Koh was one of the speakers, along with law professors from Columbia, Duke, Cornell, Georgetown, Villanova, and other prominent schools.[8]

These professors taught their colleagues from around the country how to instruct American law students in the legal doctrines of trans-nationalism. They did not satisfy themselves with generalities, but had specific workshops on how to teach transnationalism, instead of classes on Civil Procedure, Constitutional Law, Contracts, Criminal Law and Procedure, Property, and Torts. Still not satisfied, the AALS also held a special workshop in which the panelists discussed "the kinds of institutional support—including leave for preparation of materials, joint programs with institutions outside the United States, the role of foreign graduate students in first year courses—that may be necessary to ensure that transnational law actually becomes part of a first year curriculum."[9]

How many Americans do you think know what is going on in our law schools today? Sadly, not many. But exactly what is it that the law school elites want their students to embrace? It is critically important that we understand the answer to that question. The law professors whom I have been quoting have used various terms: *transnational, international, global.* So let's zero in on one term: *the transnationalist movement.*

Here, again, we can learn from Dean Koh. He is completely above-board about the vision he has for the world—and it's a vision that should frighten anyone who believes that national sovereignty is a good idea. The transnationalists' goal is both to understand *and commandeer* the processes whereby nations obey international norms. Koh has written that "transnational legal process provides the key, in my view, to understanding the critical issue of compliance with international law."[10]

Furthermore, Koh has written that "transnational legal process describes the theory and practice of how public and private actors—nation-states, international organizations, multinational enterprises, nongovernmental organizations, and private individuals—interact in a variety of public and private, domestic and international fora to make, interpret, enforce, and ultimately, internalize rules of transnational law."[11]

That is the radical goal of the dean of the Yale Law School and many others—forcing obedience upon nations through back channels and without anyone noticing until it is too late. But that is exactly what we must never allow to happen.

Koh has repeatedly advocated in writing that a cadre of legal and intellectual elites needs to manipulate international opinion, as well as national and international governing bodies and NGOs, to bring about the desired goal of transnationalism. For our present purposes, it is sufficient to realize that the goal of many transnationalists is to bring about the end of national sovereignty, and that to do so they intend to employ national and international courts. So some of the "domestic and international fora" that Koh referenced above are actually the courts.

In 1998, Koh delivered an address that was later turned into a *Houston Law Review* article, entitled "Bringing International Law Home." In it he wrote, "If nations do come to 'obey' international law, even if only out of a perceived self-interest that becomes institutional habit, how do we transform grudging compliance into habitual obedience?"[12]

Reading this, the first question we might rightly ask is: Who do these people think they are? I think a fair answer is: They think they are the masters of the world.

Interpreting the Transnationalist Agenda

Koh went on to lay out an agenda for self-proclaimed human rights activists who seek to manipulate nations: "For human rights activists, this suggests a simple three-pronged strategy: first, provoking interactions; second, provoking norm interpretations; and third, provoking norm-internalizations."[13]

This agenda is already being pressed, and with dangerous results. So let's try to parse the legal gobbledy-gook. This is really just an expansion of Koh's previous statement. He wants human rights activists to agitate on issues of concern until they get some national or international body to make a declaration, propose a treaty, or—most importantly here—issue a court opinion. Then, they want the activists and others to press the governments of the world to acknowledge and voluntarily adopt these norms. This is exactly what has happened with recent US Supreme Court decisions that have jettisoned American law in favor of following world opinion.

Koh illustrated how his technique has already successfully worked in the area of land mines:

> First, if transnational actors obey international law as a result of repeated interaction with other actors in the transnational legal process, one progressive step would be to empower more actors to participate in the process. The goal, therefore, should be to expand the participation of intergovernmental organizations, NGOs, private business entities, and transnational norm entrepreneurs as process-activators. The process surrounding the worldwide ban on landmines is a graphic example of how norm entrepreneurs were able to build a public-private transnational network of individuals and groups dedicated to pressing their norm, while enlisting governmental allies and building popular global support.[14]

Notice how Koh calls these activists "transnational norm entrepreneurs." These are people who make their living trying to control the legal thinking of the whole world! Koh continues to develop his game plan as follows:

> Second, if the goal of interaction is to produce interpretation of human rights norms that may be applied against violators, activists must seek new fora for the enunciation and elaboration of norms.

Once again, the landmines case shows how a transnational issue network, stymied in the existing Geneva Process, first enlisted the aid of the smaller governmental players, then created a new intergovernmental forum—the Ottawa Process—in which to promote development of the norm. Intergovernmental organizations play key roles, not just as instigators of interaction, but also as creators of new interpretive fora. For example, existing intergovernmental organizations have created new law-declaring arenas, as the UN Security Council did by creating international criminal tribunals for Rwanda and the former Yugoslavia, or as the United Nations has recently done by laying the foundations for a new International Criminal Court.[15]

It is important to notice that the ICC is just one of various courts the transnationalists are manipulating.

Koh also notes that

[I]n other cases in which dedicated fora do not already exist, intergovernmental organizations have sought to adapt existing fora, so that international human rights issues can be raised before the European Court of Justice, or international environmental issues raised before GATT Panels. By promoting development of these fora, human rights activists can also seek to expand the interpretive community that determines the contours of a legal norm and whether that norm has been violated in particular instances.[16]

Koh also readily admits that courts should be manipulated to lull citizens and legislators to sleep. He suggests that if radical ideas are forced on us through our courts, eventually the ideas will come to feel "familiar" and will be more readily accepted:

Third and finally, human rights activists need to develop techniques to provoke legal norm-internalization as a starting point for political and social internalization. . . . [P]ersistent activists can combine strategies of judicial internalization with strategies of political, social, and legislative internalization, with an eye toward making international norms "feel familiar" to political actors. Even when explicit ratification efforts fail, as in the landmines and UNCLOS III episodes, *activists inside and outside of participating governments can act to conform governmental conduct to unratified treaties.* Such action sets the stage for eventual ratification of these treaties by the abstaining nations on the ground that de facto internalization has already become a *fait accompli.*[17]

As we have already seen in other chapters, this tactic of conforming the activities and regulations of government agencies to international standards—even when the treaties establishing those standards have not been officially ratified or accepted—is already far advanced here in America. This process, which has been carefully followed by the UN and its supporters for forty years, is one of intentionally seeking consensus reports, convention agendas, plans of action, legal decisions, and so on, and one that is intended to build up an impressive edifice of perceived "international norms" that everyone else would then be intimidated into accepting. This sophisticated process is called creating "soft law," which the activists hope to get converted into positive law later.

Koh concluded his *HLR* article with this rallying cry to his troops:

I have argued that transnational legal process is not self-activating. Our action influences that process; our inaction ratifies the status quo. By this reasoning, those who favor application of international norms to state behavior cannot afford to be passive observers. To the contrary, they must seek self-consciously to participate in, influence, and ultimately enforce transnational legal process, by promoting the interaction, interpretation, and internalization of international norms into domestic law. If our aim is to promote obedience to international law, we have a duty not simply to observe transnational legal process, but to try to influence it.[18]

I believe that the transnationalists' soft law agenda is an evil that must be stopped. In fact, there are some transnationalists who seek nothing less than the complete elimination of national sovereignty—the elimination of the nation-state itself. And they are no less shy about committing their views to paper than are Dean Koh or the AALS.

For example, Gordon A. Christenson, professor of law at the University of Cincinnati College of Law, wrote an article in 1997 telling federal judges how they should incorporate transnationalist principles into their opinions in such a way that they could avoid "making a hard choice between loyalty to a sovereign political community, to some vague allegiance to a states system that is changing, or a new loyalty to a cosmopolitan world community not yet here."[19]

Of course, all the federal judges whom he was addressing had taken an oath to uphold the Constitution of the United States. Yet Christenson cites and endorses other professors who claim that sovereignty is "obsolete."[20]

Is Sovereignty Obsolete?

Numerous other American law professors have mocked the very idea of nation-states in print. As usual, we can turn to Dean Koh for a flagrant example. In this case, he quotes US Supreme Court Justice Stephen Breyer and references recent Supreme Court cases that have relied upon international law, namely *Lawrence v. Texas*,[21] which struck down the Texas anti-sodomy law, and *Atkins v. Virginia*,[22] in which the Supreme Court disallowed the execution of a murderer whom a witness had characterized as being "mildly mentally retarded."

While men and women of good faith can disagree over whether the mentally retarded should be executed, it is no business of the United States Supreme Court to rely on international law to so conclude. Unless perhaps they are the dupes or willing puppets of the aforementioned "transnational norm entrepreneurs."

In any event, *Lawrence* and *Atkins* may signal that the nationalists' heyday has finally passed. As Justice Breyer recently noted:

> By now . . . it should be clear that the chicken has broken out of the egg. Like it or not, both foreign and international law are already part of our law. In time, I expect, those who continue to deny that reality will be remembered like those who assumed the attitude once ascribed . . . to the British: when told how things are done in another country they simply say, "How funny."[23]

The Multifaceted International Judicial System

The ICC is in fact just one of the judicial vehicles used by the transnationlists to achieve their international soft law agenda.

Stanford law professor Jenny S. Martinez has recently written, "Is there an international judicial system? Talk of globalization is everywhere, but it still comes as a surprise to many lawyers and scholars who do not specialize in international law to learn that there are now more than fifty international courts, tribunals, and quasi-judicial bodies, most of which have been established in the past twenty years."[24]

Martinez goes on to write:

> It is no longer possible to dismiss the topic of international adjudication with a version of the cynical critique that "international law is not really law" along the lines that "international courts are not really courts." International courts are acting more and more like, well, courts: they are convicting people of international crimes and sending them to prison; they are exercising compulsory jurisdiction over trade disputes; they are enforcing the rights of individuals against governments. Compliance with the decisions of international courts is not perfect, to be sure, but the reputational and other consequences of noncompliance are factors that political actors cannot simply ignore. Moreover, in a world of global

commerce and communications, national courts cannot avoid interactions with the larger world, and lawyers and scholars cannot ignore the transnational aspects of modern litigation.[25]

In a similar vein, Roger P. Alford has documented the rise of international judicial and quasi-judicial bodies, and he is in a position to know. Now a law professor at Pepperdine, he has previously served as a senior legal advisor in Switzerland to a tribunal set up to deal with claims to dormant Holocaust-era Swiss bank accounts. He also clerked for a federal judge and served as a legal assistant to the Honorable Richard C. Allison, Iran-United States Claims Tribunal, in The Hague.

In 2000, Professor Alford wrote of the many new courts and tribunals that had been created in the past twenty years:

> The rate of growth has been so furious that government leaders now express concern over "tribunal fatigue." Among the more noteworthy developments in this field in the past two decades are the establishment of two new UN criminal tribunals, one new tribunal relating to the law of the sea, four new or reinvigorated trade and investment tribunals, five new mass claim reparation tribunals, several new regional economic integration tribunals, numerous new human rights tribunals, and one soon-to-be-established international criminal court.[26]

Professor Alford noted, moreover, that it is not just the *number* of tribunals that has increased. It is also the frequency with which individuals and nations are turning to these tribunals that has radically increased. Knowing that this phenomenon is exactly what the transnationalists want, we should not be surprised. However, we should be alarmed—because their desired agenda is unfolding right before our eyes.

Professor Alford documented the developments. And remember, this was in 2000.

International courts and tribunals are being utilized with greater and greater frequency. . . . In its first forty years of existence, the ICJ [International Court of Justice] handled seventy-two cases and rendered forty-five judgments. In the past three years, the ICJ has rendered more than twenty contentious and advisory opinions and currently has twenty-four pending cases on its docket.

Likewise, in its first five years of existence, the World Trade Organization's Dispute Settlement Body has been notified of 190 complaints and has rendered thirty-two decisions. Even more astounding, the mass claims tribunals have been rendering decisions that number in the thousands. The Iran-US Claims Tribunal has resolved more than 3,000 claims, the Claims Resolution Tribunal for Dormant Accounts in Switzerland has rendered more than 7,500 decisions, the Commission for Real Property Claims in Bosnia and Herzegovina has rendered more than 25,000 decisions, and the United Nations Compensation Commission (UNCC) has resolved in excess of 125,000 claims.[27]

NGO and the ICC

The creation of the International Criminal Court was a long-term goal of the transnationalists. Not surprisingly, the ICC employs numerous personnel whose job it is to interact with NGOs. In fact, the ICC is in the debt of numerous NGOs for its very existence. That is not a healthy situation.

For example, an organization called the NGO Coalition for an International Criminal Court was instrumental in pushing for the formation of the ICC. It now continues to push its agenda, which includes agitating that nations sign the Roman Statute, thereby bringing more nations unequivocally under the jurisdiction of the ICC; agitating that more nations sign the Agreement on the Privileges and Immunities of the International Criminal Court; and heaping a steady stream of ridicule on the United States for failing to do either.[28]

This NGO has been credited by those in the know with being

instrumental in the creation of the ICC. In November 1998, just months after the Rome Statute went into effect, Silvia Fernández, legal adviser to the Permanent Mission of Argentina to the United Nations, praised the NGO Coalition for an International Criminal Court:

> I am convinced that the successful adoption of the Rome Statute is largely due to the work of the Coalition and the partnership that you managed to develop between NGOs and governments during the four years of our work. The fluid dialogue between delegations and representatives of civil society was indeed essential to identify goals and preoccupations and to design the best strategy to achieve them.[29]

To fully understand Fernández's praise, we need to understand that the phrase *civil society* is a term of art with a distinct meaning. To understand what civil society means to the transnationalists, we can look once again at the scholarship of Gordon A. Christenson. Borrowing from others, Christenson defines *civil society* as "all that part of society which is not the state. It is residue."[30]

So Fernández is praising the Coalition for an International Criminal Court for facilitating the "fluid dialogue," not between delegations and governments, but between delegations and nongovernmental actors, very likely some of Koh's "transnational norm entrepreneurs."

We now have a criminal court that is politically beholden to numerous NGOs loose on the world scene. This court employs personnel to interface with the NGOs, and the NGOs engage in full-time propaganda on behalf of the court. Meanwhile, this court's entire history has the fingerprints of the transnationalists all over it.

The US and the International Criminal Court

The United States has not agreed to participate in the ICC. However, many legal experts of the transnationalist persuasion would contend that we Americans are subject to the court's jurisdiction anyway.

So far, the United States has taken a fairly consistent stand against the ICC—but not without some significant exceptions.

First, the US Senate has refused to ratify the Rome Statute. Yet President Clinton signed the treaty on 31 December 2000, the last day that would allow any nation to participate in further ICC discussions. He signed the treaty so that the United States would be "in a position to influence the evolution of the court," Clinton claimed.[31]

"I will not, and do not recommend that my successor submit the treaty to the Senate for advice and consent until our fundamental concerns are satisfied," the president continued.[32] Clinton also admitted to being worried about what he called "significant flaws in the treaty." He specifically said, "In particular, we are concerned that when the court comes into existence, it will not only exercise authority over personnel of states that have ratified the treaty, but also claim jurisdiction over personnel of states that have not."[33]

Of course, such are precisely the fears of those who oppose the ICC. How could a United States president who had such legitimate concerns still sign the treaty? That is what Senator Jesse Helms wanted to know. Helms immediately issued a press release with the bold headline: "THIS DECISION WILL NOT STAND." Helms denounced the ICC as an "international kangaroo court" and a "global Star Chamber" and soundly rebuked Clinton's lame-duck action:

> President Clinton's decision to sign the Rome Treaty establishing an International Criminal Court in his final days in office is as outrageous as it is inexplicable. Two years ago, the president refused to sign the Rome Treaty, citing the threat the Court posed to American service members and officials.
>
> At the time, his chief negotiator Ambassador David Scheffer told Congress: "The [Rome] treaty purports to establish an arrangement whereby United States armed forces operating overseas could be conceivably prosecuted by the International Criminal Court, even if the

United States has not agreed to be bound by the treaty. Not only is this contrary to the most fundamental principles of treaty law, it could inhibit the ability of the United States to use its military to meet alliance obligations and participate in multinational operations. . . ."

Nothing—I repeat, nothing—has changed since then to justify U.S. signature. To the contrary, for two years, the administration has tried in vain to secure additional protections for American citizens, but was rebuffed at every turn by our so-called allies.[34]

The Bush administration has been saddled with this albatross since day one. President Bush has done his best to undo the damage and has even attempted to "unsign" the treaty. A letter from John R. Bolton, then undersecretary of state for arms control and international security, to UN Secretary-General Kofi Annan, dated 6 May 2002, states:

This is to inform you, in connection with the Rome Statute of the International Criminal Court adopted on July 17, 1998, that the United States does not intend to become a party to the treaty. Accordingly, the United States has no legal obligations arising from its signature on 31 December 2000. The United States requests that its intention not to become a party, as expressed in this letter, be reflected in the depository's status lists relating to this treaty.[35]

Organizational Structure of the ICC

Other concerns about the ICC are manifold. Law professors Diane Marie Amann and M. N. S. Sellers summarized these concerns in an article written a few months before the ICC opened its doors in March 2003. Let's look at them one-by-one. The professors organized these concerns into two main groups with subgroups under each. Their framework is very helpful, and I will follow it here.[36]

The first group of concerns relate to problems with the design of the

ICC itself. Within this group, the first subissue is that the ICC operates largely outside the control of the Security Council. Thus, unlike Security Council measures that are subject to US or other permanent member veto, the ICC operates unchecked. The only way the Security Council can block an ICC investigation is if all permanent members of the Security Council and a majority of the nonpermanent members vote to do so.[37]

To understand the significance of this, you need to understand that the ICC is not just a court, as you and I understand courts. That's why it seems strange to us to hear of ICC investigations. Ordinary courts don't investigate; law enforcement officials investigate. But the ICC is no ordinary court; rather it is a mammoth group of people doing not only the traditional job of judging, but also police work and prosecutorial work. That is why we speak of ICC investigations.

According to German national Hans-Peter Kaul, one of the inaugural judges of the ICC, the staff grew from an "advance team" of five in July 2002, to about four hundred by April of 2005. Like so many UN-related agencies, the ICC is composed of four organs: the presidency, the judicial divisions, the office of the prosecutor, and the registry.[38]

According to Kaul, the registry takes care of the ICC's support and administrative functions and is responsible for representing both defendants and victims in all ICC proceedings. It especially helps victims who seek reparations.[39]

The office of the prosecutor has two main functions: to investigate and to prosecute crimes. Kaul is quick to point out that in individual nations, the investigatory function is usually carried out by the police, not the prosecutors. Additionally, Kaul claims that the office of the prosecutor also negotiates "cooperation agreements with relevant states, entities, and intergovernmental and nongovernmental organizations that will enable the prosecutor to fulfill his mandate."[40]

Yet the authority that Kaul cites does not stand up. Neither the Rome Treaty nor the ICC's rules authorize the ICC to enter into agreements with NGOs.[41] But apparently it is doing so, or is prepared to do so!

What is more, the NGOs are already busy pushing their respective agendas through the ICC. In his report to the second assembly of the member states, the prosecutor, Luis Mereno-Ocampo, told the states:

> My office has so far received no referrals from the UN Security Council or States Parties. We have received 499 communications between July 2002 and July 2003, sent by nongovernmental organizations and individuals from 66 different countries. I wish to thank this expression of interest by civil society in the office of the prosecutor and take this opportunity to also welcome continued cooperation with nongovernmental organizations. Their collaboration, especially that of those nongovernmental organizations that prepared detailed reports, is essential for the current work of my office.[42]

Dean Koh must be jumping for joy. Any NGO with a soapbox can do a little "interaction" or "interpretation" at the ICC.

Immediately after the final draft of the Rome Statute was completed, the Coalition for an International Criminal Court's publication, *International Criminal Court Monitor*, ran a story entitled simply "We Won!" in which it reported, "Gustavo Gallon of the Colombian Commission of Jurists voiced the feelings of many NGOs when he stated at a press conference that 'we feel that this is not the court . . . that we would have liked to have. But we feel that this is an embryo that can be improved to be a strong, independent, and effective court.'"[43]

The transnationalist NGOs have every intent to manipulate this court, and the court is giving every indication that it wants to be manipulated. Note again the phrase "civil society" that Prosecutor Moreno-Ocampo used. If the ICC is about anything, it is about doing an end-run around the governments of the world. And why not? According to the transnationalists, they must be forced to obey anyway.

The office of the prosecutor is also responsible for arresting defendants.[44] One can only have nightmares about where this could go. Imagine a few arrests gone bad. Or a few uncooperative governments. The ICC will undoubtedly clamor for more power. Does anyone really believe that they will ever want to stop until they obtain the unequivocal right to arrest whomever they want, whenever they want, and wherever they want?

The presidency is responsible for the overall management of the court. It is composed of the president and the first and second vice presidents, each of whom is elected from among the judges of the court.[45] In addition to supervising the registry, the presidency assigns investigations to the various pretrial chambers and exercises other authority over the judges.[46]

The judges themselves are the last organ. On 7 February 2003, the first eighteen judges were elected.[47] In the short time that the ICC has been in existence, the judges have already engaged in some controversial decisions. Since the Rome Statute authorized the judges to create their own governing rules[48] (so much for checks and balances), in so doing, they rejected both the common law adversarial approach and the inquisitorial approach.[49]

A Stark Contrast with American Jurisprudence

The adversarial approach is what we use here in America: both the plaintiff and the defendant rely on their lawyers to present their cases to their best ability, and the judge's role is to preside and make rulings on questions of law, leaving the outcome in the hands of the jury.

The inquisitorial approach may be familiar if you have ever seen any British courtroom scenes in movies or on television, although the criminal systems of continental Europe are even more inquisitorial. Under this system, which sometimes may still have a jury, it is the judge's job to seek the truth. The problem, of course—at least from the American point of view—is that the judge may not be impartial or may make up his mind too soon. However, it is a tried and true method, familiar throughout the world.

But neither of these systems was good enough for the ICC. It created its own system, which Judge Kaul admits is *sui generis*, a judge's way of saying "one-of-a-kind." Yet Kaul is clear that it is much more inquisitorial than adversarial in nature.[50] And of course there are no juries. What would we expect from a court that seeks to enforce human rights norms on the entire world? It will get to decide for itself what the truth is.

Judge Kaul freely admits that when the ICC set up its rules, it had before it the recent examples of the International Criminal Tribunals for the Former Yugoslavia (ICTY) and the International Criminal Tribunals for Rwanda (ICTR), which were in the American common law tradition, and that the judges deliberately rejected that approach:

> Whereas the ICTY and the ICTR were initially strongly oriented toward the party-driven model of adversarial trials typical of the common law tradition, the starting point for the Rome Statute was different from the outset. The Statute creates strong incentives for the judge to play an active role in running the trial and seeking the truth. This orientation becomes most apparent in Article 69, paragraph 3, the second sentence of which states: "The Court shall have the authority to request the submission of all evidence that it considers necessary for the determination of the truth." The trial judges are thus endowed with a large measure of influence and investigative autonomy during the trial.[51]

The judges are organized into three divisions: the pretrial division, the trial division, and the appeals division. The president serves on the last chamber. Within the divisions, the judges are organized into chambers, or working groups of judges (although some tasks in the pretrial division can be done by a single judge).[52]

Time will tell how much mischief the ICC will unleash on the world. The ICC has the authority to impose penalties of life imprisonment, fines, forfeiture of property, and reparations. These tools—or should I say weapons?—could wreak havoc with American interests, and indeed with the interests of every sovereign nation on the face of the planet.

Concerns about the ICC

Returning to the concerns that have been summarized by Professors Amann and Sellers, remember that they pointed out that the ICC operates largely outside of the control of the UN Security Council. I want to emphasize that little word *largely*.

There *is* an on-going relationship between the UN and the ICC. This is important because some people, including Judge Kaul, have tried to paint the ICC as independent of the UN. So, for example, Kaul has been careful to use the word *independent* when describing the two organizations, even though what he describes doesn't sound very independent to most people.

Kaul acknowledges that the Relationship Agreement, which went into effect on 4 October 2004, allows the ICC to present matters to the UN for its attention, and allows the ICC not only to attend but even to "participate in the work of the Security Council."[53]

Kaul even pointed out that the UN has agreed to allow its officials to waive confidentiality when testifying before the ICC. More generally, the two organizations have agreed to share information and, whenever possible, facilities.[54] And, of course, the Security Council can refer cases to the ICC.[55]

That doesn't sound very independent to me. And that's just the current "snapshot." Don't forget that the ICC was birthed out of the UN, that it was the UN that created the Preparatory Committee on the Establishment of an International Criminal Court, which met over fifty times, and that it was the UN, under the authority of its Resolution 52/160, that convened the United Nations Diplomatic Conference of Plenipotentiaries on the Establishment of an International Criminal Court in Rome in June 1998.[56]

Furthermore, Article 2 of the Rome Statute reads in its entirety,

"The Court shall be brought into relationship with the United Nations through an agreement to be approved by the Assembly of States Parties to this Statute and thereafter concluded by the President of the Court on its behalf."[57]

Finally, the United Nations Secretariat served as the Secretariat of the Assembly of States Parties to the Rome Statute (that is, the ICC member nations) until 31 December 2003.[58]

So while the ICC may now be *technically* independent of the UN, it is not *truly* independent in any normal sense of that word.

The second sub-issue related to the ICC is that the Rome Statute grants jurisdiction to the ICC even over the citizens of nations (like the United States) that have refused to ratify the treaty, when those citizens are accused of committing crimes within the territory of nations that have signed the treaty.[59] This is of concern because our soldiers, whether serving in our own armed forces or serving as UN peacekeepers, would be at risk of arrest, prosecution, and judgment, not by a jury of their peers as granted in the Bill of Rights, but by the ICC.

The third cluster of concerns deals with politically motivated prosecutions. Summarizing the concerns of US senator Rod Grams and others, the professors note that every member nation has an equal vote in the Assembly of States Parties. The Assembly has the authority to elect and remove the prosecutors and all of the judges. It also has the ability to alter some of the rules governing the Court. Finally, and most dangerously, it has the power to amend the Rome Statute itself.[60] Senator Grams was worried that, because any nation can join the Assembly, nations with no commitment to the rule of law could lead the ICC in dangerous directions.[61]

Of course, it's not just non-rule-of-law nations that we need to worry about. Remember, the NGOs consider this court just an "embryo" that they intend to grow into a more useful tool for their transnationalist agenda.

Another concern here is that ICC prosecutors have the authority to initiate investigations on their own authority.[62] The legal term here is *proprio motu,* and this was one of the provisions that the Coalition for an International Criminal Court crowed about.[63]

Finally, the professors note that the crime of "aggression," which the ICC will be authorized to prosecute, remains undefined.[64] This is one of the most dangerous provisions since it could become the primary mechanism by which the United States comes under attack by the ICC. The ICC has been authorized by the Rome Statute to prosecute the crime of aggression, once it gets around to defining it.

So what we have with the ICC is an unaccountable judiciary trying cases without juries on the basis of evidence submitted by prosecutors with unlimited authority for crimes that have not been defined. Why would anyone worry about that?

US Constitution vs. Rome Statute

The preceding issues are due process concerns. Due process is a loaded expression with many different meanings in the legal world. But here it is used in the original literal sense: the process that is due someone accused of a crime. We are particularly concerned about American citizens, especially members of the military who may be falsely accused of NGO-defined crimes against humanity, or of aggression. Here the most important concern is the lack of trial by jury.[65]

While the professors dismiss all of these concerns, they are honest enough to admit that many people are not concerned about just one of these issues, but rather that the real problem is the cumulative impact of all of these things combined. The old adage comes to mind, "The whole is greater than the sum of the parts."

Another major group of concerns deals with conflicts between the Rome Statute and the US Constitution.[66] Several of the subcategories here overlap with the issues identified earlier, and I won't belabor those. These include concerns about the power of the office of the prosecutor and due process.

Other conflicts include a loss of immunity for officials, including the president of the United States![67] In a similar vein, there is a likely conflict that could arise because an American president could issue a pardon that would not be honored by the ICC.[68]

At this point in Professors Amann's and Sellers's analysis, one is in for a real shock. While I disagreed with almost every position that the professors took, I found their research to be competent and level-headed. It was detailed and documented. Then I read their suggestion that, had the ICC existed, President Nixon might have been hauled before it for his actions in Vietnam and the coup in Chile.[69]

Then I "chased the footnote" and found that they had even cited *The Trial of Henry Kissinger* by Christopher Hitchens, in which he accuses the former Secretary of State and national security advisor of war crimes that would subject Kissinger to stand trial at the ICC. This scenario may be a harbinger of the future for us, if we don't stand up to the ICC now.

Ironically, for a court that is supposed to be about ridding the world of its most animalistic members, the normal sentence is thirty years in prison, and only in exceptional cases, life in prison.[70] While this is assuredly not the worst problem about the ICC, it is another conflict with the US Constitution, which allows the death penalty. On the flip side of the coin, US citizens could end up imprisoned in hell-on-earth Third World prisons.[71]

The final concern deals with fugitives. But don't let the word fool you. While a fugitive could truly be a war criminal, it could just as easily be your son or daughter or grandson or granddaughter, who is serving or has served our country in uniform. The ICC requires that fugitives be handed over without extradition treaties.[72]

When a federal court refused to turn over a fugitive to the International Criminal Tribunal for Rwanda, citing the constitutional requirement of an extradition treaty, the Fifth Circuit Court of Appeals reversed that decision.[73] Furthermore, you need to know that if they come after your children and grandchildren—which apparently our courts are now willing to allow—there is no statute of limitations for any ICC crime.[74]

The transnationalists have answers for these conflicts with the US Constitution. One answer is for the United States to just give up every constitutional protection—and that sounds like patent nonsense to me. But that is exactly what is proposed by Amnesty International, which has called for the United States to establish "domestic laws with the same crimes, the same universal jurisdiction, the same concepts of penal responsibility, the same limits on defenses, and the same punishments."[75]

ICC judge Kaul has another solution: forced compliance. He has made numerous disturbing suggestions, or left hanging certain questions, that seem to permit more disturbing questions. All these questions center around the cooperation of member and nonmember states regarding investigations and arrests. Kaul has called this "the question to end all questions."[76]

I believe that the ICC ultimately wants every nation on earth at its beck and call. Kaul noted that International Criminal Tribunal for Yugoslavia arrests were largely made by NATO and UN troops. He was worried that by comparison no such troops were available in Uganda or the Congo, where the ICC had investigations underway at the time of his comments.[77]

Kaul noted that under the Rome Statute, "States are not entitled to refuse to cooperate with the court on any grounds." And he whined that "the credibility of the court would suffer if an arrest warrant issued by the judges of the pretrial chamber at the request of the prosecutor pursuant to Article 58 remained ineffective over a long period because the states parties were slow, or failed to execute it."[78]

Judge Kaul dropped another hint. He said that member states and the court need to develop a standard of "best practices" regarding his concerns. According to him, "These include fast and reliable communication channels for relevant information, the use of military or intelligence sources, and perhaps national contact units or focal points to ensure the immediate cooperation with the ICC when it issues a request."[79]

Judge Kaul also turned his attention to the nonmember states. He ominously noted that "a resolution containing the same obligations to cooperate as Resolutions 827 and 955 [the UN Resolutions creating the ICTY and the ICTR] would clearly be mandatory for all UN member states, including nonstate parties to the Rome Statute. . . . States would also be aware of certain measures the council might take to ensure compliance, if necessary."[80]

I am persuaded that the ICC *is* one of the most dangerous of all the UN-affiliated entities. Surely, the fact that it is "technically" independent of the UN can do nothing to assuage our concerns. And surely the fact that, as of this writing, it has undertaken only three investigations cannot be allowed to mollify us. Quite to the contrary, now is the time to act, while we still have a chance.

Wavering US Response

The Bush administration has largely taken the right approach, being very hostile to the court from the outset. The primary shield against the ICC is the American Service Members' Protection Act, which was introduced by Senator Jesse Helms. This law states that the United States shall not become a member of the ICC, except by ratification of a treaty pursuant to the US Constitution.[81] Thus, it clearly states that President Clinton's eleventh-hour signature means nothing.

This law also denies US funding to the ICC, unless we become a member by means of a ratified treaty. It also prevents extradition of US citizens; states that we are not bound by the Rome Statute and that we do not recognize its jurisdiction over our citizens; shuts down all aid, funding, cooperation, and direct or indirect sharing of information by any federal, state, or local branch of American governments; and denies ICC investigators the right to operate within the United States. It authorizes the president "to use all means necessary and appropriate to bring about the release of" our citizens and our allies' citizens and authorizes legal assistance.[82]

A number of stronger bills have been introduced and some have even passed the House, but as of this date none have made it out of the Senate. In addition, the United States has engaged in some good arm twisting at the UN.[83] (For example, the United States has periodically sought immunity for its armed forces personnel until, as is widely believed, it decided it no longer could after the Abu Ghraib prison scandal.)[84]

Furthermore, the United States has negotiated Article 98 bilateral agreements with numerous nations. These articles, named after the provision of the Rome Statute that makes them possible, states that the United States will not give the signatory country any aid unless they agree to grant US personnel protection from the ICC.[85] At the time of this writing, about one hundred such agreements have been entered into.[86]

But not all is rosy. The American Service Members' Protection Act also authorizes the president to waive some of its own provisions under certain circumstances.[87] Thus, to a certain extent, we are at the mercy of whomever occupies the Oval Office. Plus, even the Bush administration has conceded a few issues, as in backing off on its demand for immunity after Abu Ghraib.

Even more alarmingly, the United States blinked on the very first referral from the Security Council to the ICC. On 31 March 2005, the United States, along with Algeria, Brazil, and China, abstained from voting on the resolution, allowing it to pass 11 to 0.[88] The United States reportedly felt compelled to abstain due to the enormity of the Darfur tragedy in Sudan.

The *Washington Post* immediately pounced on the American vacillation, calling it a "dramatic policy reversal" for the United States and "the first time in four years that the Bush administration had departed from its practice of opposing anything having to do with the ICC." It was essentially the same politically correct scenario that Hollywood offered up in *The Interpreter*.[89]

Elena Baylis, one of Dean Koh's Yale Law graduates, who is now teaching on the law faculty at the University of Pittsburgh, has stated in the title of an op-ed that the "International Criminal Court Needs

Darfur (More Than Darfur Needs the ICC)." She contends that "while the Darfur referral is a crucial development for the ICC, and for both its proponents and opponents, it represents only an uncertain opportunity for justice in Darfur."[90]

That being the case, it seems especially egregious that the United States abstained. Two other facts make the US abstention doubly regrettable. First, we have allowed the ICC to exercise jurisdiction of the Sudan, a nonsignatory nation.[91] Thus, we have given away the very heart of our opposition. This is exactly what we have maintained the ICC cannot do.

Second, under the terms of the Rome Statute, the ICC is only supposed to have jurisdiction when the courts of the nation being investigated have done nothing.[92] This limitation on the ICC, called complementarity, has long been touted by NGOs and others as the key safeguard against ICC tyranny.[93] Yet I have long suspected that this is one of the ICC's biggest lies. While one might justly be skeptical of the Sudanese's sincerity in their very minimal efforts to bring the Darfur criminals to justice,[94] it is still frightening to see just how quickly the ICC has pulled the mask off.

Again, Judge Kaul has been honest enough to help us understand. He complains that "this principle [of complementarity] creates a curious pair of conflicting forces and hence a dilemma for the court itself: if the states generally discharge their overriding duty to prosecute crimes, the court will not be given anything to do and will have no cases. On the other hand, the court needs exemplary and successfully handled cases, because the global public and the states parties legitimately desire to see concrete evidence that the International Criminal Court is a meaningful and useful institution."[95]

I guess the Court's "needs" very quickly prevailed over the purported key check upon the ICC's power. And the United States allowed this to happen, when we had the power to stop it with a Security Council veto. This shameful failure to stand up for our professed national principles illustrates why many feel that Americans are being lulled into a sense of false security regarding the very real dangers of the ICC.

I have given you a fair amount of detail about the first three years of the ICC. But don't forget about how it all fits within the transnationalists' larger agenda. Remember the words of Professor Martinez: "There are now more than fifty international courts, tribunals, and quasi-judicial bodies, most of which have been established in the past twenty years."[96]

The point of all of these international legal entities is to eliminate national sovereignty. Even if nations continue to exist as shells, the transnationalists want "civil society" to reign. Of course, civil society will have to live by the "human rights values" that the transnationalist elites will have forced the now-meaningless governments to obey.

Already the AALS, which includes nearly every law school in America, is training the next generation of lawyers to make us vulnerable to these international legal adventures by the ICC. Our only hope for America is to expose and resist them.

While liberal activist groups like Human Rights Watch have hailed the ICC as "potentially the most important human rights organization created in fifty years," other legal experts view it quite differently.

Professor Charles Rice, the noted conservative legal scholar from Notre Dame University Law School, has described the ICC as "a monster" that "repudiates the Constitution, the Bill of Rights, and the Declaration of Independence."[97]

Defeating this monster will be a crucial battle for Americans of the 21st century.

7

GLOBAL GUN CONTROL AND
A STANDING WORLD ARMY

An able and ready army is a prerequisite for any ruler who expects to control his subjects. Whether on the local, state, national, or international level, any government is only as powerful as the military machine that it commands and controls.

As we have previously discussed, governments require three things in order to function: the ability to raise independent revenue through taxation, the ability to impose legal order through a court system, and the ability to project military force, whether defensively or offensively. For the United Nations to assume the role of a genuine world government, then, it would have to have its own independent military force.

Those who fear the rise of a global tyranny look with great suspicion on the desire of the UN elite to control a military force capable of imposing their will on the nations of the world, while simultaneously disarming the general citizenry and reducing each nation's military powers to essentially the level of a high-tech domestic police force.

One of the great constitutional controversies of the 1990s was the decision by president Bill Clinton to place American troops under the command of UN leaders in Somalia, Bosnia, Haiti, and elsewhere—often with disastrous consequences, as in the tragic "Black Hawk Down" debacle at Mogadishu in 1993. What Clinton was doing, with his then highly controversial and still–top secret Presidential Decision Directive 25 (PDD-25), was to take those first tentative steps toward establishing a standing UN army.[1]

Before we delve into some of these shadowy documents, however, let me be clear on this one point: another not-so-shadowy document, the Bill of Rights to our US Constitution, stands as one of our last bastions of defense against global tyranny. For today, as throughout history, the greatest check on the power of any tyrant is an armed citizenry jealous of preserving their fundamental rights and liberties.

Most of the critics of American gun laws have never experienced the kind of individual liberty and personal responsibility that Americans enjoy. They have lived their lives, for the most part, in oppressive authoritarian societies that emphasize conformity and cooperation rather than free expression and independent thought. They do not understand the principles of freedom that generations of Americans have learned from birth, nor do they understand that the price of keeping that freedom is eternal vigilance.

Those who would rule the world must first disarm its peoples, and the move to accomplish that goal is already far advanced. Thus we will consider in tandem these two topics: the drive toward global gun control and disarmament, and the push to establish a standing UN military force.

Inconvenient Truths about Gun Control

Back before the November 2004 election, many mainstream media pundits—trying desperately to help John Kerry get elected—began to harp on President Bush's unwillingness to stop certain federal gun control laws from expiring as scheduled. But their propaganda efforts came to naught because this issue was a nonstarter with the American people.

The fact is, in this day of increased security consciousness, post-911, most average Americans simply don't want more gun control. They want more guns on hand to defend themselves and their loved ones in the face of possible life-threatening danger. Soccer moms are now taking handgun proficiency courses down at the local firing range.

To set the record straight and dispel a few of the more common myths with some hard facts, let's look first at an interesting set of statistics. According the US Department of Health and Human Services, there is an inverse correlation between the number of accidental deaths caused by guns and those caused by doctors. Consider these facts.

Doctors: (A) There are 700,000 physicians in the United States. (B) Accidental deaths caused by physicians total 120,000 per year. (C) The accidental death percentage per physician is 0.171.

Guns: (A) There are 80 million gun owners in the United States. (B) There are 1,500 accidental gun deaths per year, counting all age groups. (C) The percentage of accidental deaths per gun owner is 0.0000188.

Statistically, then, doctors are 9,000 times more dangerous to the public health than gun owners are.

Some might call the foregoing comparison a specious argument. But it is certainly just as legitimate as some of the more hysterical rants directed against gun owners by the disarmament crowd on the Left.

Dr. Glen Otero of the Claremont Institute has published an enlightening article entitled "Ten Myths About Gun Control." Here are just a few of his well-documented findings:

- Approximately 80 percent of all adult American citizens own firearms, and a gun can be found in nearly half of American households.
- Between 1974 and 1995, the total number of privately owned firearms in America increased by 75 percent, to 236 million. During the same period, national homicide and robbery rates did NOT significantly increase.
- Less than one percent of all guns are involved in any type of crime, which means that 99 percent of all guns are NOT used to commit any crime.

- In 1987, the National Crime Victimization Survey estimated that about 83 percent of Americans would become the victims of violent crime during the course of their lifetimes.
- The National Self-Defense Survey found that between 1988 and 1993, American civilians used firearms in self-defense almost 2.5 million times per year, saving as many as 400,000 lives per year in the process.
- Guns in the hands of law-abiding citizens deter crime. Where US counties have enacted concealed-carry gun laws, murder rates fell by 8 percent, rape by 5 percent, and aggravated assault by 7 percent. Urban counties recorded the largest decreases demographically.[2]

You get the picture: Guns don't kill people. People kill people. But sometimes law-abiding citizens with guns can save the lives of other innocent people. It's time to restore some common sense to the hysterical debate over gun control. We need to enforce our criminal laws against murder, robbery, and assault, not disarm honest citizens and leave them defenseless.

I will cite the testimony of just one more expert witness. No, it's not another politician or media pundit. Here's what former Mafia underboss, self-confessed hit man, and government informant Sammy "The Bull" Gravano had to say:

Gun control? It's the best thing you can do for crooks and gangsters. I want you to have nothing. If I'm a bad guy, I'm always gonna have a gun. Safety locks? You pull the trigger with a lock on, and I'll pull the trigger. We'll see who wins.[3]

This isn't a collection of random hits from a Google search. These are hard facts that liberals in this country simply refuse to accept. Why?

Because taking guns out of the hands of law-abiding American citizens is on a decades-old globalist checklist for world domination.

Disarming Law-Abiding Citizens

The Second Amendment to the US Constitution reads as follows:

> A well regulated Militia, being necessary to the security of a free State, the right of the people to keep and bear Arms, shall not be infringed.

Advocates of disarming law-abiding Americans tend to focus on the first four words, but our Founding Fathers were wiser than that. Having just expelled Great Britain from our shores, those early American heroes understood by very recent example that, in fact, the right of the people to keep and bear arms is necessary to the security of a free state.

Nevertheless, as Congressman Ron Paul of Texas points out, even as gun-control advocates seem to be losing ground on the home front, globalist bureaucrats continue working behind the scenes (and sometimes, shockingly, in plain view) to override our national sovereignty and to force America to accept international gun control laws.[4]

UN Secretary-General Kofi Annan has called on members of the Security Council to address the "easy availability" of small arms and light weapons, which many in the United States perceive as including all privately owned firearms. In response, the Security Council released a report calling for a comprehensive program of worldwide gun control, a report that admonishes the United States and praises the restrictive gun laws of Red China.

"This conflict between the UN position on private ownership of firearms and our Second Amendment cannot be reconciled," Representative Paul said. "How can we as a nation justify our membership in an organization that is actively hostile to one of our most fundamental constitutional rights? What if the UN decided that free speech was too inflammatory and should be restricted? Would we discard the First Amendment to comply with the UN agenda?"[5]

In 2003, former congressman Bob Barr of Georgia attended a UN-sponsored meeting of the states on the "Implementation of the Program of Action on Small Arms and Light Weapons in All Its Aspects"—a lofty-sounding organization, he warns, out to outlaw personal ownership of guns altogether. Barr told WorldNetDaily that many member nations, including the UK, Netherlands, and India, want to set up a legally binding protocol requiring all UN countries to start registration of firearms. That, Barr warned, is not far from the ultimate nightmare of "the UN knocking on our door to get our firearms."[6]

"If we were to allow in any way, shape, or form the UN to begin the process of registering and regulating firearms—ultimately their goal of doing away with personal firearms—we would have dealt a blow to our sovereignty," Barr insisted.[7]

Though the UN's international gun grab dates almost to the organization's charter, the current push for worldwide gun control dates to 1995, when the General Assembly asked then-Secretary-General Boutros Boutros-Ghali to appoint a "Panel of Governmental Experts on Small Arms." These experts eventually submitted their report to the next secretary-general, Kofi Annan. In 1997, Annan forwarded that report to the General Assembly, which went on to endorse its conclusions.

The *Small Arms Report* claimed that "the excessive and destabilizing accumulation and transfer of small arms and light weapons is closely related to the increased incidence of internal conflicts and high levels of crime and violence" and that "it is, therefore, an issue of legitimate concern for the international community." The report characterized as small arms not only such modern weapons as revolvers, self-loading pistols, rifles, and carbines, but also the more primitive clubs, knives, and machetes.

The report's recommendations included:

- "The United Nations should support all appropriate post-conflict initiatives related to disarmament and demobilization, such as the disposal and destruction of weapons, including weapons turn-in programs."
- "All weapons which are not under legal civilian possession, and which are not required for the purposes of national defense and internal security, should be collected and destroyed by States as expeditiously as possible."
- "All States should determine in their national laws and regulations which arms are permitted for civilian possession and the conditions under which they can be used."
- "All States should ensure that they have in place adequate laws, regulations, and administrative procedures to exercise effective control over the legal possession of small arms and light weapons and over their transfer."
- "States emerging from conflict should, as soon as practicable, impose or re-impose licensing requirements on all civilian possession of small arms and light weapons."[8]

The US government could not implement the proposals in the *Small Arms Report* without violating the Second Amendment. Nevertheless, the US representative on the panel, Dr. Herbert L. Calhoun of the US Arms Control and Disarmament Agency, joined the other panel members in unanimously adopting the *Small Arms Report*.

In 1999, Annan asked members of the UN Security Council to "tackle one of the key challenges in preventing conflict in the next century"—the proliferation and "easy availability" of small arms and light weapons. Annan identified these weapons as the "primary tools of violence" in conflicts throughout the world.

"Even in societies not beset by civil war, the easy availability of small arms has in many cases contributed to violence and political instability," said Annan. "Controlling that easy availability is a prerequisite for a successful peace-building process."[9]

The UN's official website for its 2001 conference on small arms carries the following quote from Annan: "In an era where the world will no longer stand by in silence when gross and systematic violations of human rights are being committed, the United Nations is dedicated to addressing both the supply and demand aspects of the trade in small arms."[10]

The United Nations defines small arms as weapons designed for personal use, while light weapons are those designed for use by several persons operating as a crew. Together, however, such weapons account for virtually every kind of firearm from revolvers, pistols, rifles, carbines, and light machine guns all the way to heavy machine guns, grenade launchers, portable anti-aircraft and antitank guns, mortars up to 100-mm caliber, and land mines.

In February 2000, US State Department senior advisor John Holum of the Arms Control and Disarmament Agency, addressing a Small Arms Working Group Meeting in Washington DC, credited the United States with being "a leader on this issue" and pointed out that "the US has destroyed or assisted in the destruction of weapons stockpiles in a number of countries, including Liberia, Albania, Kuwait, Haiti, and Panama."[11]

The 2001 conference—in which member nations agreed to an ominous "plan of action" that combined commitments to tracking illegal gun sales with tracking "officially held guns" and the "maintenance of gun manufacturer records"—was followed by a second in 2003.[12]

Apparently, the United Nations believes that the best way to stop "illicit" gun sales is to know the name and address of every gun owner. Fortunately, their international gun control agenda continues to run into road blocks.

The UN Small Arms Review Conference met 26 June to 7 July 2006, in New York City. Gun control advocates had high hopes for the conference, which was intended as a five-year review of the progress made since the 2001 plan of action was launched. But the event was met with such concerted opposition from an American public, aroused by warnings from the National Rifle Association and other pro-gun groups, that the gun controllers were able to make little substantive progress.[13]

The conference delegates were unable to reach agreement on a final document. Much of the credit for that unexpected outcome goes to the US delegation, which refused to compromise on America's Second Amendment protections. Robert G. Joseph, undersecretary of state for arms control and security, made the US position crystal clear in his 27 June speech to the General Assembly.

> The US Constitution guarantees the rights of our citizens to keep and bear arms, and there will be no infringement of those rights. The United States will not agree to any provisions restricting civilian possession, use, or legal trade of firearms inconsistent with our laws and practices. Many millions of American citizens enjoy hunting and the full range of firearm sports, and our work will not affect their rights and opportunities. As an officer of the executive branch of my government, I took an oath to protect the Constitution—a duty that it is an honor to uphold.[14]

It is gratifying to see our nation's leaders take a stand in defense of our Constitution and sovereignty. However, this encouraging victory was just one small skirmish in an ongoing war to preserve our constitutional freedoms.

The UN's final conference press release noted that some delegates from the European Union "deplored the lack of progress on the priority areas." The Canadian representative called for an informal week-long follow-up conference to be held in Geneva in 2007 "to discuss concrete measures to accelerate implementation" of the small arms gun control plan of action.[15]

Freedom from War: The Kennedy-American Plan

The UN's push for civilian disarmament, writes Gary Benoit in the July 2000 issue of the *New American*, is an increasingly transparent and aggressive element in a broader, step-by-step program to grant a monopoly of power to a UN "peace" force and to render subservient to the UN the national security forces of all nation-states.

The totalitarian objective behind all of the UN's disarmament schemes, both international and domestic, is the same. That objective is not, as many believe, simply to eliminate all weapons (be they nuclear bombs or small arms), but rather to transfer the control of those weapons to the custodians of the emerging UN global police state.[16]

The UN-funded Commission on Global Governance (CGG) explicitly addressed civilian disarmament in its influential 1995 report entitled *Our Global Neighborhood.* Under the chapter heading "Promoting Security," the CGG claimed:

> Militarization today not only involves governments spending more than necessary to build up their military arsenals. It has increasingly become a global societal phenomenon, as witnessed by the rampant acquisition and use of increasingly lethal weapons by civilians—whether individuals seeking a means of self-defense, street gangs, criminals, political opposition groups, or terrorist organizations.[17]

So, according to the United Nations, civilians "seeking a means of self-defense" are no different from street gangs, criminals, rebel guerillas, and terrorists. Not exactly the American way. Yet this global gun control agenda has received our government's seal of approval! Most Americans would be shocked to learn that the US government has established as official US policy the foolhardy goal of simultaneously strengthening the UN military machine while disarming the forces of all the sovereign nations of the world, as well as their private citizens.

In September of 1961, newly elected President John F. Kennedy presented a radical disarmament plan to the United Nations General Assembly, meeting at UN headquarters in New York City. Kennedy challenged the nations of the world "not to an arms race, but to a peace race—to advance together step by step, stage by stage, until general and complete disarmament has been achieved."[18]

Kennedy's controversial plan, titled *Freedom from War: The United States Program for General and Complete Disarmament in a Peaceful World*, was subsequently published by the US Government Printing Office and widely distributed as State Department Document 7277.

The Kennedy plan called for worldwide disarmament in three phases, gradually transferring not only US military power but also all other global war-making capability to the United Nations. *Freedom From War* called for all nations to follow the US lead and gradually disarm themselves simultaneously until the world had reached "a point where no state would have the military power to challenge the progressively strengthened UN Peace Force."[19]

President Kennedy's utopian vision for "a program of general and complete disarmament in a peaceful world," as outlined on the first pages of State Department Document 7277, included the following objectives:

- The disbanding of all national forces and the prohibition of their reestablishment in any form whatsoever other than those required to preserve internal order and for contributions to a United Nations Peace Force.
- The elimination from national arsenals of all armaments, including all weapons of mass destruction and the means for their delivery, other than those required for a United Nations Peace Force and for maintaining internal order.
- The establishment and effective operation of an International Disarmament Organization within the framework of the United Nations to ensure compliance at all times with all disarmament obligations.
- To develop a plan for general and complete disarmament.
- Verification arrangements shall be instituted progressively and in such a manner as to verify not only that agreed limitations or

reductions take place but also that retained armed forces and armaments do not exceed agreed levels at any stage.

• As states relinquish their arms, the United Nations shall be progressively strengthened in order to improve its capacity to assure international security as well as to facilitate the development of international cooperation in common tasks for the benefit of mankind.[20]

Article 11 of the UN Charter gives the General Assembly the authority to "consider" and "recommend" principles governing disarmament and the regulation of armaments, but virtually no authority to enforce disarmament. Kennedy's radical proposal, also known as the American Plan—which mirrored a similar initiative being offered by the Soviet Union at about the same time—was a bold first step toward giving the UN the power that early, necessary compromises had stripped from the globalists' original vision of a world government.

Though modified and delayed by political necessity during the Cold War and afterward, the basic Kennedy global disarmament scheme has never been revoked and so remains in force. The essential principle of relinquishing arms to the UN, as well as control of the production and distribution of arms, has guided the invisible disarmament policy of almost every American presidential administration since the days of JFK.[21]

Since *Freedom from War*, the number of UN peacekeeping operations has steadily increased. Although the State Department documents mentioned above do not directly address the question of civilian disarmament, it is notable that both the 1997 and 1999 reports of UN experts on small arms place that subject under the broader UN agenda of "general and complete disarmament"—a phrase that stands out in the subtitle of *Freedom from War* and other State Department documents.[22]

In 1982, while President Ronald Reagan was orchestrating the US military build-up that eventually drove the Soviet Union into bankruptcy, the Independent Commission on Disarmament and Security (also known as the Palme Commission after its chairman, Swedish social-ist Olof Palme) released a report entitled *Common Security: A Blueprint for Survival*. This document combined the State Department's 1962-vintage *Blueprint for the Peace Race* with the 1974 *Charter of the New International Economic Order*, thereby linking global disarmament with economic development.[23]

Article 13 of the *Charter of the New International Economic Order*—an unabashedly socialistic document that clearly advocates the global redistribution of wealth from the developed nations like the United States to aid less fortunate, poverty-stricken Third World regimes—authoritatively declares:

> *All States have the duty to promote the achievement of general and com-plete disarmament under effective international control* and to utilize the resources released by effective disarmament measures for the eco-nomic and social development of countries, allocating a substantial portion of such resources as additional means for the development needs of developing countries.[24]

What this is really saying, of course, is that the United States has the alleged duty to surrender its superior military power to the Communist-dominated United Nations organization.

The Palme Commission report stressed that the costly ongoing arms race between the United States and the Soviet Union wasted valuable and limited resources and thus damaged prospects for Third World develop-ment. The members of the Commission claimed to believe that war was imminent, and that there was a "drift towards war." The world, in their view, seemed to be "marching towards the brink of a new abyss."[25]

The Palme Commission's official report further stated:

> Nations must strive for objectives more ambitious than stability, the goal of the present system in which security is based on armaments.

For stability based on armaments cannot be sustained indefinitely. There is always the danger that the fragile stability of an international system based on armaments will suddenly crumble, and that nuclear confrontation will take its place. A more effective way to ensure security is to create positive processes that can lead to peace and disarmament. *It is essential to create an irreversible process, with a momentum such that all nations cooperate for their common survival.*[26]

Note their demand for an "irreversible process" that places supreme military power in the United Nations. Although the Palme Commission did not appear to be taken very seriously at the time, it successfully introduced into the world community's collective consciousness the trendy new concept of "common security," as opposed to the old-fashioned idea of "collective security."

Collective security, the original organizing principle of the United Nations, is based on the idea that sovereign nation-states should band together and use their collective military might to enforce accepted international standards prohibiting unprovoked military aggression by any rogue nation.

The doctrine of common security goes the extra mile, calling for the complete disarmament of the world's nation-states and their national interdependence under the auspices of an international controlling authority such as the United Nations. Those who want to see the UN achieve global hegemony now emphasize the supposed duty of all the nation-states to embrace the common security model.[27]

It's really just another way to look at a global government whose rule is enforced under the threat of a UN-controlled military machine.

Changing Roles for UN Peacekeepers

Under the UN Charter's Article 43, member nations are required "to make available to the Security Council, on its call and in accordance with a special agreement or agreements, armed forces, assistance, and facilities—for the purpose of maintaining international peace and security."[28]

Transfers of US military personnel are regularly mandated in and out of the North Atlantic Treaty Organization (NATO) without informing the troops that they have been assigned to a UN regional affiliate. Chapter VIII of the UN Charter states, "The Security Council shall, where appropriate, utilize such regional arrangements for enforcement action under its authority."[29]

Since 1950, all US military personnel serving in South Korea, whether they knew it or not, have served in the United Nations Command. No blue helmets or UN insignia have as yet been required. But in 1982, Army General Robert W. Sennewald was identified as "Commander-in-Chief, United Nations Command."[30]

US military activities in Korea, Vietnam, Haiti, Bosnia, Somalia, and Iraq have all been carried out under the legal auspices of the United Nations. For example, when Saddam Hussein invaded Kuwait in 1990, US president George H.W. Bush didn't ask Congress for authorization to go to war, according to the clear requirements of the Constitution. He merely asked permission from the UN Security Council.

In April 1994, a British troop commander (General Sir Michael Rose), a UN diplomat from Japan (Yashusi Akashi), and the UN secretary-general (Boutros Boutros-Ghali) ordered US fighter planes from NATO to attack positions in Bosnia. US Admiral Leighton Smith expressed great delight that his men were "carrying out the mandates of the secretary-general."[31]

And in June of 1994, when fifteen US military personnel were killed in a helicopter crash while enforcing a "no-fly-zone" in Iraq, Vice President Al Gore said, "I want to extend my condolences to the families of those who died in the service of the United Nations."[32]

Thus by the early 1990s, the idea of US troops serving as UN soldiers was becoming more and more commonly accepted by folks both at home and abroad. But up until that time, those US troop deployments had been facilitated under the 1945 United Nations Participation

Act, which granted the president broad authority to send US troops into action in response to a call for help from the UN Security Council in response to actual military aggression.

When Bill Clinton took office in 1993, that situation changed rapidly and radically. Acting in a clandestine fashion, without any accountability to Congress, Clinton introduced a series of top secret Presidential Decision Directives by means of which he single-handedly changed the way US foreign policy was implemented.

"I Am Not a United Nations Fighting Person. . . ."

In 1995, one young man named Michael New, a twice-decorated US Army Specialist E-4, refused to don the blue helmet when President Bill Clinton ordered US troops into UN service in Macedonia. New had been in the army for two-and-one-half years, had served honorably as a medic in Kuwait during Operation Desert Storm, and was credited with saving one man's life and another's eyesight.

Nevertheless, for upholding his sworn oath to protect and defend the US Constitution, and for refusing to alter his uniform (*against military regulations*), New was first threatened, then court-martialed and quickly convicted in a military kangaroo court that refused even to allow him to present his side of the story, and summarily drummed out of the armed services with a dishonorable discharge.

Michael New wasn't looking for publicity. He wasn't trying to avoid a dangerous assignment. From the time that New learned in July 1995 that his unit, Company A, Third Infantry Division, would be seconded to the United Nations, he took steps to reconcile his military duty with the fact that the proposed deployment and the orders to wear UN uniforms were not legal. In September 2005, New sent a letter to his chain of command outlining his objections and again asking for clarification of orders.

"As an American soldier I fully intend to obey all lawful orders, and I again request that the Army through appropriate channels provide for my review the legal justification for the change of uniform and the justification for pending deployment orders," New wrote to his superiors. In the letter, New outlined his specific objections of conscience, yet he stated that he did not want to draw attention to himself or to cause the military any embarrassment. Here is part of what he said in that letter:

> On August 21, 1995, my seniors in the US Army chain of command informed me that my unit and I would soon be ordered to significantly alter our uniform by sewing a United Nations patch on my right shoulder and wearing the blue beret and/or helmet of the UN. These are important insignia. If they were unimportant, then I would not have been threatened with courts-martial, imprisonment, or less than dishonorable discharge when I expressed my reservations about wearing them. I interpret the wearing of a uniform, or the accoutrements of a uniform, as a sign of allegiance and faithfulness to the authority or power so signified, or which issues that uniform. I am an American citizen who was recruited for and voluntarily joined the US Army to serve as an American soldier. *I am not a citizen of the United Nations. I am not a United Nations Fighting Person.* I have never taken an oath to the United Nations, but I have taken the required oath to support and defend the Constitution of the United States.[33]

Michael New's efforts to placate his superiors and defuse the explosive situation proved fruitless. His concerns, which were rooted in principles of law and conscience, were dismissed as frivolous and insubordinate. He was threatened with severe punishment unless he agreed to accept the unlawful orders he had been given.

On 10 October 1995, when 550 soldiers arrived at formation wearing UN insignia and light-blue baseball caps, only one soldier showed up wearing his regulation US Army uniform. New was removed from the parade field, read his rights, and told that he would be court-martialed. The rest of his unit, meanwhile, saluted their new commanding officer, General Jehu Engstrom of Finland.

New's court-martial opened almost three months later, with a preliminary ruling that, frankly, makes no sense. Lieutenant Colonel Gary Jewell arbitrarily declared New's orders to be "lawful" and instructed the soldier's defense counsel to argue only the "obedience" issue. Remarkably, the prosecution and the court-martial panel *agreed* with New's assertion that altering his uniform to UN standards *was against regulations*.

On 9 January 1996, a Stipulation of Fact was entered into the court record that stated the UN insignia that New was ordered to wear on his shoulder "has not been approved by the Director of the Institute of Heraldry, US Army, as required and mandated under the provisions of paragraphs 27-16a and b of Army Regulation 670-1." The document added, "Both the Department of Defense and Department of the Army have not authorized, either formally or informally, the United Nations insignia and accouterments."[34]

Nevertheless, on 25 January 1996, a seven-member military panel in Germany deliberated for only twenty minutes before they convicted New on a charge of disobedience. Although the military prosecutor wanted to send New to prison, the panel determined that a Bad Conduct Discharge was punishment enough. New lost his promising military career, his veteran's benefits, and his reputation.

Here's the part of Michael New's story that really gets to me. The Clinton administration took the time to write a letter purporting to explain the alleged legality of the president's troop deployment order. Section 7 of the United Nations Participation Act authorizes the president to detail US military personnel to UN peacekeeping operations authorized under Chapter VI of the UN Charter to serve in any non-combatant capacity.[35]

It turns out that the troop deployment to Macedonia was not a Chapter VI deployment at all, but a Chapter VII deployment, according to a memorandum from the Joint Chiefs of Staff. Any assignment or deployment of US troops under Chapter VII of the UN Charter requires *prior* congressional approval. Congress never gave that approval. So the Clinton administration actually broke the law when it sent Michael New—and every other American service member—into Macedonia. Thus, not only was it constitutionally wrong to order Michael New into Macedonia as a UN soldier, it also violated the letter of the law in ordering all of the other US soldiers to serve there, in the absence of prior congressional approval.

But the Clinton administration's campaign of lies didn't stop there. The letter went on to imply that the US soldiers in Macedonia actually were serving under US command. Not so. Our soldiers reported to General Engstrom, and Engstrom reported to the UN Security Council. The UN Security Council does *not* report to the president of the United States (who is supposedly the commander-in-chief of all US military personnel).

At the time of his conviction in 1996, New was the conquering hero of the counterculture conservatives who seemingly lived in the alternate reality of hard-right newsletters, conservative radio talk shows, and Internet chat rooms. They rallied to his defense and supported his one-man crusade against the new world order with their words and their checkbooks.

One fairly typical, if particularly accurate and articulate accolade, was the following supportive commentary from syndicated columnist Samuel Francis. Since it would be hard for me to improve on it, I'll just quote a portion of it for you.

> Aside from the legal merits of his case, there's a much larger issue involved in it than military discipline, military justice, or even wearing the blue berets and shoulder patches of the UN forces. The larger issue concerns what the American armed forces are for. . . . Legislation now in Congress proposes forbidding any American soldier from wearing the UN uniform, and the bill has a lot of cosponsors. But the uniform is not really the point.

The point is that American soldiers should not come under the command of foreign powers, nor should they serve foreign interests. When Spec. New and his comrades became part of the UN Force, that's exactly what they were being ordered to do. Wearing a different uniform is only a symbol, but not the substance, of the issue.

In the New World Order, you see, uniforms don't much matter. Multinational corporations can call themselves American companies, but they merely wear the uniform of a post office box in Manhattan. Governments wedded to globalism and the new transnational order may call themselves American and keep wearing American uniforms, too, but if they serve transnational powers and interests, they're no more American than the general from Finland who would have been Spec. New's commanding officer in merry old Macedonia.

What Republican lawmakers who grasp this point (if any such there are) need to do is craft a bill that would forbid any US soldier from coming under foreign command or engaging in any foreign mission not explicitly approved by Congress.

That way we would withdraw our troops from future peacekeeping follies, curb the power of the executive to involve us in wars we don't want to fight and keep the New World Order's armies as toothless as they should be.[36]

Sam Francis's astute analysis of the substance behind the symbol was right on target. Unfortunately, the prudent limiting legislation that he advocated has not yet made its way into law.

Michael New has been in and out of court for more than ten years now, attempting to reverse his wrongful conviction. Federal courts have heard his case and agreed that his arguments had some merit, but nevertheless repeatedly sent him back to exhaust his remedies in the military courts. The military courts refused to consider New's principled arguments based on the Constitution because they said that they couldn't rule on political issues. So one court after another has effectively affirmed New's conviction and dishonorable discharge—for the heinous crime of trying to honor his solemn oath to defend the US Constitution.

Constitutional scholar Herb Titus, who is Michael New's lead attorney in the continuing quest to clear his good name and military reputation on appeal, says that even more is riding on Michael's eventually getting his day in court:

> At stake is whether Michael New—or any American soldier—can get justice in a military court when challenging a direct order of the president of the United States. Also at stake is Michael New's oath as a soldier to defend the Constitution of the United States. If a soldier cannot defend himself in the courtroom against a charge of disobedience of an unlawful order, simply because it has been issued by the White House, then the American military will have been reduced to a dangerous mercenary force serving the political interests of one man. That is not the American way.[37]

At the time of this writing, New's defense team was preparing for oral arguments on his behalf in the US Court of Appeals for the District of Columbia Circuit.[38] Since even the last US district judge to rule against New has conceded that President Clinton probably did break the law, I am hopeful that justice—for Michael New and every other man and woman who wears an American military uniform—will ultimately prevail.

Bill Clinton and Black Hawk Down

You have to ask yourself: What's the big deal? Why didn't Michael New's chain of command, from his company commander all the way up to the White House, just transfer him out of his unit and sweep the whole messy situation under the proverbial rug? The answer to that question, unfortunately, points back to an American leader willfully working in secret to sign away our national sovereignty.

I'm talking specifically about Presidential Decision Directives 13 and 25, a pair of secret documents intended by the Clinton administration to parse the Constitution and create a legalistic loophole that would allow a president to place US troops under UN control for any reason he might choose.

Our Constitution doesn't allow US troops to serve foreign commanders. It's pretty straightforward, actually. Article 2, Section 2, states: "The President shall be Commander in Chief of the Army and Navy of the United States, and of the Militia of the several States, when called into the actual Service of the United States."

This means that a soldier's chain of command, from the squad leader on up, stops with the president of the United States. When US troops put on the UN's blue hats, they answer to a foreign chain of command that does not include the president.

That's not just wrong. It's unconstitutional, and it's illegal.

But Clinton's policy position was not one that emerged out of nowhere in 1995. It had been in the works for a long time. When Bill Clinton was still merely Candidate Clinton, the foreign policy part of his presidential campaign had focused pointedly on expanding the UN's military role.[39]

In a 1991 speech at his alma mater, Georgetown University, Clinton introduced his plan to shift "the burden of maintaining peace to a wider coalition of nations of which America will be a part." Clinton even then advocated establishing a UN rapid deployment force "that could be used for purposes beyond traditional peacekeeping, such as standing guard at the borders of countries threatened by aggression; preventing attacks on civilians; providing humanitarian relief; and combating terrorism and drug trafficking."[40]

UN Secretary-General Boutros Boutros-Ghali issued his "Agenda for Peace" proposal on 31 January 1992, in which he demanded that member states should enter into Article 43 agreements with the UN and "earmark" certain military forces for participation in UN peacekeeping operations. In apparent response to Boutros-Ghali's proposal, Clinton made it known that if elected, his administration was going to explore the possibility of implementing such a plan.[41]

Shortly after taking office in 1993, President Clinton quickly announced a new foreign policy approach that he referred to as "assertive multilateralism."[42] Translated, that really meant that he wanted to use US troops to meddle in other people's business all over the world, any time he felt like it. That decision ultimately led to some disastrous consequences in Somalia.

"UN Orders US-Led Force Into Somalia" screamed the front-page banner headline of the *Washington Post* in early December 1992. By unanimous vote, the Security Council had authorized sending in troops to protect humanitarian relief operations that were being disrupted by warring factions within the poverty-stricken country. Their ostensible goal was to help as many as two million Somalis who were suffering from disease and starvation.

"The decision constitutes the first United Nations intervention in a country's internal affairs with a mandate to use offensive force, if necessary," the *Post* story correctly explained. President George H.W. Bush expressed his optimistic hope that the Somali police operation would be quick and easy, and the estimated twenty-seven thousand American troops would be home before he left office the following January.[43]

In 1993, following up on the plans begun under his predecessor, newly inaugurated President Clinton proceeded to authorize thousands of Americans to serve in Somalia under the auspices of United Nations Operations, while he also prepared to send other US troops to serve under foreign commanders as UN peacekeepers in Macedonia. It was this explicit decision by Clinton to place US troops under foreign command that distinguished his actions from those of previous presidents.

Early on in Clinton's tenure, the top secret draft document *Presidential Decision Directive 13* (PDD-13) was generated by the Clinton administration to pave the way for US troops to serve under UN commanders on a regular basis.[44]

The full text of that controversial decision has never been released, but understanding its basic intent is essential to understanding what happened next. According to informed sources, the United States recognized the United Nations as the world's "primary peacekeeping organization" and agreed to supply US troops for UN nation-building and police actions.

Harry Summers, a syndicated columnist, retired US army colonel, and distinguished fellow of the Army War College, has observed that "as originally written, the Clinton Administration's PDD-13 would once again have sidetracked the military from its fundamental reason for being, turning it, as JFK had attempted to do, into an instrument for social change."[45]

PDD-13 was first brought to the public's attention in August 1993 when the *Washington Post*, relying on leaked information, reported that the document "endorses the United Nations as ersatz world policeman and commits Washington to support multinational nation-building and peacekeeping operations politically, militarily, and financially."[46]

Two weeks later, the *New York Times* reported that "the Clinton Administration is considering an expanded role in United Nations peacekeeping operations that would include having Americans serve under foreign commanders on a regular basis."[47] Then in October 1993, Clinton lost eighteen American soldiers—and whatever public support he'd built for UN peacekeeping operations—when a team of outgunned US Army Rangers was ambushed in Mogadishu while trying to capture renegade Somali warlord Mohamed Farrah Aidid.

Their defeat in the infamous "Black Hawk Down" incident was blamed on an incompetent UN command structure that sent them into battle without the necessary armor, and then ignored their desperate calls for backup support while the battle raged. Images of dead American soldiers being dragged through the streets of Mogadishu blanketed the news channels, and public criticism of both Clinton and the United Nations was widespread.

"The Clinton administration appears dedicated to sending the US military into the dangerous seas of multinational peacekeeping in an effort to elevate the status of the United Nations into the guardian arbiter of the new world order," declared Mississippi senator Trent Lott two days later on the Senate floor. "Key to this new vision of the world is a vision of a new world army whose singular purpose is to enforce the whims of the arcane United Nations Security Council."[48]

In the aftermath of the Black Hawk Down debacle, as more and more influential people became aware of the existence of PDD-13, the public criticism of the policy escalated. Pat Buchanan called it "a surrender of US sovereignty, [and] a betrayal of the ideas upon which our republic was founded." With an amazing prescience, Buchanan warned, "It is a formula for making American soldiers Hessians of an imperial army, whose interventions could make America the most hated nation on earth."[49]

The Clinton administration quickly changed its official public attitude toward UN troop deployments. Just days after the Black Hawk Down incident, Clinton addressed the United Nations, sanctimoniously warning the assembled delegates, "If the American people are to say yes to UN peacekeeping, the United Nations must know when to say no." Shortly thereafter, the president announced that US troops would participate in UN peacekeeping operations only if they served under a US chain of command.[50]

On 2 March 1995, after twenty-seven grueling months, the last US Marines finally left Somalia. The United States had been humiliated and disgraced, and 42 Americans were counted among the 120 UN troops who had died. The war-torn country (where an estimated 350,000 Somalis had died in 1992 alone) was still in political turmoil and gripped by famine, disease, and internal fighting.[51]

Examining Clinton's Treasonous PDD-25

Yet somehow that unfortunate Somali experience didn't stop soldiers in the US Third Infantry Division from deploying to Macedonia as peacekeepers, almost a year to the day after the Mogadishu debacle.

And it didn't stop Michael New from being court-martialed, despite his written agreement with the public statements emanating from the White House! In my view, Michael New's legal predicament is tied to Clinton's PDD-13 and its later revised version, PDD-25, which was signed by Clinton on 3 May 1994.

PDD-25 was presented to the public as a "reform" of the still–top secret PDD-13 and was supposed to be a clarification of US foreign policy and a limitation upon the exposure of US troops to the dangers inherent in UN service. But many observers feel that it was really just another public relations spin designed by the Clinton White House to disarm their opponents and further confuse the issue in the minds of the general populace.

I personally believe the former administration drew a top secret line in the sand over how, when, and where US troops would be deployed. According to the publicly available executive summary that our government has declassified, PDD-25 attempts to define "command" and "operational control" in such a manner as to broaden the president's ability to send American kids into harm's way on behalf of the United Nations.

Under PDD-25, the president retains his status as commander-in-chief. But the directive allows the president to assign US troops to a foreign commander for specific "operational control." US troop commanders do have the right to protest illegal orders from their foreign leadership back to their American chain of command. Here, specifically, is part of what President Clinton's PDD-25 executive summary has to say about military command and control:

- Definition of Command: No president has ever relinquished command over US forces. Command constitutes the authority to issue orders covering every aspect of military operations and administration. *The sole source of legitimacy for US commanders originates from the US Constitution, federal law and the Uniform Code of Military Justice* and flows from the president to the lowest US commander in the field. The chain of command from the president to the lowest US commander in the field remains inviolate.

- Definition of Operational Control: It is sometimes prudent or advantageous (for reasons such as maximizing military effectiveness and ensuring unity of command) to place US forces under the operational control of a foreign commander to achieve specified military objectives. In making this determination, factors such as the mission, the size of the proposed US force, the risks involved, anticipated duration, and rules of engagement will be carefully considered.

- Operational control is a subset of command. It is given for a specific time frame or mission and includes the authority to assign tasks to US forces already deployed by the president, and assign tasks to US units led by US officers. Within the limits of operational control, a foreign UN commander cannot: change the mission or deploy US forces outside the area of responsibility agreed to by the president, separate units, divide their supplies, administer discipline, promote anyone, or change their internal organization.

- Fundamental Elements of US Command Always Apply: If it is to our advantage to place US forces under the operational control of a UN commander, the fundamental elements of US command still apply. US commanders will maintain the capability to report separately to higher US military authorities, as well as the UN commander. Commanders of US military units participating in UN operations will refer to higher US authorities' orders that are illegal under US or international law, or are outside the mandate of the mission to which the United States agreed with the UN, if they are unable to resolve the matter with the UN commander.

- There is no intention to use these conditions to subvert the operational chain of command. Unity of command remains a vital concern. Questions of legality, mission mandate, and prudence will continue to be worked out "on the ground" before the orders are issued. The United States will continue to work with the UN and other member states to streamline command and control procedures and maximize effective coordination on the ground.[52]

If all that seems a little confusing to you, maybe even somewhat disingenuous, you're not alone. John R. Bolton, our current ambassador to the UN who was at the time the senior vice president of the American Enterprise Institute, testified before the House Committee on International Relations in October 2000. His comments then mirror what I am thinking now.

"The central deficiency of PDD-25 is that it really provides no policy guidance at all," Bolton testified. "Despite rhetorical gestures in the direction of limiting and rigorously analyzing proposed peacekeeping operations, loose language throughout the document permits justification of nearly anything the Administration ultimately decides to do."[53]

Some members of Congress didn't like it either. Texas congressman Ron Paul was particularly upset over what he referred to as a "presidential power-grab." He went on: "Do you want our military to be moved under the United Nations command without congressional approval? Unfortunately, Presidential Decision Directive 25 takes the matter of US troops in UN operations completely out of the hands of Congress. PDD-25 is classified and the exact text has not been made available even when requested by members of Congress, but from the 'summary' of each PDD we have been allowed to see, and sources familiar with the actual documents, that is what they appear to say."[54]

President Clinton also issued other secret, far-reaching Presidential Decision Directives before leaving office. Journalist Cliff Kincaid has reported that Clinton issued more than eighty still-classified PDDs while in office. One reportedly establishes the questionable premise that UN treaties take precedent over US law. Another supposedly exempts UN personnel from prosecution for violating US laws.[55]

We Already Have a UN Army

Many liberals see the United Nations as a benevolent global authority from which may someday flow all the blessings of human love, peace, and brotherhood. They view those who mistrust the motives of the UN as being paranoid and reactionary. People who fear and thus oppose the rise of a global dictatorship or a malevolent police state are derisively dismissed as "the black helicopter crowd." The fact is, though, the black helicopters are real. And so is the UN army, although most folks don't know it yet.

Back in 1992, as we have already mentioned, UN Secretary-General Boutros Boutros-Ghali unveiled his new "Agenda for Peace," which called for the establishment of a permanent UN rapid deployment force to move quickly in time of emergency. Similar suggestions had been made by previous UN officials and also by a variety of NGOs, including, among others, the World Federalist Association (WFA), the Campaign for UN Reform (CUNR), and the Commission for Global Governance (CGG).

In 1993, the Canadian senate specifically endorsed the creation of a "standing UN army" to deter and repel threats by "a military force of a lesser order." Two years later, after the tragic loss of life in Rwanda, the Canadian government issued a major report titled *Toward a Rapid Reaction Capability for the United Nations*. The Danish government meanwhile produced a similar document, *Report by the Working Group on a Multinational United Nations Stand-by Forces High Readiness Brigade*. Both reports endorsed "a permanent standing UN police force" that would instantly be "available for use worldwide" in times of emergency.

By late 1996, the governments of Canada, Denmark, Austria, the

Netherlands, Norway, Poland, and Sweden had pledged to send troops. In 1997, the Multinational Stand-by High Readiness Brigade for United Nations Operations—or SHIRBRIG for short—was born, with operational headquarters based near Copenhagen.[56]

This clandestine mobilization of the first permanent UN military force in history was conducted quietly until 1998, when the media finally got wind of a secret $200,000 donation by the US State Department to help establish a $2.3 million trust fund to finance the operation's headquarters. According to the *Washington Times*, "The administration gave 'backdoor support' last September because of the political sensitivity over creating an army under UN command and political authority, said a UN secretariat official close to the process who asked not to be named."[57]

Once again, the Clinton administration was caught with its pants down, so to speak. Both the UN and the White House denied that any standing army had been created. But their critics weren't buying those denials.

"The key thing is having the headquarters, the command-and-control system, and the logistical infrastructure, and once you have that you can plug in your troop units with relative ease," said Thomas G. Moore, the director of international studies at the Heritage Foundation and a former Army officer. "You don't need a standing army. It serves the same purpose without standing. The political benefits are you can deny you have created a standing army, even though you have created an equivalent."[58]

SHIRBRIG, with at least 4,000 to 5,000 troops under arms, was declared fully operational in March 2000. At that time eighty-eight nations had pledged to designate troops for the force, representing a potential pool of 147,500 available military personnel.[59]

Since that time SHIRBRIG soldiers have served in Ethiopia, Eritrea, and elsewhere. The principal limiting factor to the SHIRBRIG model is the fact that its troops are supplied by the various participating nation-states, and those troops can be recalled by those states at will. Each individual state may pick and choose which UN operation it will allow its soldiers to participate in.

Those who advocate the expansion of the UN's military power are now calling for the creation of an all-volunteer fighting force under permanent UN command, something like the old French Foreign Legion used to be. This would enable the UN to act immediately whenever its leaders might feel the need to use military force, without waiting on the various nation-states to agree to provide it with troops.

According to the 1995 report of the Commission on Global Governance, "The very existence of an immediately available and effective UN volunteer force could be a deterrent in itself. It could also give important support for negotiation and the peaceful settlement of disputes."[60]

Once again, the doctrine of incrementalism rules the day. The globalists know that over time, the accumulation of many small incremental gains will result in the attainment of their goals. This idea was unmistakably expressed in William R. Frye's seminal 1957 study, *A United Nations Peace Force.*

> Establishment of a small, permanent peace force, or the machinery for one, could be the first step on the long road toward order and stability. Progress cannot be forced, but it can be helped to evolve. That which is radical one year can become conservative and accepted the next.[61]

Clinton's Legacy is Binding on Bush

Speaking to the assembled leaders of the world at the Millennium Summit in 2000, President Bill Clinton called publicly for a larger UN standing army that would be able to "project credible force" into tense international crises. And he said plainly that to him, the United Nations represents the shape of things to come.

"Those who believe we can either do without the UN, or impose our will upon it, have not learned from history and do not understand the future," Clinton declared.[62]

Although I have harshly criticized Bill Clinton for his anti-American actions as president and his obvious affection for internationalist agendas, I have to acknowledge that neither Clinton nor the Democrats have a monopoly on foreign policy folly. In fact, our last two Republican presidents have not been much better. We all remember that it was the first President Bush who popularized the phrase "new world order" during the first Gulf War in 1991, and who gave renewed legitimacy to the United Nations by fawning before it for permission to attack Saddam Hussein. After that war he both radically reduced the size of the US military and endorsed Boutros-Ghali's call for a strengthened UN military power.

Now the second President Bush has decided to follow closely in the footsteps of both his father and his immediate predecessor in the Oval Office. According to conservative columnist Chuck Baldwin, "The president of the United States is pushing for a standing UN army."[63]

Baldwin's charge comes following the May 2004 revelation by Bill Gertz in the *Washington Times* that "the Pentagon and State Department are planning to set up a 75,000-member international peacekeeping force for Africa." Most of the peacekeepers will be soldiers from various Third World nations. The program will cost US taxpayers more than $600 million over five years.[64]

Bush's plan, known as the Global Peace Operations Initiative (GPOI), closely tracks the recommendations of the UN's Millennium Declaration—which in turn affirms the set of principles articulated in the August 2000 *Report of the Panel on United Nations Peace Operations*, also known as the *Brahimi Report.*[65] (Lakhdar Brahimi, the chairman of the panel that produced the report, has been a close associate of Kofi Annan for years. Recently in Iraq, it was Brahimi, described by Annan as "my own envoy," who was instrumental in setting up the post-Saddam government structure there, with US assistance.)

The *Brahimi Report* calls for strengthening the UN Standby Arrangements System (UNSAS) "to include several coherent, multinational, brigade-size forces and the necessary enabling forces, created by Member States working in partnership, in order to better meet the need for robust peacekeeping forces that the Panel has advocated."[66]

A brigade, according to Brahimi, consists of five thousand troops. Bush's new GPOI plan to train and equip seventy-five thousand troops would thus increase the original SHIRBRIG task force by fifteen-fold and would greatly enhance the UN's permanent, independent military presence not only in Africa but around the globe.

President George W. Bush is actively working to strengthen the standing UN army, while simultaneously unilaterally cutting back on the strategic nuclear weapons arsenal of the United States. These actions line up perfectly, if somewhat belatedly, with the overall JFK plan for "General and Complete Disarmament" described in *Freedom from War* more than forty-five years ago. The shape of things to come is gradually emerging.

Globalists note these developments and rejoice, because they see George W. Bush doing for the UN today what Richard Nixon did for Communist China thirty years ago. Using his so-called conservative credentials to dispel criticism from the Right, Bush is advancing anti-American objectives that an unabashed liberal like John Kerry or Hillary Clinton never could accomplish.[67]

8

THE UN'S GOAL REALLY *IS* WORLD GOVERNMENT

Most people in the world today probably believe that the ultimate goals of the UN are benign. Even when it is ineffective in its efforts, its intentions are good, the pro-UN public relations spin declares. But I suggest that this optimistic Panglossian vision of a benign United Nations engaged in a noble, utopian mission simply doesn't match the hard facts of reality.

We have seen so far that there are disturbing trends in the globalist movement, leading in various directions that many, and perhaps most, Americans might not approve. But does this fact alone constitute an indictment of the whole United Nations system?

To many, the answer to this vital question is a resounding *yes*. Why? Because the harshest critics of the UN are convinced that its ultimate agenda is the establishment of an overarching world government.

One such critic is Henry Lamb, who has been monitoring both world trends and UN activities for more than three decades. Lamb sees a very clear, if at times clever and subtle, agenda at work. In his pointed opinion:

> Virtually every activity, conference, and action plan devised by the UN since the early 1970s has been aiming toward the ultimate objective of eventual global governance, founded upon principles of collec-

tivism, central planning, and omnipotent enforcement, disguised by the language of equity, social justice, and environmental protection.[1]

There is a great deal of hard historical evidence to prove that Lamb is right.

Back in 1945, the US State Department promised the senators who voted to ratify the United Nations that the new international organization "in no sense constituted a form of World Government and that neither the Senate nor the American people need be concerned that the United Nations or any of its agencies would interfere with the sovereignty of the United States or with the domestic affairs of the American People."[2]

But a mere five years after the United Nations came into existence, globalist James Warburg told the Senate Foreign Relations Subcommittee, "We shall have world government whether or not we like it. The question is only whether world government will be achieved by conquest or by consent."[3]

This explains why US senator Robert Taft, who voted in 1945 to approve US membership in the United Nations, was by 1951 calling the organization "a trap." This salient fact alone would support the logical conclusion that—from the very beginning—there were certain highly influential people whose secret vision for the UN was far different from that disingenuous facade which was presented to the world for public consumption.

Then in 1962, the State Department financed a study entitled "A World Effectively Controlled by the United Nations." The study was undertaken by Lincoln Bloomfield, a professor at M.I.T. His conclusions are shocking to those who love America, because they reveal a cynical plan to enslave our people against their will.

A world effectively controlled by the United Nations is one in which *"world government" would come about through the establishment of supranational institutions,* characterized by mandatory universal membership and some ability to employ physical force. Effective control would thus entail a preponderance of political power in the hands of a supranational organization. . . . The present UN Charter could theoretically be revised in order to erect such an organization equal to the task envisaged, *thereby codifying a radical rearrangement of power in the world.*[4]

That report outlined what would be needed for such a total world government: a mandatory universal membership, an ability to use physical force, and compulsory jurisdiction of its courts. One of the UN's "principle features," stated the report, would be "enforceable taxing powers."[5]

As we have already discovered, the movement to establish the UN's autonomous military power, independent funding and taxing authority, and global legal authority is already far advanced. The inescapable conclusion to be drawn is that the UN and its supporters both desire and intend ultimately to transform the organization from being merely a voluntary forum of peace-loving nations into a sovereign, supranational world government. It seeks to usurp absolute legal and political authority over the sovereign nations of the world and to acquire irresistible military power.

I have become convinced that the United Nations is a thoroughly corrupt bureaucratic organization whose operations around the globe are typically characterized by waste, negligence, and incompetence. What's more, the UN has demonstrated repeatedly that its overall attitude is hostile to American interests. And finally, I am persuaded that the totalitarian global agenda that the UN seeks to advance is inherently evil.

Allowing the UN to achieve its goals of world hegemony under a global socialist dictatorship could prove disastrous—not only for Americans but also for all the other peoples of the earth.

The Most Trusted Man in America

When someone whom they know and respect begins to give sage and solemn advice, most people tend to listen, even if they don't necessarily like what they are hearing. So when someone with the reputation of being "the most trusted man in America" advocates world government, it's bound to have an impact—even if the reaction occurs below the surface of human mental consciousness, at some deeper subliminal level.

Walter Cronkite, the longtime anchorman for *CBS Evening News*, was known for his dispassionate news delivery and grandfatherly public persona. For almost two decades, from 1962 to 1981, a whole generation of Americans grew up getting their perception of reality from kindly "Uncle Walter." Every night at six o'clock, families all across America would tune in after dinner to hear the popular newscaster tell them what was happening in their world that day. Whether it was the Cuban missile crisis, the 1963 JFK assassination, the 1968 Tet Offensive during the Vietnam War, the Apollo 11 moon landing, or the Nixon Watergate scandal, Cronkite told the official version of the story—"and that's the way it is," he would solemnly intone at the close of each broadcast.[6]

But after Cronkite retired from the news desk, he began to manifest a different philosophical and political side, one that most folks had not seen before. He quickly emerged as a champion of liberal socialism and global governance.

In 1989, for example, Cronkite spoke to a dinner meeting of the People for the American Way, an organization devoted to banning the free expression of religious faith from the public square under the misguided notion of separation of church and state. After expressing his disappointment in the 1988 presidential election and his hope that "liberalism isn't dead in this country," but rather had temporarily "lost its voice," Cronkite turned his attention to the loathsome Religious Right.

"We know that religious beliefs cannot define patriotism," Cronkite opined. "God almighty, we've got to shout these truths in which we believe from the housetops. Like that scene in the movie *Network*, we've got to throw open our windows and shout these truths to the streets and the heavens."[7] (Ironically, many conservatives today believe that the central character in that movie, a popular TV newsman who is "chosen" to deliver the official message of the powerful ruling elites who control the world, may have been based on Cronkite himself.)

Cronkite was even more outspoken, however, speaking at the United Nations in 1999, when he accepted the Norman Cousins Global Governance Award from the World Federalists Association. After being introduced by Hillary Rodham Clinton, Cronkite told the group about his personal dream of world government.

> It seems to many of us that if we are to avoid the eventual catastrophic world conflict *we must strengthen the United Nations as a first step toward a world government* patterned after our own government with a legislature, executive, and judiciary, and police to enforce its international laws and keep the peace. *To do that, of course, we Americans will have to yield up some of our sovereignty.* That would be a bitter pill. It would take a lot of courage, a lot of faith in the new order. But the American colonists did it once and brought forth one of the most nearly perfect unions the world has ever seen.[8]

Apparently Cronkite was not prepared to preserve that "nearly perfect union," but rather wanted to trade it in on a new and improved model of global governance. In reality, he missed the point of the War for Independence entirely—those early American colonists were fighting to shake off the yoke of an oppressive tyranny, not for the right to surrender to one.

In the same speech, Cronkite then launched a broadside against the "Christian Coalition and the rest of the religious right wing," whom he blamed for the failure of the United States to ratify certain international treaties. Cronkite characterized their views this way:

> Their leader, Pat Robertson, has written that we should have a world government but only when the Messiah arrives. Any attempt to achieve world order before that time must be the work of the devil.

This small but well-organized group has intimidated both the Republican Party and the Clinton administration. It has attacked each of our presidents since FDR for supporting the United Nations. Robertson explains that these presidents were and are unwitting agents of Lucifer.[9]

Well, nobody can say that the other side hasn't heard what their critics are saying.

After his speech to the World Federalists, Cronkite also spoke with reporters, where he further amplified his remarks by calling for an omnipotent global police state.

"I wouldn't give up on the UN yet," he told the press. "I think we are realizing that we are going to have to have an international rule of law. We need not only an executive to make international law, but we need the military forces to enforce that law and the judicial system to bring the criminals to justice. . . . American people are going to begin to realize that they are going to have to yield some sovereignty to an international body to enforce world law, and I think that's going to come to other people as well."[10]

In 2002, Cronkite authored a controversial fund-raising letter for the World Federalist Association's "Campaign for Global Change." In that letter he called for, among other things, a standing UN army and the ratification of the International Criminal Court by the US Senate, because "until we have effective international law to forge genuine, enforceable international solutions, many of the most vexing problems we face will continue to defy change." The 9-11 terrorist attacks showed us that "united citizens of the world" must stand together to "create a world free of intolerance, injustice, and violence," Cronkite's letter said. "*An empowered UN is our best hope for achieving such a goal*—a global community that can solve our problems effectively, democratically and peacefully."[11]

It is informative to learn belatedly that Cronkite's anchorman career with CBS originally came about through the influence of Blair Clark, a longtime liberal Democratic Party insider, Harvard classmate of JFK, and editor of the socialist magazine the *Nation*. Thus Cronkite was all along among the cadre of committed fellow travelers whose mission was to move America subtly to the left. His highly touted dispassionate journalistic impartiality was just a newsroom facade for public consumption; he came out of the liberal closet, so to speak, after his retirement from CBS.[12]

Walter Cronkite was just one voice among the many that have been slyly and subversively working among us for years to undermine the legal, historical, and philosophical foundations of the republic. What we need to realize is that not only was he not alone, his ideology did not arise in a vacuum. It was carefully crafted and nurtured over time by an interrelated group of very patient people with an end result in mind.

The Poet's Vision: A Federation of the World

The year 2005 marked the UN's sixtieth anniversary—and its internationalist agenda is clearer today and its globalist goals much further advanced than at any time in its six decades of existence.

The history of the UN is a case study in the Leninist doctrine of gradualism, where large accumulated gains are the result of many small incremental advances over time, and there is nothing new under the sun. Walter Cronkite was both a participant in and a product of that ongoing process of gradual social change. But the history of the ideas that produced the United Nations actually predates the organization's own existence by at least twenty-five years, and some would argue by more far than a century.

For those with the time and inclination, it may be both enlightening and edifying to poke around in the past. Our necessarily brief historical survey will start out with a fairly famous poem, entitled "Locksley Hall," written in 1842 by Alfred, Lord Tennyson. It reads in part:

> For I dipt into the future, far as human eye could see,
> Saw the Vision of the world, and all the wonder that would be;

Saw the heavens fill with commerce, argosies of magic sails,

Pilots of the purple twilight, dropping down with costly bales;

Heard the heavens fill with shouting, and there rained a ghastly dew

From the nations' airy navies grappling in the central blue;

Far along the world-wide whisper of the south-wind rushing warm,

With the standards of the peoples plunging thro' the thunder-storm;

Till the war drum throbb'd no longer, and the battle-flags were furl'd

In the Parliament of Man, the Federation of the World.

There the common sense of most shall hold a fretful realm in awe,

And the kindly earth shall slumber, lapt in universal law.[13]

The most obvious initial observation to make here is that the poet apparently did have some kind of vision of the future, for he describes things that did not exist in his day, like "airy navies" fighting in the heavens. The phrase "there rained a ghastly dew" could well imply a variety of frightening modern warfare scenarios that would make men legitimately long for peace.

Finally, the poet sees that desirable result of peaceful slumber coming about through "the common sense of most," which will hold in check the evil tendencies of the rest. (Parenthetically, the earth is "kindly"; it is the humans who are "fretful.") Thus, in the poet's vision, through "the Parliament of Man, the Federation of the World" will come forth a system of "universal law" that produces global peace.

This outcome, of course, is the stated goal and vision of men such as Walter Cronkite and all the others like him, both famous and obscure, who labor patiently to bring a true world government into existence. To them, the beneficent end clearly justifies the absolutist means.[14] Whatever the sacrifices of national sovereignty, individual liberty, and/or economic prosperity that may be necessary to attain such an end, these are seen as being really minimal by comparison, and so they are clearly worth the cost.

Now, I have no way of knowing whether Walter Cronkite was influenced by this poem, or whether he ever read it or even heard of it. Many other prominent people, however, most certainly have done so. For example, according to Pulitzer Prize-winning historian Arthur Schlesinger Jr., British prime-minister Winston Churchill referred to this poem as "the most wonderful of modern prophecies." And US president Harry Truman reportedly carried a copy of the poem in his wallet all throughout his adult life. These wartime leaders of the two great English-speaking Allied powers also just happened to be instrumental in planning and establishing the postwar United Nations system.[15]

What's more, the nineteenth-century steel magnate Andrew Carnegie had previously praised the poem in his own book, *Triumphant Democracy.* "The Parliament of Man and the Federation of the World have already been hailed by the poet," Carnegie wrote, "and these mean a step much further in advance of the proposed reunion of Britain and America."[16]

Carnegie, after embracing philanthropy and "spiritual studies" later in life, left his vast fortune to tax-exempt charitable foundations with the goal of promoting world peace and social progress. Whether by those terms Carnegie meant to imply world government and international socialism, as some have suggested, is a question that I can't answer. However, the projects funded today by his Carnegie Foundation do often appear to fit into those categories.[17]

Writing in the *Wall Street Journal* more than a decade ago, at a time of intense disagreement between some members of Congress and the Clinton administration over the course of US foreign policy—and specifically whether or not US soldiers would be sent off to serve under UN command in far-flung peacekeeping operations around the globe— Professor Schlesinger made some astute observations on the larger implications of the question.

> If this reaction prevails, *Woodrow Wilson's vision of a peace system based on collective security will be dead,* or at least indefinitely deferred. This was the vision revived by Franklin Roosevelt, reaffirmed by all succeeding

presidents of both parties, renewed by George Bush in his call for a "new world order" and by Bill Clinton in his address to the United Nations, and generally applauded by the American people. *But collective security means a world of law*; it means the prevention and punishment of aggression; it means military enforcement; it means sending troops, including American troops, into combat *not always in support of US interests narrowly construed but in support of international order.*[18]

Schlesinger, a brilliant historian, has accurately summed up almost a century of American foreign policy in one succinct paragraph. Some of the historical facts he mentioned will be discussed in more detail later. What we need to consider at the moment are the implications of these facts—both from his perspective and from our own.

First, he points to "Woodrow Wilson's vision of a peace system based on collective security." That was ostensibly the driving idea behind Wilson's proposed League of Nations after World War I: to establish an international organization that could control aggression and eliminate wars through collective action. So it is the death of this noble vision that is at stake, according to Schlesinger, if the process already begun long ago does not continue to its predetermined end.

Second, he imparts legitimacy to this "revived vision" by claiming that it has been "reaffirmed by every US president of both parties" up until 1993, which is when his *Wall Street Journal* editorial essay was written. It is true that the idea of collective security was not repudiated by any American president. However, the crucial point of contention— and one that I feel it is absolutely imperative to make at this juncture— is simply this: merely expressing agreement with the general premise of using a collective security treaty to promote peace by limiting aggressive warfare is decidedly *not* the same thing as accepting either the need for or the desirability of an overarching world government.

Finally, Schlesinger draws what to him is a logical conclusion from those two preceding premises: "But collective security means a world of law"—and all else then derives from that particular concept of law. Then he bluntly explains exactly what that will mean in the real world.

> The world of law will not be attained by exhortation. Law requires enforcement. *Let us not kid ourselves that we can have a new world order without paying for it in blood as well as in money.* Maybe the costs of enforcement are too great. National interests narrowly construed may well be the safer rule. But let us recognize that we are surrendering a noble dream. Remember those lines of Tennyson that Churchill called "the most wonderful of modern prophecies" and that Harry Truman carried in his wallet throughout his life.[19]

Then he quotes the poem "Locksley Hall."

From this presentation it would certainly appear that the utopian "noble dream" expressed in this poem constitutes the philosophical and emotional underpinning of the whole internationalist movement. In the worldview of Professor Schlesinger and other committed globalists, the "world of law" means not merely the acceptance by sovereign nations of agreed standards of justice, but rather the establishment of an elaborate legal edifice and a global system of enforcement, that is, a planetary police state.

They are perfectly willing to sacrifice the liberty, autonomy, and sovereignty of both nations and individuals to achieve this "noble dream." To that end, Schlesinger also floated the idea of establishing a standing UN army composed of mercenaries, rather than the current system using troops temporarily donated by the member nations.

"Can the president persuade the nation to let our armed forces do their job in the interests of a new world order?" he asked rhetorically. If not, then

> perhaps we should promote the proposal recently made by that distinguished international civil servant Sir Brian Urquhart for a UN volunteer army, a foreign legion made up of people moved by idealism or

by a desire for adventure, that could serve the Security Council as a rapid deployment peacemaking force. In the meantime, we must seize every small opportunity to strengthen international law and international institutions.[20]

So it turns out that the internationalists' poetic vision for our world's future is an entire planet "lapt in universal law," which will be administered from UN headquarters and enforced by an army of mercenaries seeking thrills and adventure in the UN's "foreign legion." This euphemistically named "peacemaking force," with no allegiance to any nation, sounds a lot like the modern Gestapo of a tyrannical dictatorship to me.

What all this really means is that there has been a secret and sinister agenda at work all along, hidden behind the poetic rhetoric of universal peace and brotherhood. People have to learn to discern the difference between perception and reality, because what some people mean by certain words is not necessarily the same thing that other people may think they hear them saying. My mother is pretty smart. She always told me, "You can't always believe what people say, but you can always believe what they do."

We can see where the UN and its supporters are heading by looking at both what they have said and what they have done.

A Brief History of Globalism
in the Twentieth Century

For all practical purposes, we can accept the assumption that the drive for some kind of an international peacekeeping organization arose in the aftermath of World War I. The world was shocked by the massive human carnage produced in that prolonged and bloody conflict. Machine guns, tanks, heavy artillery, poison gas—the new weaponry that made its debut in WWI forever changed the complexion of modern warfare.

The British poet T.S. Eliot captured the world's grim postwar mood of innocence lost in his long poem "The Wasteland." Meanwhile, in the

cafés and garrets of Paris, a self-described "Lost Generation" of disillusioned artists and writers embraced the empty, hopeless doctrines of
nihilism and existentialism. The specter of enduring more ghastly wars
like the latest one made men cringe in fear, and they looked for new
solutions that held out the hope of peace.

One such solution appeared in December 1918, when an article
entitled "The League of Nations: A Practical Suggestion" was printed in
the *Round Table*, a British periodical published by Alfred Milner's secret
society, which parenthetically had been created by Cecil Rhodes before
his death. The authors of this article were an Englishman named Lionel
Curtis and an American, Col. Edward Mandell House, who for several
years had been President Woodrow Wilson's chief political adviser.

In 1919, the Paris Peace Conference convened to negotiate the
treaty that would conclude World War I. House attended as Wilson's
chief deputy, along with a contingent of American delegates. On 30
May, House and his cohorts met at the Majestic Hotel in Paris with
Milner and the members of his British Round Table group.

Out of that meeting came a decision to establish sister foreign policy organizations on both sides of the Atlantic, to promote world peace
and Anglo-American unity. The subsequent result was the eventual
founding of the Royal Institute of International Affairs in London and
the Council on Foreign Relations in New York.

The Treaty of Versailles that ended World War I was signed on 28 June
1919. The Covenant of the League of Nations comprised its first thirty
articles, essentially as they had been outlined previously in the *Round
Table* article by Curtis and House.

In America, President Wilson actively and enthusiastically promoted the League. According to most accounts, Wilson was guided to a
large degree by House, a man who believed in progressive socialism and
who saw the US Constitution as an impediment to the establishment of
his desired new international order.

Senator Henry Cabot Lodge and others opposed ratification of the

League of Nations treaty, but Lodge agreed to accept it if Wilson would guarantee that the new organization would not threaten American autonomy and sovereignty, and also promise that any decision to commit American troops to war would have to be approved by Congress. When Wilson refused to compromise in 1920, the Senate rejected the treaty. Wilson, already very ill, was crushed, and died dejected.

The Royal Institute for International Affairs (RIIA) was founded in London in 1920. The group was headquartered at Chatham House, from which they took their informal name, the Chatham House crowd. The following year, the Council on Foreign Relations (CFR) opened its doors at Pratt House in New York City.

The first president of the CFR was J.P. Morgan's lawyer, John W. Davis. The group was initially funded by American oilman John D. Rockefeller and Paul Warburg, whose family owned the Reichsbank in Germany and who in 1913 had been instrumental in creating the Federal Reserve System in America.

The first issue of the CFR quarterly journal *Foreign Affairs* was published in 1922. In the lead article, Charles W. Eliot, then president of Harvard University, deplored what he called the "dubious doctrines of 'safety first' and 'America first.'"

> The next American contribution to civilization should be full participation in the safe conduct of those world affairs through which the enlightened common interests of mankind are served, first, by joining heartily in the League of Nations for the immediate salvation of Europe and the Near East, and *then by advocating steadily for all the world Federalism, elastic and progressive Law.*[21]

The following December, the second issue of *Foreign Affairs* contained an article by Philip Kerr, a leader of the Round Table group. Kerr's article, "From Commonwealth to Empire," challenged the traditional system of nation-states in the world. Kerr insisted that

obviously there is going to be no peace or prosperity for mankind so
long as it remains divided into fifty or sixty independent states. . . .
Equally obviously there is going to be no steady progress in civilization or self-government among the more backward peoples
until some kind of an international system is created which put
an end to the diplomatic struggling incident to the attempt of
every nation to make itself secure. . . . *The real problem today is*
that of world government.[22]

From this short chronology and these brief quotes, we can clearly
discern certain obvious facts that should be accepted by all without dispute. First, some very wealthy, powerful, and influential people on both
sides of the Atlantic had developed a deep and abiding interest in the
establishment of some kind of an international federation or world government. Second, they saw the sovereignty of individual nation-states as
an obstacle to the achievement of those goals and the existence of traditional, patriotic "Fortress America" and "America First" attitudes as
being particularly objectionable.

What the true motives of these men were, whether altruistic or otherwise, is beyond the scope of this book; but this might be a question that
an inquiring person would want to explore more deeply. I believe that
any open-minded researcher would be astounded by the wealth of facts
that such a diligent study would reveal.[23]

Whether the continuing efforts, over the course of the next eighty
years or so, of these men and their disciples and minions constitute an
actual conspiracy to eliminate national sovereignty and to gain acceptance for a new world order system of World Government—that is
another question that each person will have to decide individually. But
conspiracy or not, those directly affiliated with the CFR and RIIA, and
many more within their widespread sphere of influence, continued to
make these internationalist goals a top priority during the years between
the two World Wars.

In 1931, for example, the famous British historian Arnold Toynbee of the RIIA candidly admitted, "We are working discreetly with all our might to wrest this mysterious force called sovereignty out of the clutches of the local nation-states of the world."[24]

While World War II was still in progress, but in anticipation of the end of hostilities and the expected founding of the United Nations, the CFR published a report called *American Public Opinion and Post-War Security Commitments*. This somewhat cynical 1944 study advocated the indoctrination of the American people into the acceptance of world government, but acknowledged the significant difficulties still to be overcome due to their "sovereignty fetish."

> The sovereignty fetish is still so strong in the public mind that there would appear to be little chance of winning popular assent to American membership in anything approaching a super-state organization. Much will depend upon the kind of approach that is used in further popular education.[25]

Recognition of these obstacles, however, didn't stop the CFR policymakers from continuing with their efforts to establish a "super-state organization." By 1948, a Rockefeller Foundation-funded committee of top-flight scholars at the University of Chicago had produced a *Preliminary Draft of a World Constitution*, authored by Robert M. Hutchins and Rexford G. Tugwell, which would have established a "Federal Republic of the World."[26]

The proposed world constitution, which was actually submitted to Congress in 1949 and 1950 by Sen. Glenn Taylor (D-Idaho), demanded that all nations "surrender their arms" and declared that "iniquity and war inseparably spring from the competitive anarchy of the national states . . . therefore the age of nations must end."[27]

Things happened fast after World War II, as the Soviet Union stole the atomic bomb from America and thus plunged the fearful world into a protracted Cold War. Anti-Communist sentiment ran high in the 1950s, and revelations that a number of the principle architects of the UN were Communist sympathizers, spies, or worse, served to tarnish the UN's reputation with many patriotic Americans.

It was within this time frame that the following academic analysis was completed.

Comparing the Three Models for "Global Governance"

As we study the latest trends toward turning the United Nations into a full-fledged world government, we need to understand that none of these arguments are new; they have all been around for more than three generations, in one form or another. But most people have never really heard these issues articulated and debated. That had already been done before most of us were born, and a large part of our nation seems to have lost its historical memory.

From the very beginning, there were certainly those who wished to see the United Nations transformed eventually into a world government. This is clear from some of the statements we have already read. But in fact, according to its own Charter, the UN organization was established as something quite different—it was merely a voluntary association of sovereign nations.

It is vitally important to understand the difference, because we need to realize that the nations who agreed to join this treaty in 1945 certainly did not intend, at the time they did so, to be perpetually signing away their national sovereignty.

According to Inis Claude, who was for many years a distinguished professor of government and foreign affairs at the University of Virginia and also the author of several books on these topics, there have been three predominant schools of thought among those seeking supranational solutions to global problems. In his definitive work, *Swords into*

Plowshares, which at one time was widely used as a textbook, Claude listed these three options as: international organization, world federalism, and world government.

As an international organization, Claude said, the UN's original job was to work "within the national state system to achieve the redemption of man from the evils of anarchy." Claude then describes the UN's intended goals as follows:

> Its objectives are these: to prevail upon governments to settle their quarrels peacefully, persuade them to behave reasonably, and deter them from acting aggressively; . . . to facilitate the development of national societies characterized by such economic and social well-being, respect for human rights, and political maturity that they will produce decent, cooperative, responsible governments; and to educate human beings to renounce nationalistic arrogance and ideological intolerance, helping them to become spiritually and morally fit for participation in the *collaborative enterprises of a world community of separate but independent states*. By such means, international organization purports to offer hope of *making the multi-state system work reasonably well*.[28]

The other two options are world federalism, which implies a stronger form of central government but still one that is endowed only with certain limited powers, and global government *per se*, which implies a unitary government holding unlimited power.

> In strict theory, *world government offers a distinctive approach to the central problem of peace and security*. It sees war as a necessary, natural, and inescapable product of the multi-state system; consequently, it proposes to abolish and replace the system, rather than to tinker with it.[29]

Claude points out that those who want to transform the UN from its original role almost always tend to emphasize the federalist approach—

even if what they ultimately hope to achieve is absolute global control. Why? Because of semantics, primarily. They don't want to scare people away. "*Government* is the big, brave word," Claude explains. "*Federalism* is the little, cautious word."[30]

Federalism implies a government with limited powers, and therefore people think that they are being asked to pay a limited price for world peace. Hence, the World *Federalist* Association rather than Greens for Global *Government*, for example.

But in fact, the distinction is more artificial than real. Those who want an expanded role for the UN have adopted what Claude calls a method of "patient gradualism" wherein they seek to transform the organization gradually over time, first into a federal system and ultimately into a unitary global government. "Since the federal form of government is so overwhelmingly the choice of those who pursue this line," Claude explains, "*I shall treat world federalism as synonymous with world government.*"[31]

Thus, according to Claude, the whole push toward world government "is preeminently a campaign to persuade human beings to accept and support the federalist solution." That campaign "tends to rely heavily upon the persuasive potency of three major themes: the imminent peril of atomic destruction, the utter inadequacy and ultimate futility of international organization, and the availability of salvation through the transformation of international anarchy into international government."[32]

But Claude flatly rejects the notion that global government is a desirable goal merely because some assert that it is necessary for the preservation of mankind.

> The case for world government must rest on something more than the grim reminder that civilization is in danger, a citation of the fact that the United Nations has failed to exorcise that danger, a doctrinaire assertion that *international organization, not being government,* offers the world no significant hope, and a glib assumption that *world fed-*

eration, being government, provides the exclusive and sufficient means to a solution of the problem of war. *The case has not been proved.*[33]

What is more, Claude also sounds a cautionary note to anyone who might be tempted to heed the siren song of those promoting world federalism as a safer destination than something that is openly identified as world government. It simply isn't true.

> *When the world federalist tells the wary nationalist that his project is safe,* because it involves the delegation of clearly defined powers to a global regime and the careful reservation of residual powers to the national state, *he is talking through his hat.* . . . A federal formula for the distribution of powers and functions is merely a starting point. It is quite possibly true that the gradual transformation of a federal into a unitary system is the only course of development compatible with its survival; . . . *What is certain is that changes would take place and that they would not be determined by those who had agitated for establishment of the federation.*[34]

For Claude, then, the choice was clear. Either nation-states would retain their autonomy and work together as a voluntary association, as the UN's original structure contemplated, or they would surrender their sovereignty and accept a unitary world government. There was no middle ground: the choice was all or nothing.

And that choice was fraught with danger, because in Claude's view, "The only theoretically adequate government is a Leviathan, an omnipotent dictatorship."

> If a global regime is to have sufficient power to fulfill its task, *questions of profound gravity arise:* who will exercise and control the force of the community, in accordance with what conception of justice, within what constitutional limits, with what guarantees that the limits will be observed? These are not questions that can be readily answered, but

they are crucial—*for the threat of global tyranny lurks in unsatisfactory answers.*[35]

Inis Claude was an acknowledged authority on foreign affairs and international organizations, and the author of several books on these topics. What he wrote back in the 1950s and the 1970s is still relevant today, because the basic issues remain the same now as they were back then.

The fundamental question remains: will we have personal independence and national sovereignty, or will we have world government? This is a question to ponder as we weigh the arguments advanced by those who see world government as being both desirable and inevitable.

World Federalists—Pushing for World Government

The World Federalist movement officially began in 1947 with headquarters in Switzerland. The American branch, called United World Federalists (UWF), was formed that same year at a conference held in Asheville, North Carolina. According to Wikipedia, the organization accepted any American "except persons Communist or Fascist oriented." Some of its members were open advocates of centralized world government.

The World Federalists grew rapidly, reaching a peak membership of more than fifty-thousand during the 1950s. Prominent people from all walks of life were associated with the group, including Albert Einstein, Kurt Vonnegut, Mortimer Adler, E. B. White, Oscar Hammerstein, and Sen. Alan Cranston. The group's longtime president and most conspicuous spokesman was Norman Cousins, who was editor of the *Saturday Review* and also a CFR member.

In 1970, speaking on the very first observance of Earth Day, Cousins declared, "Humanity needs world order. The fully sovereign nation is incapable of dealing with the poisoning of the environment. . . . The management of the planet . . . requires a world government."[36]

The UWF organization changed its name twice during the Cold

War, first in 1969 to World Federalists, USA, and later in the mid-1970s to the World Federalist Association (WFA). Today, after a 2003 facelift and merger with another pro-UN group, they are called Citizens for Global Solutions.[37]

The World Federalists' ongoing agenda in America has been to "build political will" for a more powerful United Nations to solve the world's problems. They have been particularly active in promoting the Law of the Sea Treaty and various disarmament schemes, including the Nuclear Test Ban Treaty, as well as pushing for UN "reform."

John Logue, vice president of the World Federalist Association, testified in December 1985 before the House Foreign Affairs Committee's subcommittee on Human Rights and International Organizations. He was talking about the United Nations when he made the following comments about himself and other peace people:

> Peace people—and all people—must see that if we really want to stop the arms race we must have effective world political institutions. . . . Yes, peace people must stop patronizing the people of the world. It is time to tell the world's people not what they want to hear, but what they ought to hear. What they ought to hear is that if we really want to have peace and promote justice, *we must reform, restructure and strengthen the United Nations and give it the power and authority and funds to keep the peace and promote justice.* The Security Council veto must go. One-nation, one-vote must go. *The United Nations must have taxing power or some other dependable form of revenue. It must have a large peacekeeping force.* It must be able to supervise the dismantling and destruction of nuclear and other major weapons systems. In appropriate areas, particularly in the areas of peace and security, *it must be able to make and enforce law on the individual.*[38]

Clearly, what the World Federalists have wanted to accomplish all along is the transformation of the current United Nations into an actual world government. From the 1970s on, the WFA has been a powerful voice for the expansion of UN authority and one of the most influential of the proliferation of globalist-oriented nongovernmental organizations.

The WFA has at times bestowed its annual Norman Cousins Global Governance Award on prominent media figures like CNN founder Ted Turner, who donated $10 billion to establish the United Nations Foundation, and longtime CBS News anchorman Walter Cronkite, whose leftist ideology was mentioned earlier.

In 1993, that coveted World Federalist award went to Strobe Talbot, who was then Bill Clinton's deputy secretary of state, for an essay that he had written the year before while he was still editor-at-large for *Time* magazine. In "The Birth of the Global Nation," Talbot had expressed his opinion that

> within the next hundred years . . . *nationhood as we know it will be obsolete; all states will recognize a single, global authority.* A phrase briefly fashionable in the mid-twentieth century—"citizen of the world"— will have assumed real meaning by the end of the twenty-first century.
>
> All countries are basically social arrangements, accommodations to changing circumstances. No matter how permanent and even sacred they may seem at any one time, in fact they are all artificial and temporary. Through the ages, there has been an overall trend toward larger units claiming sovereignty and paradoxically, a gradual diminution of how much true sovereignty any one country actually has. . . .
>
> *The best mechanism for democracy,* whether at the level of the multinational state or that of the planet as a whole, is not an all-powerful Leviathan or centralized superstate, but *a federation, a union of separate states that allocate certain powers to a central government while retaining many others for themselves.*
>
> Federalism has already proved the most successful of all political experiments, and organizations like the World Federalist Association have for decades advocated it as the basis for global government.[39]

Talbot, who like Clinton had been a Rhodes scholar, clearly says that he disavows establishing a leviathan superstate. Instead he supports a milder, safer form of federalism "as the basis for global government." Now, where have we heard that line before? According to Inis Claude's expert analysis, Talbot is talking through his hat.

Today, the new twenty-first century face of World Federalism, operating under the name Citizens for Global Solutions, is orchestrating the Stop Bolton Campaign, the Washington Working Group on the ICC, the Partnership for Effective Peacekeeping, and the Center for UN Reform Education, among their other projects and initiatives.

Milestone: President Bush Announces the New World Order, 1990

On 11 September 1990, as the United States prepared to mobilize a massive military force in Operation Desert Shield, President George H.W. Bush addressed a Joint Session of Congress and dramatically announced the birth of a new world order.

> We stand today at a unique and extraordinary moment. The crisis in the Persian Gulf, as grave as it is, also offers a rare opportunity to move toward an historic period of cooperation. Out of these troubled times, our fifth objective—*a new world order*—can emerge: a new era—freer from the threat of terror, stronger in the pursuit of justice, and more secure in the quest for peace. An era in which the nations of the world, east and west, north and south, can prosper and live in harmony.
>
> A hundred generations have searched for this elusive path to peace, while a thousand wars have raged across the span of human endeavor. *Today that new world is struggling to be born. A world quite different from the one we've known. A world where the rule of law supplants the rule of the jungle.* A world in which nations recognize the

shared responsibility for freedom and justice. A world where the strong respect the rights of the weak.[40]

Later, in March 1991, after we had invaded Iraq and Operation Desert Storm had been brought to its swift one-hundred-hour conclusion, Bush again addressed the Congress. He proclaimed victory in the Gulf War—"a victory for the rule of law"—but also explained the significance of that victory.

> Now, we can see *a new world coming into view*. A world in which there
> is a very real possibility of *a new world order*. In the words of Winston
> Churchill, a world order in which "the principles of justice and fair
> play protect the weak against the strong." *A world where the United
> Nations*—freed from Cold War stalemate—*is poised to fulfill the his-
> toric vision of its founders*. A world in which freedom and respect for
> human rights find a home among all nations,
> The Gulf War put this new world order to its first test. And, my fel-
> low Americans, we passed that test.[41]

These bold public pronouncements by Bush alarmed those people who saw an emerging world government as a threat rather than a blessing, and that number included most conservative evangelical Christians. In his 1991 book *New World Order*, the prominent Christian broadcaster Pat Robertson, host of CBN's *700 Club*, explained his own reaction at the time.

> I know George Bush. I have met with him in the White House, and
> I personally believe that President Bush is an honorable man and a
> man of integrity. Nevertheless, I believe that he has become con-
> vinced, as Woodrow Wilson was before him, of the idealistic possi-
> bilities of a world at peace under the benign leadership of a forum for
> all nations.

But I am equally convinced that for the past two hundred years the term *new world order* has been the code phrase of those who desire to destroy the Christian faith and what Pope Pius XI termed "the Christian social order." They wish to replace it with an occult-inspired world socialist dictatorship.[42]

Some have suggested that since the elder President Bush was a member of the Council on Foreign Relations, and a longtime government insider, he was simply doing the will of his CFR masters, both in launching the first Gulf War against Iraq and in cloaking that attack in globalist terms that would strengthen the UN.

Bush himself disavowed any conspiratorial intent in his "new world order" phraseology, emphasizing his essentially moral purpose in the war. He told the National Religious Broadcasters convention, while the air war was still raging over Iraq, that this was indeed a just war.

> The war in the Gulf is not a Christian war, a Jewish war, or a Moslem war—it is a just war. And it is a war in which good will prevail. Every war—every war—is fought for a reason. But a just war is fought for the right reasons—for moral, not selfish reasons.
>
> Some ask whether it's moral to use force to stop the rape, the pillage, the plunder of Kuwait. And my answer: extraordinary diplomatic efforts having been exhausted to resolve the matter peacefully, then the use of force is moral.[43]

Whether the first Gulf War was launched for reasons of high moral purpose or for more mundane geopolitical expediency, only God really knows and history will reveal. One thing is certain, however, and that is the fact that President Bush made the term *new world order* part of the everyday vocabulary of most Americans, virtually overnight. And lots of things have happened very fast since then.

The Globalist Express Is Picking Up Speed

The fall of the Berlin Wall in 1989 and the subsequent collapse of the Soviet Union had two major impacts on the world.

First, it ended what George H.W. Bush referred to as the "Cold War stalemate," so that we no longer had Evil Empire Communists for our mortal enemies. Theoretically, this would instantly enable us all to live in harmony under some beneficent "brotherhood of man" umbrella organization.

Second, it brought the self-described "convinced Communist" Mikhail Gorbachev to America, to ply his booming environmental disaster trade among the decadent Western capitalists. Theoretically, this would enable us all to join arms to fight our common environmental threat and save our endangered planet.

A major UN conference held in 1991, the Stockholm Initiative on Global Security and Governance, led directly to the establishment of the Commission on Global Governance in 1992. The word *governance* emerged as the semantic term of choice for use in common parlance among globalists, as it was perceived to be a "softer" word than *government*, and thus less likely to be rejected by the unconverted.

In 1992, former Soviet dictator Mikhail Gorbachev spoke at the Churchill Memorial in Fulton, Missouri, calling for a "democratically organized world community" and a "restructured" United Nations with more money and its own army.

In 1993, the First Meridian Conference on Global Governance was held in Bolinas, California. That same year, Gorbachev—along with financier Maurice Strong—established his environmental foundation, Green Cross International. This group is devoted to spreading the UN's pagan Earth Charter worldwide.

Then in 1995, on the fiftieth anniversary of the UN, Gorbachev hosted his first annual State of World Forum at the historic Fairmont Hotel in San Francisco, where the UN Charter had been negotiated. According to Jim Garrison, president of the Gorbachev Foundation,

"We have to empower the United Nations and . . . we have to govern and regulate human interaction." That's the conventional wisdom from the State of the World Forum.

"Over the next twenty to thirty years, we are going to end up with world government. It's inevitable," Garrison told the *San Francisco Weekly* magazine in 1995. "There's going to be conflict, coercion, and consensus. That's all part of what will be required as we give birth to the first global civilization."[44] If Garrison is right, we're already about ten years closer to our date with destiny.

Also in 1995, the 410-page *Our Global Neighborhood* was released by the Commission on Global Governance. It contained recommendations for empowering the UN, including giving the organization its own taxing power and eliminating the veto in the Security Council—both moves that would reduce America's ability to control the direction of the organization in any significant way.

In 1996, the Campaign for UN Reform was established by the World Federalists to lobby for expanded global governance.

In 1999, in preparation for the UN's upcoming Millennium Assembly, the *Charter for Global Democracy* was released with the support of most prominent NGOs, particularly the International Progress organization. This charter, which would modify and expand the powers of the existing UN Charter, codified the 1995 recommendations of the CGG into twelve principles for the "process of democratizing global governance."

The 1999 World NGO Conference in Canada was billed as a "People's Parliament" to promote world democracy. The push by NGOs to promote their own "Civil Society" influence in the UN represented a major new trend.

The year 2000 featured Gorbachev's ritzy State of the World Forum, which was held the 4th through the 10th of September at the New York Hilton. The central feature of that meeting was Gorbachev's controversial demand that the UN institute Marxist economic controls globally and also establish a top-level authority over the environment.

"In 1988, I spoke of a new role for the UN, a new body," Gorbachev announced, raising the ante. "In addition to the Security Council, we must have an Economic Council and an Environmental Council, with authority equal to that of the Security Council."[45]

Meanwhile, the Millennium Assembly was held the 5th through the 8th of September, and the Millennium Summit, the 6th through the 8th of September, at UN headquarters in New York. The result of those meetings was the Millennium Declaration, which pushed for most of the expanded UN powers described in the Charter for Global Democracy.

The anti-American sentiments openly expressed at these assemblies, whether at the UN itself or at the related off-site gatherings, is clear and evident. The status quo will not hold much longer. Either America will bend to the international pressure and assent to the power now being both demanded and asserted by the UN, or we will stand our ground for sovereignty and independence.

The Hard Road to World Order

Three decades ago, way back in 1974, Richard N. Gardner wrote an important essay in *Foreign Affairs,* the highly influential magazine on US international policy published by the Council on Foreign Relations. That essay, "The Hard Road to World Order," has been widely quoted ever since—primarily because of what it reveals about the ardent internationalists' mind-set and game plan.

Gardner, a professor of international law at Columbia University and formerly a JFK/LBJ deputy assistant secretary of state for International Organization Affairs (1961–65), lamented the lack of US commitment to world law. He complained that

we are witnessing an outbreak of shortsighted nationalism that seems oblivious to the economic, political, and moral implications of interdependence. Yet never has there been such a widespread recognition by the world's intellectual leadership of the necessity for cooperation and planning on a truly global basis, beyond country, beyond region, especially beyond social system.[46]

As a result, Gardner explained, "the 'house of world order' will have to be built from the bottom up rather than the top down." The sly, incrementalist solution that he proposed was simple: "An end-run around national sovereignty, eroding it piece by piece, will accomplish much more than the old-fashioned frontal assault."[47]

Gardner's end-run formula of patient gradualism has been followed by the globalists for the past thirty years, as they have been building their "house of world order," brick by brick. Now the edifice of world government is almost complete.

Unless America tears that house down, the globalists are going to move inside—and take us in with them. As we contemplate that prospect, let's remember this sage admonition: "Liberty has never come from the government," a former president wisely warned. "The history of liberty is the history of the limitation of governmental power, not the increase of it."

Who said that? Why, Woodrow Wilson, of course.

9

SAVING AMERICAN SOVEREIGNTY IN THE 21ST CENTURY

Many powerful forces are propelling the UN toward its apparent destiny as the undisputed ruler of the world. Special interests with incredible wealth and influence support its ascension to global power.

The common perception among people worldwide is that these trends toward global governance are the turning tides of history, and as such are inexorable and can be neither stopped nor reversed. As Victor Hugo once said, "An invasion of armies can be resisted, but not an idea whose time has come."[1]

Indeed, there are some people who believe that the rise of a global tyrant is predicted by the Bible and is therefore inevitable. But while this latter premise may be true, it is equally true that no man knows "the day or the hour" when this prophetic event will occur. For individuals to acquiesce in the ascendancy of this evil without putting up any kind of resistance, therefore, is not a moral act of obedience to the Scriptures but rather, like suicide, the ultimate faithless response of hopelessness and despair.

This question about whether or not we should passively accept a dictatorial world government is *not* exclusively nor even predominately a Christian issue. In fact, the non-Christian seer Nostradamus is said to have predicted the rise of an evil world ruler, a "Master of Mohammed," who would come into Europe from Greater Arabia wearing a blue turban.[2] In the post-911 world of radical Islamic conflict and terrorism, such a specific reference makes many people wonder just what might be coming next.

As a practical matter, in today's world, despite all of the support it receives from other sources, the UN cannot possibly achieve its globalist goals without the active cooperation of the United States of America. In fact, were the United States merely to withhold its annual funding, the UN would soon face bankruptcy, or irrelevance, or both.

Conservatives in America need to assert their leadership in the long-term best interests of this nation, and starve the ever-growing appetites of this voracious UN beast. Whether the best course is to tame it, cage it, or kill it, only time will tell. But to let this snarling beast run wild, grow stronger, and ultimately wreak havoc on the earth—this course is clearly unacceptable to American patriots.

Jesse Helms Throws Down the Gauntlet

In the year 2000, while the United Nations was gearing up for its high-profile Millennium Summit in New York, there was ongoing debate here in the United States about the future of our country's involvement with that organization. There was legitimate concern not only about the wastefulness and inefficiency of the international organization but also about the growing anti-American attitudes it manifested.

The UN was in dire straits financially at that point in time because the GOP-controlled Congress, over the fruitless objections of the politically impotent lame-duck Clinton administration, was withholding the payment of back US dues until significant reforms were accomplished by the UN—whose leadership arrogantly complained that the United States "owed" them about $1.7 billion. The United States calculated the figure of its voluntary arrears dues at closer to $1 billion.

The one man in America most personally responsible for blocking the payment of those UN dues was the five-term senior senator from North Carolina—Jesse Helms, the powerful chairman of the Senate

Foreign Relations Committee. Helms was considered by many sophisticated internationalists to be an inconvenient anachronism, merely a right-wing holdover from an earlier era of American isolationism. Yet Helms had proved to be a painful thorn in the side of the UN bureaucrats, primarily because he had his finger on the pulse of the American people right down at the grassroots.

On 30 March 2002, Senator Helms hosted the fifteen national delegates of the UN Security Council at the Capitol in Washington DC. He served them lunch and gave them a tour of the Senate, all the while explaining to them that, unlike some other countries, in America the president could not act independently in matters of foreign policy and treaties, but required the advice and consent of the Senate.

Helms was cordial but direct. He pointed out that the Congress had agreed to pay the UN $926 million in arrears dues over a period of three years—but there were strings attached. The money would be given only if about a dozen significant internal reforms were adopted by the UN. Those reforms included reducing the percentage of the UN's budget that the United States was required to pay. The US share of the UN's regular annual budget was to be reduced from 25 percent to 22 percent, and of the UN's separate peacekeeping budget, from 31 to 25 percent. The delegates chafed at the US demands and complained about being forced to act under duress, but in the end they capitulated. Because after all, they had no choice.[3]

In any event, the lunch meeting and Capitol tour was mostly for show. The senator's terms had already been delivered two months prior, on 20 January, when he had addressed the UN Security Council in New York. That was the bare-knuckle, no-holds-barred speech that finally put the UN in its place—for the first time in a long time.[4]

America "Will Not Countenance" UN Global Governance

Sen. Jesse Helms' speech to the UN Security Council on 20 January 2000 was also attended by the assembled delegates of the General

Assembly, and it was broadcast live on C-Span. It was the first time a US senator had ever addressed the UN. So it qualified as a unique event, both historically and philosophically.

After Helms had offered the assembled delegates his personal "hand of friendship," he proceeded to explain the "deep frustration" that the American people have felt toward the UN. "They know instinctively that the UN lives and breathes on the hard-earned money of the American taxpayers," Helms explained, and Americans resent what they perceive to be the organization's basic "lack of gratitude."

Despite the fact that the United States had voluntarily contributed more than $10 billion to the UN in 1999—which was far more than any other nation in the world—they were still being called a deadbeat nation, a suggestion that many Americans rejected. "I resent it, too," Helms added.

Helms said that the money the US taxpayers give to the UN is not viewed by them as charity, but as "an investment from which the American people rightly expect a return. They expect a reformed UN that works more efficiently, and which respects the sovereignty of the United States."

Helms warned the assembled UN delegates that the alternative to "common-sense reforms" of the type America demanded would be "a breach in US-UN relations." And the possible nonpayment of $926 million in arrears dues.

Helms reminded the delegates that the fundamental reason why America had not joined the League of Nations eighty years ago was because of President Woodrow Wilson's stubborn refusal to compromise with Senator Henry Cabot Lodge and guarantee the continued sovereignty of the United States and the individual rights of its citizens.

"Most Americans do not regard the United Nations as an end in and of itself. They see it as just one part of America's diplomatic arsenal," Helms explained. "To the extent that the UN is effective, the American people will support it. To the extent that it becomes ineffective—or worse, a burden—the American people will cast it aside."

Therefore, he warned, the UN needs to "serve the purpose for which it was designed," which includes providing a diplomatic forum to "keep open the channels of communication in times of crisis," facilitating collective military action when needed by "coalitions of the willing," and providing "important services, such as peacekeeping, weapons inspections, and humanitarian relief."

Helms minced no words as to the consequences of doing otherwise, and this following passage reflects the heart of his speech.

> But if the UN seeks to move beyond these core tasks, if it seeks to impose the UN's power and authority over nation-states, I guarantee that the United Nations will meet stiff resistance from the American people.
>
> As matters now stand, *many Americans sense that the UN has greater ambitions* than simply being an efficient deliverer of humanitarian aid, a more effective peacekeeper, a better weapons inspector, and a more effective tool of great power diplomacy. *They see the UN aspiring to establish itself as the central authority of a new international order of global laws and global governance. This is an international order the American people will not countenance, I guarantee you.*
>
> The UN must respect national sovereignty. *The UN serves nation-states, not the other way around. This principle is central to the legitimacy and ultimate survival of the United Nations,* and it is a principle that must be protected (emphasis added).

While it is true that under the American system, all treaties signed by the United States do become the domestic law of the land, they can be revoked at any time by "a simple act of Congress," Helms informed the UN delegates. "But no treaty or law can ever supersede the one document that all Americans hold sacred: the Constitution of the United States of America."

Helms stated candidly that Americans flatly reject all "UN claims to a monopoly on international moral legitimacy," and he argued that the only real hope for peace and security in the world remains what it has always been: the capacity of sovereign nations to deliver "the principled projection of force."

By contrast, he said, "More often than not, 'international law' has been used as a make-believe justification for hindering the march of freedom." Therefore, most Americans will *not* be willing to "sacrifice some of their sovereignty for the noble cause of international justice."

Noting that Americans have "a profound distrust of accumulated power," Helms rejected the notion that the International Criminal Court has any legal or moral authority over private American citizens. In fact, he labeled it "nonsense."

What's more, he insisted, "no UN institution—not the Security Council, not the Yugoslav tribunal, not a future ICC—is competent to judge the foreign policy and national security decisions of the United States."

America did ratify the United Nations Charter, Helms admitted, then elaborated, "But in doing so, *we did not cede one syllable of American sovereignty*, not one syllable. We didn't cede it to the United Nations or anybody else" (emphasis added).

And Helms pointed out that "while our friends in Europe concede more and more power upwards to supra-national institutions like the European Union, Americans are heading in precisely the opposite direction," toward decentralization of power.

Then he wrapped up his speech with both a challenge and a threat.

That is why Americans reject the idea of a sovereign United Nations that presumes to be the source of legitimacy for the United States' Government's policies, foreign and domestic. There is only one source of legitimacy of the American government's policies—and that is the consent of the American people.

If the United Nations is to survive into the twenty-first century, it must recognize its limitations. The demands of the United States have not changed much since Henry Cabot Lodge laid out his conditions for joining the League of Nations eighty years ago: Americans want to ensure that the United States of America remains the sole judge of its own internal affairs, that the United Nations is not allowed to restrict the individual rights of US citizens, and that the United States retains sole authority over the deployment of United States forces around the world.

This is what Americans ask of the United Nations; it is what Americans expect of the United Nations. . . . If the United Nations respects the sovereign rights of the American people, and serves them as an effective tool of diplomacy, it will earn and deserve their respect and support. *But a United Nations that seeks to impose its presumed authority on the American people without their consent begs for confrontation and,* I want to be candid, *eventual US withdrawal.*[5]

What Helms was saying was clearly understood by all, for he spoke plainly and directly. If the UN wanted to function as it was intended to do, America would support it, he promised. But if the UN wanted to transform itself into a world government that would threaten American sovereignty, then the United States would simply walk out. He did not have to explain that US withdrawal would signal the death knell of the organization. Such a statement was unnecessary, because everyone listening already knew that fact full well.

The delegates rushed to the podium to respond. Most emphatically disagreed with Helms, some diplomatically and others heatedly. The Cuban delegate, for example, hotly complained to reporters that Helms had slandered his country because he had referred in passing to Fidel Castro's dictatorial oppression of his people.

Most resented the idea that the United States wanted to impose its own conditions on the UN. Some said that the United States was actually hindering UN reform efforts by withholding its arrears dues payments. Agam Hasmy, the Malaysian ambassador, said that the real reform needed at the UN was a change in the structure of the Security

Council. Back in 1995, the Commission on Global Governance had proposed expansion of the council to twenty-three members and elimination of the veto power. This move, of course, would effectively remove the Security Council from the control of the five permanent members, and would further erode US influence.

The Canadian ambassador, Robert Fowler, essentially characterized Helms' views of the organization as obsolete. "We need a UN for 2000, not 1945," Fowler said.[6] Madelyn Albright, the secretary of state and herself a former UN ambassador, was quick to announce that the only person who was authorized to speak for the United States on foreign policy matters was President Bill Clinton, while media pundits pointed out that Helms' comments did not necessarily reflect the beliefs of all Americans.

Nevertheless, the deed was done and the die was cast. Helms had spoken boldly and unapologetically, both to the people and the power brokers of the world, and he had expressed the heartfelt sentiments of millions of conservative and patriotic grassroots Americans. Reading his speech, even today, sends chills of truth down my spine.

Pat Buchanan Still Puts "America First"

Just three days after Jesse Helms delivered his blockbuster address to the UN Security Council in New York City, the veteran archconservative Pat Buchanan dropped a similar bombshell in Boston, in a political speech to the Boston World Affairs Council.

He was campaigning for president for the third time—this time as the candidate of the Reform Party, after having twice been rejected by the Republicans. And Buchanan chose to define his contrarian candidacy by his unwavering commitment to continued American sovereignty and independence, in a time of rapidly rising internationalism.

"This, then, is the millennial struggle that succeeds the Cold War: it is the struggle of patriots of every nation against a world government where all nations yield up their sovereignty and fade away," Buchanan declared. "It is the struggle of nationalism against globalism, and it will be fought out not only among nations, but within nations."[7]

Then Buchanan challenged his audience to make their own choice: "And the old question Dean Rusk asked in the Vietnam era is relevant anew: Whose side are you on?"

While the other candidates were promising the voters more shiny beads and trinkets in the form of future government benefits, Buchanan was the only one offering them a real choice between future freedom and certain slavery. After detailing the advanced degree to which globalism had already established itself as the reigning ideology of American politics—and in so doing, making many of his points based on the same evidence that we have already examined throughout this book—Buchanan then drew a stark contrast. "Let it be said: loyalty to the new world order is disloyalty to the republic."

Wow! Apparently someone does indeed "dare call it treason." As a former top adviser to Ronald Reagan and longtime speechwriter for the Great Communicator, Buchanan knows well how to communicate his own message to the masses. Here is how he ended his speech in Boston:

> "I believe globalization is inevitable," Bill Clinton told Larry King at year's end. Well, I don't.
>
> My vision of America is of a republic that has recaptured every trace of her lost sovereignty, independence, and liberty, a nation that is once again self-reliant in agriculture, industry, and technology, a country that can, if need be, stand alone in the world.
>
> My vision is of a republic, not an empire, a nation that does not go to war unless she is attacked, or her vital interests are imperiled, or her honor is impugned. And when she does go to war, it is only after following a constitutional declaration by the Congress of the United States.
>
> We are not imperialists; we are not interventionists; and we are not isolationists. We simply believe in America . . . first, last, and always.[8]

Like Jesse Helms, Pat Buchanan talks straight to the issue and pulls no punches. I have repeated the words of these two great men in some detail, for one fundamental reason: because these are the true voices of traditional American conservatism. They are strong voices, courageous voices, and undefeated voices. They are the authentic voices that Americans desperately need to hear and to heed.

But they are also the kinds of voices that are heard in our land with decreasing frequency with every passing day. The tides of history have already turned, we are told, and these old-fashioned ideas of American patriotism and liberty and sovereignty are no longer in vogue.

Jesse Helms retired from the Senate in 2003, and as I write these words, he is reported to be quite ill. Pat Buchanan is now in his seventies, and although he still writes cutting-edge social commentary, he will no longer stand for public office. Who will replace these aging American heroes and provide the authentic voice of freedom for the next generation of American conservatives?

Can UN Reform Efforts Work Today?

Today we have John Bolton as our US ambassador to the UN, and he talks tough in New York City and refuses to kowtow to the international powers that be. That's good, as far as it goes. But the fact is, not much has really changed at the Parliament of Man on the banks of the East River.

So, in the wake of scandals, and amid reports of rampant institutional corruption and incompetence, many voices are clamoring for reform at the United Nations. That idea has become the new watchword of the day: we'll just *reform* the UN, and all will be well.

A blue-ribbon bipartisan study commission, headed by former GOP Speaker of the House Newt Gingrich and former Democrat Senate Minority Leader George Mitchell, has recently released its 145-page report, *American Interests and UN Reform*, which recommended a laundry list of much-needed and long-overdue changes. Even Secretary-

General Kofi Annan says he agrees that significant reforms are needed at the UN.

Conservative Republican stalwart Rep. Henry Hyde of Illinois introduced H.R. 2745, the United Nations Reform Act of 2005, last year. It passed the House on 17 June by a vote of 221 to 184, which was split largely along party lines. Two competing versions of UN reform bills are now pending in the Senate, and most congressional observers expect some type of reform legislation to become law in 2006.

In September of 2005, on the sixtieth anniversary of the UN, the National Public Radio network devoted a significant amount of airtime to promoting the idea of UN reform, and to praising the bipartisan Gingrich/Mitchell commission for their outstanding work. The result of these noble reform efforts, gushed the International Affairs experts from both the liberal Brookings Institute and the ostensibly conservative Heritage Foundation, would be more "transparency and accountability" at the UN.

In touting the UN reform process, however, these experts took time to lament the American public's unhealthy tendency to lapse into "nativism and isolationism," negative attitudes that were described as being counterproductive to the common good. The core issue for the United States, they insisted, was the conflict between "bad" unilateralism and "good" multilateralism.[9]

But is this proposed UN reform law really a good thing, and will it accomplish the positive goals that so many hope for? According to Rep. Ron Paul of Texas, the answer is a resounding *no*, on both counts. This independent-minded Republican voted against the UN reform bill in the House last summer because the measure will ultimately, in his own words, "expand the power of the United Nations beyond the dreams of even the most ardent left-wing, one-world globalists."[10]

Paul contends that the bill, which threatens to drastically cut US funding to the UN unless certain mandatory reforms are accomplished, will actually strengthen the international organization and expand the scope of its activities far beyond their original boundaries. "But this time the UN power grabbers aren't European liberals," Paul observes. "They are American neoconservatives, who plan to use the UN to implement their own brand of world government."[11]

Paul is especially critical of the redefinition of terrorism that makes any resistance to an incumbent government a crime against the international community, and thus provides an excuse for the UN's uninvited intervention into the internal affairs of sovereign nations.

He also sees the establishment of the UN's planned Peacebuilding Commission as the first step in an expansion of the UN into a full-fledged new world order. Paul finds it logically inconsistent for American patriots and defenders of the Constitution to support such pro-UN legislation.

Conservatives who have been critical of the UN in the past have enthusiastically embraced this bill and the concept of UN reform. But what is the desired end of "UN reform"? The UN is an organization that was designed to undermine sovereignty and representative government. It is unelected and unaccountable to citizens by its very design. Do honest UN critics really want an expanded UN that functions more "efficiently"?

The real question is whether we should redouble our efforts to save a failed system, or admit its failures—as this legislation does— and recognize that the only reasonable option is to cease participation without further costs to the United States in blood, money, and sovereignty. Do not be fooled: it is impossible to be against the United Nations and to support "reform" of the United Nations. The only true reform of the United Nations is for the US to withdraw immediately.[12]

Representative Paul practices what he preaches. Every year he reintroduces a new and improved version of his American Sovereignty Restoration Act, which calls for repeal of the six-decades-old United

Nations Participation Act of 1945. Passage of Paul's bill would effectively remove the United States from the UN.

Organizations like the pro-Constitution, anti-Communist John Birch Society (JBS) agree with Paul's assessment of UN reform and support his legislation to withdraw our nation from the world body. For more than forty years the JBS has been demanding that America's elected leaders take decisive action to "Get the US Out of the UN and the UN Out of the US."[13]

So far that has not happened, of course. But there is some strong evidence that the pendulum of public opinion in America is finally starting to swing away from the globalist institution. According to a recent public poll, "Fully 42 percent of Americans say that the United States should 'mind its own business internationally and let other countries get along the best they can on their own.'"[14]

This finding is made even more remarkable by the fact that the poll was sponsored, not by some radical, right-wing, anti-UN group, but by the ardently internationalist Council on Foreign Relations (CFR) working in conjunction with the Pew Research Center for the People and the Press. "Public views of the United Nations have become much more negative over the past four years," the Pew poll report declared. "Only about half of Americans (48 percent) now express a positive opinion of the UN, down from 77 percent four years ago."[15]

"Don't Mend It, End It" is the current slogan of the JBS campaign to save American sovereignty by means of US withdrawal from the UN. According to William F. Jasper, a senior editor of the *New American* magazine, "Public revulsion for the UN is beginning to crystallize into genuine opposition" that has UN supporters worried.

"The current reform drive is being fueled by a series of UN scandals that have been keeping the UN's professional spinmeisters and their allies in Congress operating in the nonstop damage control mode," Jasper explained in a recent article.[16]

John Birch Society president John McManus has compared the UN to a deadly cancer attacking a vital organ, and he insists that halfway measures won't work: the only solution is to cut it out in order to save the patient's life. "Like a cancerous tumor, the United Nations is a malignant growth that cannot be reformed," McManus wrote. "The only solution is the total withdrawal of the United States from the UN."[17]

Can that really be accomplished? Is US withdrawal from the UN really a viable option in today's interdependent society? I asked McManus those questions personally, and he readily conceded that, up until this point in time, there has not been the political will to take such a drastic step. But that could change, he suggested.

"At the very least, we need a set of minimum guarantees from the United Nations, very much like the ones Senator Helms outlined to the Security Council a few years back, guaranteeing our continued national sovereignty and independence," McManus said. "But I seriously doubt that we will be able to get such a guarantee," he added. "And if we don't, we will have no choice other than to withdraw. Anything less will constitute a national suicide."[18]

It's High Time to Bring Back Bricker

I believe that we can learn some valuable lessons from history, so I want to share a true story that most people today probably do not know about.

Very few people now living will remember John Bricker, but he was an American patriot half a century ago. His most memorable claim to fame was the highly controversial Bricker Amendment of 1953, a revised version of which narrowly failed in the Senate in 1954. Had it passed, our nation would be a much safer place to live today.

John Bricker was born in Ohio in 1893 and admitted to the bar in 1917. After serving as an Army officer in World War I, Bricker entered Ohio politics as a conservative. He was elected governor in 1938 and reelected twice more. In 1944, Governor Bricker was drafted to be

Thomas Dewey's vice-presidential running mate in the GOP's unsuccessful bid to unseat FDR and Harry Truman.[19]

In 1946, Bricker was elected to the US Senate, where he served alongside another staunch Ohio conservative, Sen. Robert Taft, the son of former President William Howard Taft. Widely known as "Mr. Republican," Taft unsuccessfully sought the Republican nomination for President in both 1948 and 1952.

In July 1952, Taft entered the Republican Convention in Chicago as the clear front-runner, with almost enough delegates already pledged to secure the nomination. But the "Draft Eisenhower" forces successfully challenged the credentials of Taft's southern delegation, and so engineered his bitter last-minute defeat. According to the *Encyclopedia Britannica*, Taft's convention loss to Eisenhower "was indicative of the defeat of isolationism by the internationalist wing of the party." (While I might dispute some parts of that interpretation, the encyclopedia's identification of Eisenhower as an internationalist is dead on target.)[20]

Anti-Communist sentiment was running high in America in 1952. That's why Ike had chosen Congressman Richard Nixon, who had strong anti-Communist credentials, as his running mate. The official Republican platform blasted President Truman for his "appeasement of Communism at home and abroad." It also criticized Truman for keeping the "hordes of loafers" and "incompetents" at the State Department, which was perceived as being an agency infiltrated by Communists and catering to their insatiable demands in the United Nations.[21]

This perception was entirely understandable. In April 1952, John Foster Dulles—an "unreconstructed Wilsonian" international lawyer who had previously had a hand in the 1919 Paris Peace Conference and also in crafting the United Nations back in 1945—had stirred up considerable controversy when he addressed the American Bar Association (ABA) in Louisville, Kentucky, on the topic of international treaties.

Dulles, the son of a Presbyterian minister, had spoken on behalf of the Federal Council of Churches during World War II to generate support for the proposed UN. He was a Republican who had nevertheless worked with the Truman administration in 1945 to draft the preamble to the United Nations charter. He was appointed by Truman to serve as a US delegate to the UN General Assembly from 1945 through 1949. In 1951 Dulles had served as Truman's special ambassador at large to negotiate the postwar peace treaty with Japan.[22]

In his highly inflammatory 1952 speech to the ABA, Dulles had declared:

> The treaty-making power is an extraordinary power, liable to abuse. Treaties make international law and they also make domestic law. Under our Constitution, *treaties become the supreme law of the land.* They are indeed more supreme than ordinary laws, for Congressional laws are invalid if they do not conform to the Constitution, whereas *treaty laws can override the Constitution.* Treaties, for example, can take powers away from the Congress and give them to the president. They can take powers from the states and give them to the federal government or to some international body and *they can cut across the rights given to the people by their Constitutional Bill of Rights.*[23]

The assembled attorneys, a much more conservative bunch than is today's ABA crowd, were aghast. Dulles was speaking New Deal heresy, and they would have none of it. The ABA called loudly and long for a Constitutional amendment limiting the power of the executive branch to conclude treaties and requiring that their provisions conform to the Constitution, else they would be deemed null and void.

The specific sovereignty-preserving language demanded by the ABA read as follows: "A provision of a treaty which conflicts with any provision of this Constitution shall not be of any force and effect. A treaty shall become effective as internal law of the United States only through legislation in Congress which it could enact under its delegated powers in the absence of such a treaty."[24]

Senator John Bricker was the selfless US patriot who obliged. On 7 January 1953, he introduced the Bricker Amendment.[25] The Bricker Amendment became the focus of a political fight to the death between Eisenhower and Senator Taft, who had become Majority Leader. Like the ABA, Bricker and Taft saw the amendment—rightly, in my view— as a necessary roadblock to the subversive internationalist influences that threatened to undermine the Constitution, diminish American sovereignty, and subvert US national security.

Dulles, who was now serving as newly inaugurated President Eisenhower's Secretary of State, came to testify before the Senate Judiciary Committee on 6 April 1953, arguing that passage of the Bricker Amendment would both embarrass the president and hinder his ability to conduct foreign policy. Here is part of what Dulles argued to the senators:

> Section 1 of S.J. Res. 1 provides that no treaty shall abridge any right in the Constitution. The Constitution specifies the power of Congress to declare war. Does Section 1 of the proposed Constitutional amendment mean that the United States will never make a treaty which would outlaw war? Can we never agree, with other nations, to abridge the present unqualified right of Congress in relation to war? Surely this is no time for the United States to make itself unable to enter into treaties which would effectively ban the terrible specter of war.[26]

Dulles played the fear card and used the potential horror of nuclear war to undermine the Constitution. Eisenhower threw all the weight of the presidency and all the force of his war-hero personality into opposing Taft and Bricker. One senator said that in twenty years of public service, he had "never seen as urgent, unreasonable, and unceasing pressure exerted on the members of either body of Congress by any president for any purpose, as Eisenhower put on him and the other senators to defeat the original Bricker Amendment."[27]

The Bricker Amendment temporarily stalled in committee without coming before the Senate for a vote, and Senator Taft died that summer in New York City. In 1954, a revised version of the amendment (now called the George Amendment) failed by just one vote to get the two-thirds majority it needed for passage. If the Bricker Amendment had passed, the tangled web of international treaties—which now bind America down like the Lilliputians bound Gulliver with threads—would not exist.

The "progressive" internationalist arguments advanced by John Foster Dulles—in support of the idealistic notion of securing world peace through treaty law—and the countervailing "traditionalist" arguments of Senators Taft and Bricker—in support of the Constitution, the Bill of Rights, and American sovereignty—are not trivial or irrelevant questions. They are the very same bedrock issues still being debated today.

John Bricker should be remembered, by all who cherish our tradition of liberty and sovereignty, as the Jesse Helms of a half-century ago. It's high time we find another unapologetic American patriot made in that heroic mold today, and encourage him or her to reintroduce a modern version of the Bricker Amendment for the twenty-first century.

The US Constitution Still Rules

For all the pious talk floating around about rule of international law, the truth of the matter is, the US Constitution is still the supreme law of the land. While judicial activists don't always interpret and apply this document appropriately, their erroneous decisions are still subject to being overturned later.

Whether we pass a Constitutional amendment along the lines of the one proposed by John Bricker more than five decades ago—and I for one am all in favor of that option—or whether we simply apply the Constitution correctly and use its authority to get rid of the activist judges who would refuse to do so . . . either way, the Constitution remains our last bulwark of defense against the threat of rampant internationalism and emerging world government.

Sadly, many if not most Americans have been miseducated in the name of progress and modernism. They have not been taught the principles of moral self-government that are necessary to preserve the liberty and freedom that we have inherited from our more knowledgeable forbears. Neither the average citizen nor the average elected official in America really understands the constitutional principles of limited government and personal responsibility that are the bedrock of our republic.

Our nation needs leaders at every level who realize that government is not an end in and of itself—whether at the local, state, federal, or international level. Rather, government is a mechanism whereby free men order the affairs of their society to provide the maximum degree of liberty and opportunity for all the inhabitants of the land. The government exists to serve the needs of the people; the people do not exist to serve the needs of the state.

We need a new generation of leaders with an awareness of our unique American heritage of freedom and with a burning commitment to preserve our precious liberty from those who would steal it in the name of so-called social justice and international law. At every level, our nation's leaders should be promoting America's best interests first and foremost, above all else.

They should be protecting the people of America—from threats to our lives, yes, whether from domestic terrorists or from foreign enemies. They should be defending our nation's autonomy and sovereignty from all who would challenge, usurp, or erode it.

Instead, in far too many cases, we find our leaders driven by self-interest and personal ambition, all too willing to cop out, knuckle under, and cave in to the pressures and promises of the powerful elitists who want to move us into their socialistic system of global control.

The challenge is now and the time is short. Who will be our next Jesse Helms? Who will be this generation's John Bricker?

It is my firm belief that conservatives and Christians in America must band together and act quickly if we hope to stop the transfer of American sovereignty to a bumbling bureaucracy of avowed socialists and internationalists who hate everything decent about America.

The United Nations has declared its desire to become a true world government with sweeping global authority, replacing the God-given rights that Americans have long enjoyed under our Declaration of Independence and the Bill of Rights with the arbitrary state-conferred benefits of the UN's Universal Declaration of Human Rights.

We will either stop this transfer of sovereignty now, or later we will have to explain to our children and our grandchildren exactly why we squandered their precious birthright of liberty and allowed them to be sold into slavery.

SELECTED BIBLIOGRAPHY

Acheson, Dean, *Present at The Creation: My Years in the State Department*, Norton & Company, 1969.

Babbin, Jed, *Inside the Asylum: Why the United Nations and Old Europe Are Worse Than You Think*, Regnery, 2004.

Bom, Philip C., *The Coming Century of Commonism: The Beauty and the Beast of Global Governance*, Policy Books, 1992.

Bonta, Steve, *Inside the United Nations: A Critical Look at the U.N.*, John Birch Society, 2003.

Cain, Kenneth, Heidi Postlewait, and Andrew Thomson, *Emergency Sex and Other Desperate Measures: A True Story from Hell on Earth*, Hyperion, 1994.

Charter of the United Nations & Statute of the International Court of Justice (Signed at the United Nations Conference on International Organization in San Francisco, CA, on 26 June 1945), US State Department Publication 2353, US Government Printing Office, 1961.

Courtney, Kent and Phoebe, *Disarmament: A Blueprint for Surrender*, Conservative Society of America, 1963.

Cuddy, Dennis L., *The Globalists: The Power Elite Exposed*, Hearthstone, 2001.

———. *Secret Records Revealed: The Men, The Money & The Methods Behind the New World Order*, Hearthstone, 1994.

Encyclopedia Britannica, 15th edition, 1977.

Epperson, A. Ralph, *The Unseen Hand: An Introduction to the Conspiratorial View of History*, Publius Press, 1985.

Fasulo, Linda, *An Insider's Guide to the U.N.*, Yale University Press, 2004.

Gold, Dore, *Tower of Babble: How the United Nations Has Fueled Global Chaos*, Crown Forum, 2004.

Griffin, G. Edward, *The Fearful Master: A Second Look at the United Nations*, Western Islands, 1964.

Grigg, William Norman, *Freedom on the Altar: The UN's Crusade Against God and Family*, American Opinion Publishing, 1995.

Isaacson, Walter, and Evan Thomas, *The Wise Men: Six Friends and the World They Made*, Simon & Schuster, 1986.

Jasper, William F., *Global Tyranny . . . Step by Step: The United Nations and the Emerging New World Order*, Western Islands, 1992.

————. *The United Nations Exposed: The Internationalist Conspiracy to Rule the World*, John Birch Society, 2001.

Johnson, Paul, *Modern Times: The World from the Twenties to the Eighties*, Harper & Row, 1983.

Kah, Gary H., *En Route to Global Occupation: A High Ranking Government Liaison Exposes the Secret Agenda for World Unification*, Huntington House, 1992.

————. *The Demonic Roots of Globalism*, Huntington House, 1995.

Kincaid, Cliff, *Global Bondage: The U.N. Plan to Rule the World*, Huntington House, 1995.

————. *Global Taxes for World Government*, Huntington House, 1997.

Land, Richard D., and Louis A. Moore, eds., *The Earth Is the Lord's: Christians and the Environment*, Broadman Press, 1992.

Leo, Robert W., *The United Nations Conspiracy*, Western Islands, 1981.

McManus, John F., *Changing Commands: The Betrayal of America's Military*, John Birch Society, 1995.

Monteith, Stanley K., *Sustainable Development: An Exposé of the Origins and Goals of Modern Day Environmentalism*, Radio Liberty, 1999.

Perloff, James, *The Shadow of Power: The Council on Foreign Relations and the American Decline*, Western Islands, 1988.

Still, William T., *New World Order: The Ancient Plan of Secret Societies*, Huntington House, 1990.

Veon, Joan, *The United Nations' Global Straightjacket*, Hearthstone, 1999.

NOTES

Introduction: The Globe Is the Goal

1. Joseph Loconte, "Exploitation, Abuse, and Other Humanitarian Efforts," *Weekly Standard*, 3 January 2005.
2. "U.N. Troops Buy Sex from Teen Refugees," WorldNetDaily.com, 25 May 2004, http://www.worldnetdaily.com/news/article.asp?ARTICLE_ID=38649.
3. "U.N. Accused of Rape, Pedophilia, Prostitution: Civilians, Staff in Congo Under Internal Investigation," WorldNetDaily.com, 24 November 2004, http://www.world-netdaily.com/news/article.asp?ARTICLE_ID=41627.
4. Michelle Malkin, "The U.N.'s Rape of the Innocents," WorldNetDaily.com, 16 February 2005, http://www.worldnetdaily.com/news/article.asp?ARTICLE_ID=42877.
5. "U.N. 'Peacekeepers' Rape Women, Children: Widespread Sex Scandal Threatens to Become 'United Nations' Abu Ghraib,'" WorldNetDaily.com, 24 December 2004, http://www.worldnetdaily.com/news/article.asp?ARTICLE_ID=42088.
6. Michelle Malkin, "Who Is Didier Bourguet?" MichelleMalkin.com, 12 February 2005, (cites Brian Ross, ABC's *20/20*, 11 February 2005, and *Los Angeles Times*, 12 February 2005). See also "U.N. 'Peacekeepers' Rape Women, Children."
7. Ibid.
8. Colum Lynch, "U.N. Official Quits in Harassment Case," *Washington Post*, 21 February 2005; See also Cliff Kincaid, "Kofi Annan and the U.N. Sex Scandals," *Media Monitor*, 7 April 2005.
9. Malkin, "The U.N.'s Rape of the Innocents."
10. Loconte, "Exploitation, Abuse, and Other Humanitarian Efforts."
11. Michelle Malkin, "More U.N. Rape Allegations," MichelleMalkin.com, 23 February 2005. See also "Rape Allegations Renew Call to Evict U.N.: American Activist Group Wants World Body 'Out of the U.S.,'" WorldNetDaily.com, 24 February 2005, http://www.worldnetdaily.com/news/article.asp?ARTICLE_ID=43020.
12. Joseph Farah, "Those U.N. Peacekeeping Atrocities," WorldNetDaily.com, 25 June 1997, http://www.worldnetdaily.com/news/article.asp?ARTICLE_ID=14271.
13. Stewart Payne, "Teenagers 'Used for Sex by U.N. in Bosnia,'" *News-Telegraph* (London), 13 August 2003.
14. "U.N. Sex Abuse Scandal Gathers Momentum," *Scotsman*, 24 November 2004.
15. Kenneth Cain, Heidi Postlewaite, and Andrew Thomson, *Emergency Sex and Other Desperate Measures: A True Story from Hell on Earth* (Miramax Books/Hyperion, 1994), 252.
16. Kenneth Cain, "Death and Chaos Hold Sway Under Annan's U.N. Tenure," *Observer* (London), 11 April 2005. See also Peter Dennis, "The U.N., Preying on the Weak," *Washington Post*, 12 April 2005.

17. Cain, "Death and Chaos."

18. "U.N. 'Peacekeepers' Rape Women, Children."

19. Mary Jo Anderson, "Leaders Lean Toward Consensus on U.N.: Limited Sovereignty for Nations, Larger Power Base for Global Body" (Special Report from the State of the World Forum), WorldNetDaily.com, 8 September 2000, http://www.worldnetdaily.com/news/article.asp?ARTICLE_ID=14271.

20. Ibid.

21. Mary Jo Anderson, "Globocops Out of Africa," WorldNetDaily.com, 10 May 2001, http://www.worldnetdaily.com/news/article.asp?ARTICLE_ID=22774.

22. Dore Gold, *Tower of Babble: How the United Nations Has Fueled Global Chaos* (Crown Forum, 2004).

23. Jed Babbin, *Inside the Asylum: Why the United Nations and Old Europe Are Worse Than You Think* (Regnery, 2004).

24. Linda Fasulo, *An Insider's Guide to the U.N.* (Yale University Press, 2004).

Chapter One: Global Education Agenda

1. *Towards World Understanding, Vol. V: In the Classroom with Children Under Thirteen Years of Age,* UNESCO pamphlet (Paris, France: 1949), 54–55. Cited in William N. Grigg, *Freedom on the Altar: The U.N.'s Crusade Against God and Family* (American Opinion Publishing, 1995), 43.

2. Paul Harvey radio commentary cited in "The United Nations Wants Control of Your Child," http://www.getusout.org/artman/publish/cat_index_24.shtml.

3. Basic background information on the UN's general organizational structure comes from the *Encyclopedia Britannica,* 1977 ed., sv "United Nations," 18:894–905. See also the United Nations website, www.un.org. See also *Columbia Electronic Encyclopedia,* 6th ed., 2005, Columbia University Press, http://www.infoplease.com/ce6/history/A0850066.html.

4. *Charter of the United Nations, together with the Statute of the International Court of Justice,* signed at the United Nations Conference on International Organizations (San Francisco, California, 26 June 1945), Chapter IX, Article 55. Published as US State Department Publication 2353 (US Government Printing Office).

5. *The Millennium Development Goals Report 2005* (United Nations, 2005), http://www.unfpa.org/icpd/docs/mdgrept2005.pdf.

6. *UNESCO Constitution,* http://www.icomos.org/unesco/unesco_constitution.html.

7. *Encyclopedia Britannica,* sv "International Educational Relations," 9:740.

8. Philip C. Bom, *The Coming Age of Commonism: The Beauty and the Beast of Global Governance* (Policy Books, 1992), 45–46. Bom cites Hans Morgenthau, *Politics Among Nations: The Struggle for Power and Peace* (Alfred A. Knopf, 1973), 501.

9. "UNESCO: What It Is and What It Does," http://unesdoc.unesco.org/images/0013/001315/131585e.pdf.

10. William F. Jasper, "UNESCO's Rotten Track Record," *New American,* 19 May 2003, http://www.getusout.com/artman/publish/printer_60.shtml.

11. Sir Julian Huxley, *UNESCO: Its Purpose and Philosophy* (Public Affairs Press, 1948), 32. Cited in Grigg, *Freedom on the Altar,* 38–46.

12. Ibid., 18.

13. Ibid., 46. (Emphasis added.)

14. Ibid., 36.
15. Grigg, *Freedom on the Altar,* 37.
16. Ibid.
17. Quoted in Samuel L. Blumenfield, *NEA: Trojan Horse in American Education* (The Paradigm Company, 1984), 194. Cited in Grigg, *Freedom on the Altar,* 40–41.
18. UNESCO pamphlet, *Towards World Understanding, Vol. I: Some Suggestions on Teaching about the United Nations and its Specialized Agencies* (France: 1948), 18. Cited in Grigg, *Freedom on the Altar,* 42. (Emphasis added.)
19. *Towards World Understanding, Vol. V,* 7–9, 54–58. Cited in Grigg, *Freedom on the Altar,* 42–43.
20. "The Climate of Freedom," *Saturday Review,* 19 July 1952. Cited in Grigg, *Freedom on the Altar,* 36.
21. "Legion—Truman—UNESCO," *Washington News,* 14 October 1955. Cited in G. Edward Griffin, *The Fearful Master: A Second Look at the United Nations* (Western Islands, 1964), 140.
22. Rep. Lawrence H. Smith, "Speech to Congress," *Congressional Record* (Washington DC, 18 April 1955). Cited in Griffin, *The Fearful Master,* 139. See also William F. Jasper, "UNESCO's Rotten Track Record," *New American,* 19 May 2003.
23. Senate Internal Security Subcommittee, *Annual Report* (Washington DC, 1956). Cited in Griffin, *The Fearful Master,* 141–142.
24. Joseph Z. Kornfeder, "The Communist Pattern in the U.N.," speech to the Congress of Freedom, Veterans War Memorial Auditorium, San Francisco, April 1955. Cited in Griffin, *The Fearful Master,* 141.
25. President George W. Bush, "Address to United Nations General Assembly," 12 September 2002. Cited in William F. Jasper, "The Global School Board," *New American,* 19 May 2003.
26. Jasper, "The Global School Board."
27. William F. Jasper, *The United Nations Exposed: The International Conspiracy to Rule the World* (John Birch Society, 2001), 275. Jasper includes the following reference footnote: six goal areas arrived at in Jomtien, Thailand, reported in "Learning for All: Bridging Domestic and International Education," Conference Report, 30–31 October, 1 November 1991, Alexandria, Virginia (United States Coalition for Education for All), 1. Compare to Bush program in: Carol Innerst, "By Any Other Name: America 2000 Isn't Dead Yet," *Washington Times,* 8 February 1993.
28. Jasper, *The United Nations Exposed,* 276. Also reported in William F. Jasper, "Outcome-Based Education: Skinnerian Conditioning in the Classroom," *New American,* 23 August 1993.
29. Charlotte T. Iserbyt, "Outcome-Based Education: Conditioning for Control," *New American,* 21 July 1997.
30. Jasper, "The Global School Board."

Chapter Two: Global Land Use Regulation and Sustainable Development

1. UNESCO World Heritage Centre, "World Heritage List," http://whc.unesco.org/en/list/.
2. UNESCO World Heritage Centre, "Frequently Asked Questions," http://whc.unesco.org/en/faq/.
3. UNESCO World Heritage Centre, "World Heritage," http://whc.unesco.org/en/about/. (Emphasis added.)

4. UNESCO, "People, Biodiversity, and Ecology," http://www.unesco.org/mab.
5. Roger E. Soles, "Dear Concerned Citizen (revised 2/27/98)," US Man and Biosphere Program, http://www.mabnet.org/sovereignty.html.
6. Henry Lamb, "The Rule of International Law," WorldNetDaily.com, 19 April 2003.
7. UNESCO, "Convention Concerning the Protection of the World Cultural and Natural Heritage," Bureau of the World Heritage Committee, Nineteenth Session, 3–8 July 1995, http://whc.unesco.org/archive/repcom95.htm#yellowstone. Cited in Amy Ridenour, "Keep the Statue of Liberty Free: An Argument for Congressional Oversight of U.N. Land Designations in the U.S.," National Policy Analysis #419, July 2002, National Center for Public Policy Research.
8. Ridenour, "Keep the Statue of Liberty Free."
9. Helen Chenoweth-Hage, "The United Nation's Big Green Machine," *New American*, 3 July 2000.
10. *Report of Habitat: United Nations Conference on Human Settlements*, Vancouver, 31 May–11 June 1976 (A/Conf.70/15). Cited in Henry Lamb, "The U.N. and Property Rights," *Eco-Logic Powerhouse*, August 2005.
11. Letter from Jeane Kirkpatrick to Bruce F. Vento, 5 May 1999, downloaded from http://resourcescommittee.house.gov/archives/106cong/fullcomm/99mar18/kirkpatrick.htm, on 16 June 2002, cited in Ridenour, "Keep the Statue of Liberty Free."
12. Chenoweth-Hage, "Big Green Machine." See also Wildlands Project, "Summary of the Wildlands Project," http://wildlandsprojectrevealed.org/htm/summary.htm.
13. The Wildlands Project, "Room to Roam," http://www.twp.org.
14. Ibid.
15. Tom McDonnell, "Technical Review of the Wildlands Project and How It Is Affecting the Management of State, Federal, and Private Lands within the United States," April 2002, http://www.citizenreviewonline.org/april_2002/wildlands_project_history.htm.
16. Sen. Kay Bailey Hutchison, "Opposing Consideration of the Convention on Biodiversity," 30 September 1994, *Congressional Record S13790*. Posted online at http://www.sovereignty.net/p/land/crhutchison.htm.
17. Ricardo Bayon, "Early History of IUCN," IUCN-US Office, Washington DC, 17 December 1997.
18. IUCN chronology is from Henry Lamb, "U.N. Biosphere Reserves: Why the Government is Grabbing Our Land," *Eco-Logic Online*, 2 March 2002.
19. General information on the World Wildlife Fund is from the organization's official website, http://www.panda.org. The overall chronology of significant environmental events is from the website of Sovereignty International at http://www.sovereignty.net/timeline.html.
20. Ibid.
21. Lamb, "U.N. Biosphere Reserves."
22. World Commission on Environment and Development, *Our Common Future* (Oxford University Press, 1987).
23. Henry Lamb, "Sustainable Development: Transforming America," *Eco-Logic Powerhouse*, December 2005.

Chapter Three: Global Warming and Global Environmental Control

1. "Clinton: Climate Change World's Biggest Concern," Associated Press, 28 January 2006.
2. Charles J. Hanley, "Clinton Says Bush Is 'Flat Wrong' on Kyoto," Associated Press, 9 December 2005.
3. Ibid.
4. Marc Morano, "U.S. Called 'Only Real Problem' at U.N. Climate Conference," CNSNews, 5 December 2005.
5. Ibid.
6. Fraser Nelson, "Blair: U.S. Set for New Climate Change Treaty," *Scotsman*, 9 June 2005.
7. Henry Lamb, "Tony Blair Backs Away from Kyoto," WorldNetDaily.com, 24 September 2005.
8. Bill McKibben, "Too Hot to Handle," *Boston Globe*, 5 February 2006.
9. Ibid.
10. Wikipedia, sv "Intergovernmental Panel on Climate Change," http://en.wikipedia.org/wiki/Intergovernmental_Panel_on_Climate_Change. For official IPCC history see http://www.ipcc.ch/about/anniversarybrochure.pdf.
11. Ibid. (Emphasis added.)
12. Wikipedia, sv "United Nations Framework on Climate Change," http://en.wikipedia.org/wiki/United_Nations_Framework_on_Climate_Change. See also official UNFCCC site, http://unfccc.int/.
13. Wikipedia, sv "Intergovernmental Panel on Climate Change," http://en.wikipedia.org/wiki/Intergovernmental_Panel_on_Climate_Change.
14. Ibid. For the full text of Pachauri's remarks, see http://www.ipcc.ch/press/sp-09112004.htm.
15. Ibid.
16. Ibid.
17. Ibid.
18. Dr. Mae-Wan Ho, "Global Warming and Then the Big Freeze," Institute of Science in Society, http://www.i-sis.org.uk/LOG3.php.
19. Ian Sample, "Alarm Over Dramatic Weakening of Gulf Stream," *Guardian*, 1 December 2005.
20. McKibben, "Too Hot to Handle."
21. Andrew C. Revkin, "Climate Expert Says NASA Tried to Silence Him," *New York Times*, 29 January 2006.
22. Hansen's NASA bio is available at http://www/gsfc.nasa.gov/bios/Hansen.html. See also http://www.giss.nasa.gov/staff/jhansen.html and http://www.columbia.edu/~jeh1/.
23. Patrick Michaels (of the Cato Institute), "NASA Extinguishes Global-Warming Fire," Rense.com, 9 February 2002. See also "James Hansen Increasingly Insensitive," *World Climate Report*, 28 April 2005.
24. Sterling Burnett, "The Collapsing Scientific Cornerstones of Global Warming Theory," Brief Analysis 299, 30 June 1999, National Center for Policy Analysis, http://www.ncpa.org/ba/ba299.html.
25. Patrick J. Michaels, "Hansen's Hot Hype," *American Spectator*, 21 February 2006, http://www.spectator.org/dsp_article.asp?art_id=9433. (Emphasis added.)

26. Revkin, "Climate Expert." See also "James Hansen Acceptance Speech," The Heinz Awards, 5 March 2001, http://www.heinzawards.net/speechDetail.asp?speechID=6.
27. Wikipedia, sv "Global Warming," http://en.wikipedia.org/wiki/Global_warming. (Emphasis added.)
28. Andrew C. Revkin, "Panelist Who Dissents on Climate Change Quits," *New York Times*, 23 August 2005.
29. Ibid.
30. Robert F. Kennedy Jr., "They That Sow the Wind Shall Reap the Whirlwind," writing on the *Huffington Post*, 29 August 2005. Cited in James K. Glassman, "Hurricane Katrina and Global Warming," *Capitalism Magazine*, 3 September 2005.
31. Dan Roberts, "Buffett Links Hurricane Insurance to Climate," *Financial Times*, 6 March 2006.
32. "Poll: 70% of Evangelicals See Global Warming Threat," WorldNetDaily.com, 16 February 2006.
33. Laurie Goodstein, "Evangelical Leaders Join Global Warming Initiative," *New York Times*, 8 February 2006.
34. Ibid.
35. Michael J. McManus, "Evangelical Call to Action on Climate Change," 22 February 2006, http://www.ethicsandreligion.com/redesignedcolumns/C1278.htm.
36. Jerry Falwell, "Climate Initiative Is a Bad Idea," *Falwell Confidential Newsletter*, 10 February 2006.
37. Ibid.
38. Ibid.
39. Brannon Howse, "Evangelical Leaders Form Unholy Alliance with Pro-Gay, Pro-Abortion Globalists to Fight Global Warming?" Christian Worldview Network, 13 February 2006, http//www.ChristianWorldviewNetwork.com.
40. Goodstein, "Evangelical Leaders."
41. "Poll," WorldNetDaily.com, 16 February 2006.
42. *Report from Iron Mountain on the Possibility and Desirability of Peace*, with "Introduction" by Leonard C. Lewin (Dial Press, 1967), 66–67. (Emphasis added.)

Chapter Four: Global Population Control

1. Bahgat Elnadi and Adel Rifaat, "Interview with Jacques-Yves Cousteau," UNESCO *Courier*, November 1991. Cited in Dr. Stanley Monteith, *Radio Liberty Newsletter*, April 2003. (Emphasis added.)
2. Thomas Robert Malthus, "An Essay on the Principle of Population," printed in six editions, 1798–1826. Quoted in George Grant, *Killer Angel* (Reformer Press, 1995), 50–51. (Emphasis added.)
3. Elasha Drogin, *Margaret Sanger: Father of Modern Society* (CUL Publications, 1979), 22. Cited in Cliff Kincaid, *Global Bondage: The U.N. Plan to Rule the World* (Huntington House, 1995), 152–153.
4. For more on *The Population Bomb*, see http://www.pbs.org/population_bomb/.
5. Paul R. Ehrlich, *The Population Bomb* (Ballantine Books, 1971 ed.), xi. Cited in Brian Carnell's Blog, "Paul Ehrlich," Overpopulation.com, 1998–2001, http://www.overpopulation.com/faq/people/paul_ehrlich.html. (Emphasis added.)

6. Ibid.(Emphasis added.)

7. Ibid., 3. (Emphasis added.)

8. Ibid., xi–xii.

9. Ibid., 131-133.

10. Ibid., 146-148. (Emphasis added.)

11. Paul R. Ehrlich, "Eco-Catastrophe!" *Ramparts*, September 1969, 24–28. Cited in Wikipedia, http://en.wikipedia.org/wiki/Paul_R._Erlich.

12. Michael Fumento, "Doomsayer Paul Ehrlich Strikes Out Again," *Investor's Business Daily*, 16 December 1997, http://www.junkscience.com/news/fumento.htm. (Emphasis added.)

13. National Security Council, "Implications of Worldwide Population Growth for U.S. Security and Overseas Interests," National Security Study Memo 200 (NSSM200), 10 December 1974. Cited in Dennis L. Cuddy, *The Globalists: The Power Elite Exposed* (Hearthstone, 2001), 139–140.

14. Dr. Stanley Monteith, *Radio Liberty Newsletter*, May 2003 and July/August 2003. Also repeatedly referenced in Dr. Leonard Horowitz, *Emerging Viruses: AIDS and Ebola— Nature, Accident, or Intentional?* (Tetrahedron, 1996), 228, 238, 249, 422. (Emphasis added.)

15. "Dialogue with Archbishop Peter Proeku Dery," *National Catholic Register*, 14 December 1980. Cited in Dennis L. Cuddy, *The Globalists: The Power Elite Exposed* (Hearthstone, 2001), 152.

16. Joan Veon, *The United Nations' Global Straightjacket* (Hearthstone, 1999, 2000), 394.

17. Frederick S. Jaffe, "Activities Relevant to the Study of Population Policy for the U.S.," memo to Bernard Berelson, 11 March 1969. Cited in Cuddy, *The Globalists*, 125.

18. "Congress to Restore Funding of 'Gendercide'?" WorldNetDaily.com, 15 June 2005, http://www.worldnetdaily.com/news/article.asp?ARTICLE_ID=44774.

19. Ibid.

20. Steve Mosher, "China's One-Child Policy," Population Resource Institute, http://www.pop.org/main.cfm?EID=699.

21. American Life League, "13 Lessons in Global Population Facts," 14 March 2003, http://www.chp.ca/commentaries/LessonsInGlobalPopulation_ALL.htm.

22. "Expert Would Deny Right to Reproduce," *Los Angeles Times*, 4 September 1969. Cited in Cuddy, *The Globalists*, 125.

23. Donella Meadows, et al, *Limits to Growth* (New American Library, 1972).

24. Wikipedia, sv "Club of Rome," http://en.wikipedia.org/wiki/Club_of_Rome.

25. Wikipedia, sv "Limits to Growth," http://en.wikipedia.org/wiki/Limits_to_Growth.

26. Veon, *The United Nations Global Straightjacket*, 167.

27. Alexander King and Bertrand Schneider, *The First Global Revolution: Club of Rome* (Pantheon Books, 1991), 115. (Emphasis added.)

28. Global Environmental Facility, *Global Biodiversity Assessment: Summary for Policy-Makers*, 1992, Phase One Draft, Section 9, Rio de Janeiro, 108. Cited in Dr. Stanley Monteith, "The Population Control Agenda," *Sustainable Development: An Expose of the Origins and Goals of Modern-Day Environmentalism* (Radio Liberty, 1999), 5.

29. Laurie Goodstein, "Nations Conspire 'Against Life,' Pope Says," *Washington Post*, 31 March 1995. Cited in Cliff Kincaid, *Global Bondage: The U.N. Plan to Rule the World*

(Huntington House, 1995), 145.

30. Grant, *Grand Illusions*, 28–30, 136–137.

31. Wikipedia, sv "Mexico City Policy," http://en.wikipedia.org/wiki/Mexico_City_Policy. For detailed chronology, including reinstatement by President George W. Bush on 22 January 2001, see http://www.whitehouse.gov/news/releases/20010123-5.html.

32. Joyce Price, "Focus on Foster Endangers Planned Parenthood Funds, *Washington Times*, 6 March 1995. Cited in Kincaid, *Global Bondage*, 156.

33. Quoted in Kincaid, *Global Bondage*, 157.

34. J. Michael Waller, "What Really Happened in Cairo," *American Spectator*, 7. Cited in Kincaid, *Global Bondage*, 156–158.

35. Quoted by Alan Cowell, "Vatican Attacks Population Stand Supported by U.S.," *New York Times*, 9 August 1994. Cited in Kincaid, *Global Bondage*, 162.

36. Waller, "What Really Happened in Cairo," Quoted in Kincaid, *Global Bondage*, 157.

37. Christopher Smith, "U.N. Abortion Agenda Stopped," *Christian American*, October 1994. Cited in Kincaid, *Global Bondage*, 160–161.

38. "Man of the Year," *Time*, 26 December 1994–2 January 1995. Quoted in Kincaid, *Global Bondage*, 161.

39. To read the exact text of the final Cairo conference report, see http://www.iisd.ca/Cairo/program/p08009.html.

40. Edith Lederer, (Bloomsburg, PA) *Press Enterprise*, 1 July 1999. Quoted in Cuddy, *The Globalists*, 152.

41. "Ted Turner Names Tim Wirth to Oversee Gift in Support of U.N. Causes—Turner Takes Next Step in $1 Billion Pledge," United Nations Foundation Press Release, 19 November 1997, http://www.unfoundation.org/media_center/press/1997/11/19/pr_14007.asp.

Chapter Five: World Trade and Global Taxing Authority

1. Bob Dylan, "Jokerman," *Infidels* (Special Rider Music, 1983). Lyrics posted online at http://www.bobdylan.com/songs/jokerman.html.

2. "Socialist Was Behind U.N. Sea Treaty," WorldNetDaily.com, 3 May 2005, http://www.worldnetdaily.com/news/article.asp?ARTICLE_ID=44085. To learn more about the U.N. and the origins of LOST, visit the America's Survival, Inc. website at http://www.usasurvival.org/ck42705.shtml.

3. Ibid.

4. Ibid.

5. Ibid.

6. "Secret Agenda: Law of the Sea Treaty Will Provide Key 'Elements' of World Government," America's Survival Inc., http://www.usasurvival.org/lost.shtml.

7. *Our Global Neighborhood*, Report of the Commission on Global Governance (Oxford University Press, 1995), 251–253. Cited in Henry Lamb, "The U.N. and Property Rights," *The Eco-Logic Powerhouse*, August 2005.

8. Pat Buchanan, "Should the U.N. be Lord of the Oceans?" WorldNetDaily.com, 28 February 2005.

9. Ibid.

10. William Norman Grigg, "Sink the Law of the Sea Treaty!" *New American*, 7 March 2005.

11. Sarah Foster, "Grass Roots Force Hearing on U.N. Treaty," WorldNetDaily.com, 23

March 2004.

12. Ibid.

13. Ibid.

14. Grigg, "Sink the Law of the Sea Treaty!"

15. Ibid.

16. Ibid.

17. Ibid.

18. Ibid. (Emphasis added.)

19. Ralph Z. Hallow, "Conservatives Denounce GOP Support of Treaty," *Washington Times*, 19 February 2005.

20. Ed Feulner, "Out to Sea," *Washington Times*, 8 March 2005.

21. Ibid.

22. Jesse Helms, "Address to the United Nations Security Council," 20 January 2000. The following quoted segments are taken from the transcript of this speech posted at NewsMax.com, http://www.newsmax.com/articles/?a=2000/1/28/211810. The *New York Times* version of the transcript is posted at the Global Policy Forum's website, http://www.globalpolicy.org/finance/docs/helms4.htm.

23. All quotations taken from e-mails between Law of the Sea Committee members are found online at "INTLAWOFSEA Archives—January 2000," http://mail.abanet.org/scripts/wa/exe?A1=ind0001&L=intlawofsea. (Accessed 4/10/06.)

24. Francis Anthony Boyle, *Defending Civil Resistance Under International Law* (Transnational Publishers, Inc., 1987).

25. Walter Cronkite, "The First Priority of Humankind," address to World Federalists Association, United Nations, New York, 19 October 1999, excerpts posted online at http://www/ikosmos.com/wisdomeditions/essays/mw/cronkite01.htm. Cited in Joseph Farah, "Walter Cronkite—World Federalist," WorldNetDaily.com, 30 November 1999.

26. Henry Lamb, "Global Taxation Moves Closer," American Policy Center, 13 March 2002, http://www.americanpolicy.org/un/globaltaxation.htm. See also http://www.getusout.org/taxation/index.htm.

27. Lamb, "Global Taxation."

28. John Birch Society, "The United Nations Wants to TAX You!" (pamphlet), http://www.getusout.org/taxation/index.htm.

29. Ibid.

30. United Nations Development Program, *Human Development Report*, 1999. Cited in Lamb, "Global Taxation."

31. Joan Veon, "Africa's Poverty Driving Global Taxation," WorldNetDaily.com, 12 July 2005, http://www.worldnetdaily.com/news/article.asp?ARTICLE_ID=45238.

32. Lamb, "Global Taxation."

33. Ron Paul, "U.N. Planting the Seeds for a Coming Global Tax," *Texas Straight Talk*, 25 March 2002, http://www.house.gov/paul/tst/tst2002/tst032502.htm.

34. Paul, "U.N. Planting the Seeds."

35. United Nations High Level Panel on Financing for Development, *Report of the International Conference on Financing and Development*, Monterrey, Mexico, 18–22 March 2002, A/CONF.198/11 (United Nations, 2002), http://daccessdds.un.org.doc/UNDOC/GEN/NO2/392/67/PDF/NO239267.pdf?OpenElement. (Emphasis added.)

36. Ibid., 43, 45, 68.
37. Lamb, "Global Taxation."
38. Steve Bonta, "March Madness in Monterrey," *New American*, 22 April 2002.
30. Lamb, "Global Taxation."
40. Associated Press, "House Narrowly Approves CAFTA," CNN.com, 28 July 2005, http://www.cnn.com/2005/POLITICS/o7/27/bush.cafta.ap. (Emphasis added.)
41. Patrick J. Buchanan, "The Night They Sold America," 19 November 1993.
42. Patrick J. Buchanan, "CAFTA: Ideology vs. National Interests," WorldNetDaily.com, 27 July 2005.
43. William Norman Grigg, "CAFTA: Exporting American Jobs and Industry," *New American*, 18 April 2005. See also the John Birch Society website, http://www.stopcafta.com.
44. Grigg, "CAFTA: Exporting American Jobs and Industry."
45. Henry Kissinger, *Los Angeles Times*, 18 July 1993. Cited in "The Inside Truth About the FTAA," *New American*, 7 February 2005.
46. "The Inside Truth." (Emphasis added.)
47. Robert Bartley, "Open NAFTA Borders? Why Not?" *Wall Street Journal*, 2 July 2001. Cited in "The Inside Truth."
48. Grigg, "CAFTA: Exporting Jobs."

Chapter Six: International Criminal Court

1. Hans-Peter Kaul, "Developments at the International Criminal Court: Construction Site for More Justice: The International Criminal Court After Two Years," *American Journal of International Law* 99 (April 2005), 370–371.
2. Ibid.
3. Ibid.
4. Roger S. Clark, "Steven Spielberg's Amistad and Other Things I Have Thought about in the Past Forty Years: International (Criminal) Law, Conflict of Laws, Insurance, and Slavery," *Rutgers Law Journal* 30 (Winter 1999), 417, note 140. Clark describes Jessup's decision to use the term.
5. The Modern History Project, sv "Jessup, Philip C.," http://www.modernhistoryproject.org/mhp/EntityDisplay.php?Entity=JessupPC.
6. Harold Hongju Koh, "Letter from Dean Koh," Yale Law School, http://www.law.yale.edu/outside/html/Admissions/admis-jdfromthedean.htm.
7. American Association of Law Schools, "American Association of Law Schools [2006] Annual Meeting," http://aals.org/am2006/program.html.
8. Ibid.
9. Ibid.
10. Harold Hongju Koh, "The 1994 Roscoe Pound Lecture: Transnational Legal Process," *Nebraska Law Review* 75 (1996), 183.
11. Ibid.
12. Harold Hongju Koh, "Bringing International Law Home," *Houston Law Review* 35 (Fall 1998), 676.
13. Ibid.
14. Ibid.
15. Ibid., 677.

16. Ibid.
17. Ibid., 678. (Emphasis added.)
18. Ibid., 679.
19. Gordon A. Christenson, "Federal Courts and World Civil Society," *Florida State University Journal of Transnational Law & Policy* 6 (Summer 1997), 515.
20. Ibid., 413.
21. *Lawrence v. Texas*, 539 *US* 558 (2003).
22. *Atkins v. Virginia*, 506 *US* 604 (2002).
23. Harold Hongju Koh, "Agora: The United States Constitution and International Law: International Law as Part of Our Law," *American Journal of International Law* 98 (January 2004), 56–57.
24. Jenny S. Martinez, "Towards an International Judicial System," *Stanford Law Review* 56 (November 2003), 430.
25. Ibid., 432.
26. Roger P. Alford, "The Proliferation of International Courts and Tribunals: International Adjudication in Ascendance," *American Society of International Law Proceedings* 94 (April 2000), 160.
27. Ibid.
28. The activities of the NGO Coalition for an International Criminal Court are more than adequately represnted on its website, www.iccnow.org.
29. *The International Criminal Court Monitor* 10 (November 1998), 2, http://www.iccnow.org/publications/monitor/10/monitor10.199811.pdf.
30. Gordon A. Christenson, "Federal Courts and World Civil Society," *Florida State University Journal of Transnational Law & Policy* 6 (Summer 1997), 407.
31. William J. Clinton, "Statement on the Rome Treaty on the International Criminal Court," *Weekly Compilation of Presidential Documents* 37 (31 December 2000), 4.
32. Ibid.
33. Ibid.
34. Jesse Helms, "Helms on Clinton Signature: This Decision Will Not Stand," *Congressional Press Releases* (31 December 2000).
35. John R. Bolton, letter to UN Secretary-General Kofi Annan. http://www.state.gov/r/pa/prs/ps/2002/9968.htm. (Accessed 5 February 2006.)
36. Diane Marie Amann and M.N.S. Sellers, "American Law in a Time of Global Interdependence: US National Reports to the XVIth International Congress of Comparative Law: Section IV. The United States of America and the International Criminal Court," *American Journal of Comparative Law* 50 (Fall 2002). While I will be adding my own thoughts and interspersing information from other sources, the basic information about the two categories and their various sub-categories closely follows this article, although I have sometimes combined or divided sub-categories. (Incidentally, this is my description of their organization, not theirs.)
37. Ibid., 386–387.
38. Kaul, "Developments at the International Criminal Court," 371.
39. Ibid., 372.
40. Ibid., 373.
41. Judge Kaul's assertions can easily be checked against the sources he cites, *i.e.*, Article 54

of the Rome Statute and Rule 176. See Rome Statute of the International Criminal Court, UN Doc. A/CONF.183/9, http://www.un.org/law/icc/statute/romefra.htm.

42. Luis Moreno-Ocampo, "Report of the Prosecutor of the ICC," Second Assembly of States Parties to the Rome Statute of the International Criminal Court, 8 September 2003, http://www.iccnow.org/documents/statements/others/LMOstatementASP8Sept03.pdf.

43. Coalition for an International Criminal Court, "We Won!" *International Criminal Court Monitor* 9 (August 1998), 2.

44. Kaul, "Developments at the International Criminal Court," 375.

45. The Rome Statute, Art. 38.

46. Ibid., 39–41.

47. Kaul, "Developments at the International Criminal Court," 370.

48. Ibid., 375–376.

49. Ibid., 376.

50. Ibid.

51. Ibid.

52. The Rome Statute, Art. 39.

53. Kaul, "Developments at the International Criminal Court," 382.

54. Ibid.

55. Ibid., 374.

56. Numerous documents created during this process are linked from the UN's "old" International Criminal Court website, http://www.un.org/law/icc/. (Accessed 5 February 2006.)

57. The Rome Statute, Art. 2.

58. This is stated on the old ICC site, http://www.un.org/law/icc/.

59. Amann and Sellers, "American Law," 388.

60. Ibid.

61. Ibid., 388.

62. Ibid., 388–389.

63. Coalition for an ICC, "We Won!"

64. Amann and Sellers, "American Law," 389.

65. Ibid., 390.

66. Ibid., 391–400.

67. Ibid., 392–393.

68. Ibid., 394–395.

69. Ibid., 395.

70. Ibid., 397–398.

71. Ibid., 398.

72. Ibid., 398–399.

73. Ibid.

74. Ibid., 399.

75. Ibid., 402.

76. Kaul, "Developments at the International Criminal Court," 383.

77. Ibid.

78. Ibid.

79. Ibid.

80. Ibid., 374.

81. American Service Members' Protection Act (2002), Title 22 *US Code* Sec. 7401 *et seq.*, http://www.state.gov/t/pm/rlt/othr/misc/23425.htm.

82. Ibid.

83. Diane F. Orentlicher, "Unilateral Multilateralism: United States Policy Towards the International Criminal Court," *Cornell International Law Journal* 36 (2004), 418–427.

84. Ademola Abass, "The Competence of the Security Council to Terminate the Jurisdiction of the International Criminal Court," *Texas International Law Journal* 40 (Winter 2005), 263–265.

85. Ibid.

86. Coalition for the International Criminal Court, "Status of U.S. Bilateral Immunity Agreements (BIAs)," http://www.iccnow.org/documents/USandICC/2006/CICCFS_BIAstatus_08Jan06.pdf.

87. American Service Members' Protection Act (2002), Sec. 7422.

88. Jason McClurg, "Sudanese Government Disputes ICC Jurisdiction in Darfur," *International Enforcement Law Reporter* 21, no. 10 (October 2005).

89. Cited in Kincaid, "Hollywood Promotes the International Criminal Court."

90. Elena Baylis, "Why the International Criminal Court Needs Darfur (More Than Darfur Needs the ICC)," *Jurist: Legal News & Research* (University of Pittsburgh School of Law), http://jurist.law.pitt.edu/forumy/2005/06/why-international-criminal-court-needs.php.

91. Jason McClurg, "Sudanese Government Disputes ICC Jurisdiction in Darfur," *International Enforcement Law Reporter* 21, no. 10 (October 2005).

92. Ibid.

93. Amann and Sellers, "American Law," 389.

94. McClurg, "Sudanese Government Disputes."

95. Kaul, "Developments at the International Criminal Court," 384.

96. Martinez, "Towards an International Judicial System."

97. Cited in William F. Jasper, "Court of Injustice," *New American*, 17 June 2002.

Chapter Seven: Global Gun Control and a Standing World Army

1. Executive Summary of Presidential Decision Directive 25 (PDD-25), *Clinton Administration Policy on Reforming Multilateral Peace Operations* was unofficially released by Anthony Lake, assistant to the president for national security affairs, at a press conference on 5 May 1994; it was later released by the Bureau of International Organizational Affairs, US Department of State, 22 February 1996.

2. Dr. Glenn Otero, "Ten Myths About Gun Control," Doctors for Sensible Gun Laws.

3. Sammy "The Bull" Gravano, quoted on the website of the Maryland Citizens Defense League at http://www.mcdl.org. (Accessed 20 December 2004; now not found on site.)

4. Ron Paul, "Reject U.N. Gun control," *Texas Straight Talk*, 22 September 2003, http://www.house.gov/paul/tst/tst2003/tst092203.htm.

5. Ibid.

6. "U.N. Seeking Global Gun Control? Conference Moving Toward Plan That Would Regulate U.S. Arms," WorldNetDaily.com, 16 July 2003.

7. Ibid.

8. Kofi Annan, *Report of the Group of Government Experts on Small Arms*, Small Arms Report

to UN General Assembly (A/54/258), 19 August 1999, http://www.globalpolicy.org/security/smallarms/1999/ga_resolution258.pdf.

9. Ibid.

10. Kofi Annan, September 1999, quoted in *United Nations Conference on the Illicit Trade in Small Arms and Light Weapons in All Its Aspects*, New York, 9–20 July 2001, http://disarmament.un.org/cab/smallarms/.

11. "John Holum on Illicit Trafficking in Small Arms, Light Weapons," 4 February 2000, http://www.useu.be/ISSUES/arm0204.html.

12. UN Small Arms Conference, *Report of the United Nations Conference on the Illicit Trade in Small Arms and Light Weapons in All Its Aspects,* New York, 9–20 July 2001.

13. Jerome F. Corsi, "U.N. Gun Confab Ends in Frustration: Small Arms Conference Fails to Agree on Final Document," WorldNetDaily.com, 10 July 2006, http://www.worldnetdaily.com/news/article.asp?ARTICLE_ID=50983.

14. Ibid.

15. "Final Press Release," UN Review Conference on Illicit Small Arms Trade, 7 July 2006, http://www.un.org/new/press/docs/2006/dc3037.htm.

16. Gary Benoit, "Civilian Disarmament," *New American*, July 2003, http://www.thenewamerican.com/tna/2000/07-03-2000/vo16no14_disarm.htm.

17. UN Commission on Global Governance, *Our Global Neighborhood*, 1995.

18. John F. Kennedy, "Address to United Nations General Assembly," 25 September 1961, White House Information Office. Cited in John F. McManus, "Whose Side Are They On?" (pamphlet), John Birch Society, Appleton, WI, 1991.

19. John F. Kennedy, *Freedom from War: The United States Program for General and Complete Disarmament in a Peaceful World,* Department of State Publication 7277, Disarmament Series 5, September 1961, Office of Public Services, Bureau of Public Affairs. Cited in William F. Jasper, *Global Tyranny . . . Step by Step* (Western Islands Press, 1992), 13.

20. Kennedy, *Freedom from War*. Note: This document was allowed to go out of print and is no longer available from the US Government Printing Office. However, an exact reproduction of the original document has been printed by and is available from The John Birch Society, P.O. Box 8040, Appleton, WI 54913. The existence of the original document has been verified on Microcard records in the Government Documents Department of the Old Dominion University Library, Hampton, Virginia.

21. Henry Lamb, "Part One: Global Governance: Why? How? When?" http://www.engr.utexas.edu/cofe/governance/.

22. "The United Nations System—Peace-keeping Operations," *Eco-Logic Powerhouse*, May/June 1996. Note: A "new and improved" version of the same basic disarmament idea found in *Freedom from War* was presented in May 1962 by the newly formed US Arms Control and Disarmament Agency, entitled *Blueprint for the Peace Race: Outline of Basic Provisions of a Treaty on General and Complete Disarmament in a Peaceful World* (Publication 4, General Series 3, 3 May 1962).

23. Independent Commission on Disarmament and Security Issues, *Common Security: A Blueprint for Survival* (Simon & Schuster, 1982). This is the report of *The Independent Commission on Disarmament and Security Issues*, hereafter referred to as the *Palme Commission Report*.

24. "Charter of the New International Economic Order," 1974. Cited in Henry Lamb, "The

Rise of Global Governance," 1996, http://www/eco.freedom.org. (Emphasis added.)

25. *Palme Commission Report*, xiii, 1, 7.

26. *Palme Commission Report*, xx. (Emphasis added.)

27. Andrew Butfoy, *New Security Agendas I*, "Chapter 5: Changing Western Conceptions of Global Security," http://www.arts.monash.edu.au/ncas/teach/unit/pol/chpt05.html.

28. *UN Charter*, Article 43.

29. *UN Charter*, Chapter VIII.

30. McManus, "U.S. Defenders or U.N. Enforcers?"

31. Ibid.

32. John Birch Society, "The United Nations Wants America's Armed Forces" (pamphlet), http:// www.getusout.org.

33. Michael New, personal letter to commanding officers, September 1995, cited in Douglas W. Phillips, "Michael New v. the New World Order," *Home School Court Report*, vol. 12, no. 5, Sept./Oct./Nov. 1995. (Emphasis added.)

34. Source for court-martial records is "Record of Trial" transcript supplied to military counsel for Michael G. New, special court martial held at Leighton Barracks, Wurzburg, Germany, 24 Oct., 17 Nov., 8 and 13 Dec. 1995, and 18–19 January and 23–24 1996. See also Michael P. Farris and Herbert W. Titus, attorneys, "Brief for Appellant," US Court of Appeals for the District of Columbia Circuit, No. 96-5158, *The United States Ex. Rel. Michael G. New v. William G. Perry, Secretary of Defense, and Togo D. West, Secretary of the Army*, argued 26 September 1997. Decided 11 November 1997, for apellees.

35. US Army, Judge Adjutant General Corps., *Occupational Law Handbook (2004)*, "Chapter 23: United Nations and Peace Operations," 9–10. http://www.jagcnet.army.mil/JAGNETInternet/Homepages/AC/CLAMO_public.nsf.

36. Samuel Francis, "The Real Meaning of Spec. Michael New," *Conservative Chronicle*, 31 January 1996.

37. Herb Titus, press release, http://www.mikenew.com. See also "I Am Not a United Nations Soldier," letter from Col. Ron Ray, legal advisor to the New family, 30 September 1995.

38. Herbert W. Titus, Henry L. Hamilton, & William G. Olson, Attorneys, "Brief of Appellant Michael G. New," US Court of Appeals for the District of Columbia Circuit, No. 05-5023, *Michael G. New v. Donald H. Rumsfeld, Secretary of Defense, et al*, 6 September 2005.

39. James W. Houck, *The Command and Control of United States Forces in the Era of "Peace Enforcement*," 4 Duke J. Comp. & Int'l L. 1, 3 (1993).

40. Bill Clinton, "A New Covenant for American Security," address at Georgetown University, 11 December 1991.

41. J. William Snyder Jr., "'Command' Versus 'Operational Control': A Critical Review of PDD-25," http://www.ibiblio.org/jwsnyder/wisdom/pdd25.html.

42. Peter W. Rodman, "Declarations of Dependence," *National Review*, 13 June 1994.

43. John M. Goshko, "U.N. Orders U.S.-Led Force into Somalia," *Washington Post*, 4 December 1992.

44. William Norman Grigg, "Battle for War Powers," *New American*, 6 January 1997, http://www.trimonline.org/congress/articles/war_powers.htm.

45. Harry Summers, "Defense Decisions That Could Be Worse," *Washington Times*, 1 January 1994.

46. "Wider U.N. Police Role Supported," 5 August 1993, http://www.fas.org/irp/offdocs/pdd13.htm.

47. Stephen A. Holmes, "Clinton May Let US Troops Serve under UN Chiefs," *New York Times*, 18 August 1993. Cited in John F. McManus, "Sovereignty Sellout," *New American*, 11 July 1994.

48. Trent Lott (speech on Senate floor), *Congressional Record*, 5 October 1993. Cited in McManus, "Sovereignty Sellout."

49. Cited in McManus, "Sovereignty Sellout."

50. Snyder, "'Command' Versus 'Operational Control.'"

51. Associated Press, "Last 2,400 U.N. Troops Leave Somalia," *Virginian-Pilot* and *Ledger-Star*, 3 March 1995.

52. Executive Summary of Presidential Decision Directive 25 (PDD-25). (Emphasis added.)

53. John R. Bolton, "U.S. Policy on U.N. Peacekeeping" (statement to the House Committee on International Relations), *Congressional Record*, 11 October 2000. Also available at http://www.globalpolicy.org/security/peacekpg/us/bolton.htm.

54. Ron Paul, "Presidential Power Grab," Montgomery Citizens for a Safer Maryland, 26 October 1999, http://www.mcsm.org/ronpaul.html.

55. Miguel A. Faria Jr., "Dismantling Clinton's Scaffold of Executive Orders," NewsMax.com, 29 January 2001, http://www.newsmax.com/archives/articles/2001/1/29/104302.shtml.

56. Carl Teichrib, "World Peace Through World Force—Creating the U.N. Army," *Discerning the Times Digest*, 2000, http://www.unwatch.com/shirbrig.shtml.

57. George Archibald, "White House Backs Standby Army via Clandestine Payments," *Washington Times*, 23 April 1998.

58. Ibid.

59. H. Peter Langille, "SHIRBRIG: A Promising Step Towards a United Nations That Can Prevent Deadly Conflict," Global Policy Forum, Spring 2000, http://www.globalpolicy.org/security/peacekpg/reform/canada/htm.

60. Commission on Global Governance, *Our Global Neighborhood*, Report of the Commission on Global Governance (Oxford University Press, 1995), 21–23. Cited in Langille, "SHIRBRIG."

61. William R. Frye, *A United Nations Peace Force* (Oceana Publications, 1957), 106–107. Cited in Langille, "SHIRBRIG."

62. Austin Ruse, "Clinton Calls for U.N. Army," NewsMax.com, 6 September 2000, http://www.newsmax.com/article/archive/get2.pl?a=2000/9/6/112634.

63. Chuck Baldwin, "Our Globalist President Pushing for a Standing U.N. Army," Chuckbaldwinlive.com, 25 May 2004, http://www.chuckbaldwinlive.com/c2004/cbarchive_20040525.html.

64. Bill Gertz as cited in Baldwin, "Our Globalist President."

65. William F. Jasper, "'Hat in Hand,' on 'Bended Knee,'" *New American*, 28 June 2004, http://www.thenewamerican.com/tna/2004/06-28-2004/iraq.htm.

66. Ibid.

67. Jasper, "'Hat in Hand.'"

Chapter Eight: The UN's Goal Really *Is* World Government

1. Henry Lamb, "The U.N. and Property Rights," *Eco-Logic Powerhouse*, August 2005, 17.

2. Cliff Kincaid, *Global Bondage: The U.N. Plan to Rule the World* (Huntington House Publishers, 1995), 36.

3. "Revision of the United Nations Charter: Hearings before a Subcommittee of the Committee on Foreign Relations, United States Senate, 81st Cong., 2nd Session, on Resolutions Relative to Revision of the United Nations Charter, Atlantic Union, World Federation, etc." 2, 3, 6, 8, 9, 13, 15, 17 and 20 February 1950, 494. Cited in Gary H. Kah, *En Route to Global Occupation* (Huntington House Publishers, 1991), 33.

4. Lincoln P. Bloomfield, *A World Effectively Controlled by the United Nations: A Preliminary Survey of One Form of a Stable Military Environment,* Study Memorandum No. 7, Institute for Defense Analysis, 10 March 1962. Posted online at http://www.getusout.org/artman/publish/article_2.shtml. (Emphasis added.)

5. Ibid.

6. Wikipedia, sv "Walter Cronkite," http://en.wikipedia.org/wiki/Walter_Cronkite.

7. Walter Cronkite, "Address to People for the American Way," 1989. Cited in Joseph Farah, "Most Trusted Man in America?" WorldNetDaily.com, 20 July 2000, http://www.worldnetdaily.com/news/article/asp?ARTICLE_ID=15007.

8. Walter Cronkite, "The First Priority of Humankind," address to World Federalists Association, United Nations, New York City, 19 October 1999. Excerpts posted online at http://www/ikosmos.com/wisdomeditions/essays/mw/cronkite01.htm. Cited in Joseph Farah, "Walter Cronkite–World Federalist," WorldNetDaily.com, 30 November 1999. (Emphasis added.)

9. Ibid.

10. Ibid.

11. "Cronkite Wants Standing U.N. Army," WorldNetDaily.com, 1 July 2002, http://www.worldnetdaily.com/news/article.asp?ARTICLE_ID=28072. (Emphasis added.)

12. Blair Clark's intervention in Cronkite's behalf was revealed in the 10 July 2000 issue of the *Nation,* according to Farah, "Most Trusted Man in America."

13. Alfred, Lord Tennyson, "Locksley Hall," Charles W. Eliot, ed. *English Poetry in Three Volumes; Vol. III. From Tennyson to Whitman* (P.F. Collier & Son), 983.

14. Author's note: I should mention here that noticing the link between this poem from the distant past and internationalist agenda of the present day is not original with me. Both William F. Jasper and Dr. Stanley Monteith have previously commented on this connection in books, and I'm sure that others have as well.

15. Arthur Schlesinger Jr., "Bye, Bye, Woodrow," *Wall Street Journal,* 27 October 1993. Reproduced in Stanley K. Monteith, ed., *Sustainable Development: An Expose of the Origins and Goals of Modern-Day Environmentalism; Documentation of the Plan to Destroy Christianity, Western Civilization, Humanity* (Radio Liberty, 1999).

16. Andrew Carnegie, *Triumphant Democracy* (Charles Scribner's Sons, 1893). Cited in Monteith, *Sustainable Development.* Note: It may be permissible to mention here, just in passing, that Cecil Rhodes had almost certainly been exposed to this same poem through the influence of John Ruskin at Oxford. Carnegie's stated goal of Anglo-American reunification was also the dream of Cecil Rhodes and was one reason for his establishment of the Rhodes Scholarships.

17. Connie McLaughlin and Gordon Davidson, *Spiritual Politics* (Ballantine Books, 1994), 209. Cited in Monteith, *Sustainable Development.* For more information on foundations

see also Rene Wormser, *Foundations: Their Power and Influence* (Adair, n.d.), reprinted. by Covenant House, 1993.

18. Schlesinger, "Bye, Bye, Woodrow." (Emphasis added.)

19. Ibid. (Emphasis added.)

20. Ibid.

21. Charles W. Eliot, "The Next American Contribution to Civilization," *Foreign Affairs*, Vol. 1, no. 1, 15 September 1922, 65. (Emphasis added.)

22. Philip Kerr, "From Empire to Commonwealth," *Foreign Affairs*, Vol. 1, no. 2, December 1922, 97–98. (Emphasis added.)

23. Some recommended research sources are: Dennis L. Cuddy, *The Globalists* (Hearthstone Publishing, 2001); James Perloff, *Shadows of Power* (Western Islands, 1988); William F. Jasper, *Global Tyranny . . . Step by Step: The United Nations and the Emerging New World Order* (Western Islands, 1992); William F. Jasper, *The United Nations Exposed* (John Birch Society, 2001).

24. Arnold Toynbee, "Speech to the Institute for the Study of International Affairs," Copenhagen, Denmark, June 1931, as quoted in *New American*, 11 July 2005. Also online at http://www.saltshakers.com/midnight/mwo.html.

25. Council on Foreign Relations, *American Public Opinion and Post-War Security Commitments*, 1944. Cited in "What They Mean by the New Order of the Ages," *Newswatch Magazine*, November/December 1990.

26. Robert M. Hutchins, Rexford G. Taylor, et al, *Preliminary Draft of a World Constitution*, 1948. Cited in William F. Jasper, "Why Not World Government?" (tract), (John Birch Society, 1995). For more information on the origins of this document, see Center for the Study of Democratic Institutions, *A Constitution for the World* (The Fund for the Republic, 1965), 6–8.

27. Senate Concurrent Resolution 66 first introduced in the Senate on 13 September 1949, by Sen. Glenn Taylor. Cited in Dennis L. Cuddy, "The 'New World Order': A Critique and Chronology" (pamphlet), (America's Future, Inc., 1992), 10.

28. Inis L. Claude Jr., *Swords Into Plowshares*, 4th ed. (Random House, 1956, 1971), 412–413. (Emphasis added.)

29. Ibid., 412. (Emphasis added.)

30. Ibid., 425.

31. Ibid., 414. (Emphasis added.)

32. Ibid., 416.

33. Ibid., 422. (Emphasis added.)

34. Ibid., 426. (Emphasis added.)

35. Ibid., 429–430. (Emphasis added.)

36. Norman Cousins, Keynote Address, Earth Day, 22 April 1970. Cited in Jasper, "Why Not World Government?"

37. Wikipedia, sv "Citizens for Global Solutions," http://en.wikipedia.org/wiki/Citizens_for_Global_Solutions.

38. John Logue, testimony at the hearing on United Nations, Committee on Foreign Affairs, Subcommittee on Human Rights and International Organizations, *U.S. Policy in the United Nations*, 105th Cong., 1st Session, 4 December 1985, 162–165.

39. Strobe Talbot, "The Birth of the Global Nation," *Time*, 20 July 1992. Available at

http://www.worldbeyondborders.org/globalnation.htm. (Emphasis added.)

40. George H.W. Bush, "Address to Joint Session of Congress," 11 September 1990 (White House Information Office). (Emphasis added.)

41. George H.W. Bush, "Address to Joint Session of Congress," 6 March 1991 (White House Information Office). (Emphasis added.)

42. Pat Robertson, *New World Order* (Word, 1991), 92.

43. George H.W. Bush, "Address to the National Religious Broadcasters Convention," 28 January 1991 (White House Information Office).

44. "One World, Under Gorby," *San Francisco Weekly*, 31 May–6 June 1995.

45. Mary Jo Anderson, "Gorbachev Proposes Huge U.N. Expansion," WorldNetDaily.com, 6 September 2000, http://www.worldnetdaily.com/news/article.asp?17624.

46. Richard N. Gardner, "The Hard Road to World Order," *Foreign Affairs*, Vol. 53, No. 2, Spring 1974, 556–558.

47. Ibid.

Chapter Nine: Saving American Sovereignty in the 21st Century

1. Victor Hugo, *Historie d'un crime*, 1852.

2. Nostradamus' alleged "Third Antichrist" prophecy, cited online at http://www.armageddononline.org/nostradamus.php.

3. Tom Raum, "Helms, U.N. Security Council Spar," Associated Press Online, *CBS MarketWatch*, 30 March 2000, http://www.marketwatch.newsalert.com/.

4. Jesse Helms, "Address to the United Nations Security Council," 20 January 2000. The following quoted segments are taken from the transcript of this speech posted at NewsMax.com, http://www.newsmax.com/articles/?a=2000/1/28/211810. The *New York Times* version of the transcript is posted at the Global Policy Forum's website, http://www.globalpolicy.org/finance/docs/helms4.htm.

5. Ibid. (Emphasis added.)

6. Henry Lamb, "Helms Warns U.N. Security Council," WorldNetDaily.com, 22 January 2000.

7. Patrick. J. Buchanan, "The Millennium Conflict: America First or World Government," Speech delivered to the Boston World Affairs Council, 6 January 2000, http://www.buchanan.org/pa-00-0106-worldgovernment.html.

8. Ibid.

9. "Talk of the Nation," National Public Radio, 14 September 2005.

10. Ron Paul, M.D., "NeoCon Global Government," LewRockwell.com, 14 June 2005, http://www.lewrockwell.com/paul/paul255.html.

11. Ibid.

12. Ibid.

13. John F. McManus, "Get U.S. Out! Campaign Bears Fruit," *John Birch Society Bulletin*, January 2006, 1–3. For more information see http://www.getusout.org.

14. Poll conducted jointly by the Council on Foreign Relations and the Pew Research Center for the People and the Press, 17 November 2005. Cited in McManus, "Get U.S. Out! Campaign Bears Fruit."

15. Ibid.

16. William F. Jasper, "The U.N. 'Reform' Bandwagon," *New American*, 11 July 2005.

17. John F. McManus, "You Can't Reform a Deadly Disease," *New American*, 11 July 2005.

18. Personal conversation with John F. McManus.

19. *Encyclopedia Britannica*, 15th ed., Micropedia II: 266, sv "Bricker, John W(illiam)," (Encyclopedia Britannica Inc., 1995).

20. *Encyclopedia Britannica*, 15th ed., Micropedia IX: 763-4, sv "Taft, Robert A(lphonso)," (Encyclopedia Britannica Inc., 1995).

21. William Degregorio, *The Complete Book of U.S. Presidents: From George Washington to Bill Clinton* (Wings Books, 1993), 533.

22. Eric Froner and John A. Garraty, eds., "John Foster Douglas," *The Reader's Companion to American History*, Houghton Mifflin Company, online edition. For additional online biographical information see also Wikipedia, sv "John Foster Dulles," http://en.wiki.org/wiki/John_Foster_Dulles.

23. John Foster Dulles, "Treaty Making and National Unity," speech to the American Bar Association, Louisville, Kentucky, 11 April 1952. *John Foster Dulles Papers, 1951-59*, Vol. III. E., Box 306, 1952, Mudd Manuscript Library, Dwight D. Eisenhower Presidential Library, Abilene, Kansas. Cited in Des Griffin, *Fourth Reich of the Rich* (Emissary Publications, 1979), 138–139. (Emphasis added.)

24. Cited in Griffin, *Fourth Reich*, 139.

25. US, Congress, Senate, *The Bricker Amendment, Senate Joint Resolution 1, Proposing an Amendment to the Constitution of the United States Relative to the Making of Treaties and Executive Agreements*, 83rd Congress, 1st Session, 7 January 1953. Reprinted in Peter V. Curl, ed., *Documents on American Foreign Relations, 1953* (Harper and Bros., 1954), 101–102.

26. US, Congress, Senate, *Testimony of Secretary of State John Foster Dulles before the Committee on the Judiciary*, 83rd Congress, 1st Session, 6 April 1953. Reprinted in Curl, *Documents*, 103–108.

27. Robert Welch, *The Politician* (Belmont Publishing Company, 1964), 93.

INDEX